Violence against Women

Violence against Women

International Legal Standards and Trends

Gordana Gasmi

LEXINGTON BOOKS
Lanham • Boulder • New York • London

Lexington Books
Bloomsbury Publishing Inc, 1385 Broadway, New York, NY 10018, USA
Bloomsbury Publishing Plc, 50 Bedford Square, London, WC1B 3DP, UK
Bloomsbury Publishing Ireland, 29 Earlsfort Terrace, Dublin 2, D02 AY28, Ireland
www.rowman.com

British Library Cataloguing in Publication Information Available

Library of Congress Cataloging-in-Publication Data Available

ISBN 978-1-66696-737-1 (cloth: alk. paper)
ISBN 978-1-66696-738-8 (electronic)

For product safety related questions contact productsafety@bloomsbury.com.

♾™ The paper used in this publication meets the minimum requirements of American National Standard for Information Sciences—Permanence of Paper for Printed Library Materials, ANSI/NISO Z39.48-1992.

This book is dedicated to all women and girls in the world,
who are victims of various forms of violence in everyday life,
just because they are women and who suffer in silence,
not knowing
that there is international law and legislation,
able and available to help them,
no matter how insufficient those rules are.
—Author

Contents

Preface

The monograph deals with the international legal standards and trends in the area of violence against women seen from the perspective of human rights protection. It is based on normative-legal research, using the statute approach, conceptual approach, and case approach. The legal materials used are international legal documents. The most relevant international legal documents in this field are the UN Convention on the Elimination of All Forms of Discrimination against Women (CEDAW, 1979) with its Optional Protocol (1999), and General Recommendations No. 12 (1989), No. 19 (1992), and No. 35 (2017) of the CEDAW; Inter-American Convention on the prevention, punishment and eradication of violence against women (1994) adopted by the Organization of American States; and the Protocol to the African Charter on Human and Peoples' Rights on the Rights of Women in Africa (2003), adopted by the African Union.

The global problem of violence against women is linked to prejudice and discrimination, gender inequality in societies, harmful gender stereotypes, and gender-based power differentials. Hence, gender-based violence disproportionately affects women simply because they are women, as well as girls. Inequality is both the root cause and at the same time a consequence of gender-based violence, as it can prevent victims from seeking protection or compensation for violations of their basic human rights. Violence against women is conceptualized not only as a violation of human rights in itself but also as an extreme form of discrimination covered by the UN CEDAW. Gender-based and sexual violence can consist of the following types of violence and abuse: rape and attempted rape, sexual threats, sexual harassment, exploitation, humiliation, assault, abuse, sexual exchange, torture, and unwanted or harmful insertion of objects into the genital openings. It can also include forced pregnancy, forced sterilization, forced abortion, human trafficking for sexual exploitation, sexual slavery, forced circumcision, and forced nudity. Consequently, the consequences are disruption of physical, mental, and reproductive health, as well as a reduced possibility of using personal resources and basic human rights and freedoms.

Plethora of international legal standards in the field of violence against women is furthermore supplemented by regional ones: the European Convention for the Protection of Human Rights and Fundamental Freedoms (ETS No. 5, 1950) and its Protocols; Council of Europe (CoE) Convention on preventing and combating violence against women and domestic violence (Istanbul Convention, 2014); the Council of Europe Convention on Action against Trafficking in Human Beings (CETS No. 197, 2005); and the Council of Europe Convention on the Protection of Children against Sexual Exploitation and Sexual Abuse (CETS No. 201, 2007).

International soft law is an integral part of the international legal principles, being the predecessor of conventions, such as the United Nations General Assembly Declaration on the Elimination of Violence against Women (resolution 48/104 of 1993), the Beijing Declaration and Platform for Action, the most progressive blueprint for advancing women's rights (1995), and the CoE Recommendation Rec (2002)5 of the Committee of Ministers to member states on the protection of women against violence (2002).

The starting hypothesis of the research is that the goal of international rules and principles on violence against women is to prevent violence against women, to ensure investigation, prosecution, and punishment of perpetrators, and to provide protection and support for complainants/survivors of violence by setting international standards and providing a role model for national legislative reforms. Consequently, the research explores how and to what extent this complex goal has been achieved in relevant international legal documents. The methodology is based on legal analysis of the norms of the most important international conventions and relevant soft law documents, applied in a contextual *framework*. Furthermore, theoretical approach to the concept of law and the notion of human rights is applied, bearing in mind that violence against women represents a serious violation of women's human rights and severe discrimination of women, as being defined in the UN CEDAW Convention and in the Council of Europe (CoE) Istanbul Convention.

Taking into account that the most comprehensive international legal document in the domain of the fight against violence toward women is the CoE Convention on preventing and combating violence against women and domestic violence (Istanbul Convention, 2014), the prevalent part of the monograph focuses on the legal analysis of this Convention. The Istanbul Convention furthermore sets up the legal pattern to be followed at a global level, being voluminous legal standard for the prevention and fight against violence toward women and domestic violence as well. In addition, the CoE

Istanbul Convention made an emancipatory impulse for national legislations' reforms of the CoE member states. The Istanbul Convention has set legally binding standards in the field of prevention, protection of victims of domestic and gender-based violence, and prosecution of perpetrators. The key issue of efficiency of the legal norms established by the Istanbul Convention is dealt with through reflection on direct regulations on investigation, prosecution, and victims' protection in the area of fighting domestic and gender-based violence, which impose concrete obligations on the countries signatories of the Convention.

Relevant judgments of the European Court of Human Rights (ECtHR, Strasbourg, France) established important standards in the field of violence against women in recent years, which represented antecedents of the principle of state due diligence in the fight against violence against women and domestic violence. Therefore, the insight into the most relevant ECtHR judgments composes a separate chapter of the book.

Based on previous research assumptions, the monograph is divided into several chapters: Introductory notes; (1) Concept of law; (2) Notion of human rights; (3) Relevant universal international documents on violence against women; (4) Regional the most comprehensive international legal norms on violence to women with special emphasis on the CoE Istanbul Convention; (5) Relevant judgments of European Court of Human Rights in the area of violence against women; and (6) Concluding remarks.

The monograph brings analysis of selected international legal documents that focus on international policies and approaches to prevent and intervene in violence against women. The aim is to facilitate synthesis of different polices, programs and approaches that have been adopted internationally to address violence against women in different cultural and socioeconomic situations.

Declarations and conventions on human rights set international legal standards for the formation of public policy responses and for a legal approach to preventing violence against women. The results of the research should be used to raise the voice of women, but also to raise the awareness of the entire society about the problem of violence against women and to challenge attitudes of tolerance toward this dangerous social phenomenon by breaking negative gender stereotypes toward women and girls. In this way, the emancipatory role of international legal principles is achieved, as well as their influence on national legal reforms in the direction of modernization of relevant norms.

Introduction

> Women are in double jeopardy. Discriminated against as women, they are also as likely as men, if not more so, to become victims of human rights violations. . . . Today, what unites women internationally—transcending class, race, culture, religion, nationality and ethnic origin—is their vulnerability to the denial and violation of their fundamental human rights, and their dedicated efforts to claim those rights.
>
> (Amnesty International, Human Rights are Women's Rights)

Violence against women is a global phenomenon, which exists in all countries of the world, but not all countries recognize it as a severe violation of women's human rights even at present. Not all countries regulate violence against women as a criminal offense as it is, nor have effective legal responses to this dangerous phenomenon that threatens viable life and jeopardizes the prosperity of half population in each state. Every day in the world, women suffer various forms of violence, such as rape, genital mutilation, forced marriage, forced sterilization, physical violence, stalking, sexual harassment, and psychological violence, either in public or private space. Despite the lack of precise data at a global level, violence against women and girls remains a global pandemic—one in three women is exposed to physical and/or sexual violence at least once in their lifetime.[1] COVID-19 made the situation even worse: 45 percent of women said they or a woman they know had experienced violence during COVID-19, and six in ten women said sexual harassment in public had worsened.[2] Gender inequality and social tolerance toward violence against women are the main causes of violence against women, as well as weak legal sanctions and unreported cases.

Domestic violence against other victims (children, men, and old people) is also a negative phenomenon, which causes a high degree of concern given the level of prevalence in large number of families worldwide. Prevailing, however, is the present occurrence of violence against women, as a form of discrimination against women, which is the result of historical inequalities in power relations between women and men, leading to domination of men over women. This is particularly reflected in partnership relations. In around 80 percent of cases, the victim of domestic abuse-related crimes was female.

Those facts motivated many officials and representatives of the non-governmental organizations to inspire the adoption of relevant legal documents at the international level, which furthermore became role model for national norms in the field of prevention and punishment of violence against women in many countries. Systematic research into the problem of violence against women began in the 1970s thanks to the activities of feminist organizations. The results of these activities indicated that it is necessary to conduct permanent campaigns against violence against women, to examine various forms and manifestations of violence, and to work on the analysis of current policies and public measures to prevent and fight against violence against women for their further improvement. The better efficiency of the practice is directly related to the understanding of the origin of the problem of violence against women, with the aim of developing prevention and protection of victims.

Violence against women usually occurs within family (and at the workplace and in public) and is legally regulated under the umbrella of domestic violence, which is deeply rooted in society. Given that it takes place in the private sphere, it is often difficult to recognize and punish it in comparison with other public forms of violence (at sports stadiums, burglary, or robbery, etc.). Hence, the agencies and services which are responsible for providing assistance to victims face different forms of hiding the truth beyond the four walls of home. Punishment occurs only in cases of long-term manifestations of domestic violence and in a cruel way, sometimes with fatal consequences.[3]

Domestic abuse remains acutely underreported, however. Domestic abuse can be financial, verbal, and emotional as well as physical and sexual. Furthermore, children are explicitly identified as victims if they witness abuse. Women are exposed to different forms of violence—physical, sexual, psychological, and economic, both within the family and outside. Violence against women in the family context is a pattern of continued violence and abuse, a situation of repeated victimization, where the woman victim is vulnerable precisely because she shares a home with her abuser and also has feelings of loyalty and even love toward him.[4] Therefore, services for victims of domestic abuse, where women are prevalent victims, must be properly funded. The government's austerity policies have reduced funds for refuges for domestic violence survivors, despite analysis that shows how this violence generates significant costs to the economy in addition to the harm suffered by women.[5] Women survivors of domestic abuse face numerous internal barriers to accessing help and support and disclosing abuse. These internal barriers include a lack of recognition that the abuse is happening, feelings of guilt and shame, and lack of awareness of available support.

Violence against women is a very complex phenomenon, since it occurs not only in the family, in partnership relations, but furthermore in a public place (physical violence, rapes) or at work (through sexual harassment, mobbing, or stalking). Official statistics of the United Nations (UN) indicate that globally, 26 percent of ever-partnered women aged fifteen and older (641 million) have been subjected to physical and/or sexual violence by a husband or intimate partner at least once in their lifetime. Limited evidence from 2000 to 2018 found that 4 percent and 7 percent of women in the age group of fifty and older experienced physical and/or sexual violence by an intimate partner in the last twelve months.

Older women, however, may be vulnerable to specific forms of violence not usually measured in surveys on violence against women, such as economic exploitation or being ostracized or severely neglected. Perpetrators of such violence, aside from intimate partners, can include adult children and other relatives, strangers, caregivers, and neighbors. Some research results suggest that women from minority, marginalized, or disadvantaged communities or backgrounds, or those with protected characteristics, including black and minority women, lesbian, bisexual, and trans women, and older and disabled women, face higher rates of domestic abuse and additional barriers to support.[6]

Notwithstanding those facts, consideration of the issue of violence against women at the international level started rather late, while global legal regulation of violence against women is far from being comprehensive, as it exists only at the regional level through the Council of Europe (CoE) Convention on preventing and combating violence against women and domestic violence (Istanbul Convention, 2014). Consequently, the problem of violence against women is in many modern countries put under the regulation of criminal law, which represents the turnover from the belief that it is a private problem of the individual victim.

Furthermore, the issue of violence against women is more widely treated as a severe violation of human rights. Gender equality provides for prevention measures in relation to violence against women, but according to the UN estimates,[7] "the world is not on track to achieve gender equality by 2030, and the social and economic fallout from the pandemic has made the situation even bleaker." It is almost ninety years since the right to vote was granted to all women; almost half a century since the implementation of equal pay and anti-discrimination legislation, and today, female participation in the labor market is increasing rapidly. "Yet for all the gains made, inequality between women and men persists and what has been achieved appears easily dismantled."[8]

There needs to be far more focus on prevention, early intervention, and a more coordinated community response to violence against women, such as advocacy, safety planning, therapeutic support and counseling, support for children, and work with perpetrators to change their behavior. All these activities strongly depend on public funds and raising awareness on the need to combat violence against women. The legacy of the COVID-19 pandemic on the incidence, nature, and victims of domestic abuse is very negative, as limited data indicate an increase in the scope of violence against women globally. Limited evidence points to an intensification of violence against women during this pandemic. A 2021 rapid gender assessment survey in thirteen countries, undertaken by the United Nations Entity for Gender Equality and the Empowerment of Women (UN Women), found that 45 percent of women reported that they or a woman they know has experienced some form of violence since COVID-19.[9]

Based on the previously presented information, it is important to research on international legal frameworks of violence against women from the standpoint of the concept of law and the notion of human rights, with the aim to accentuate the most optimal approach to this issue.

NOTES

1. https://www.unwomen.org/sites/default/files/Headquarters/Attachments/Sections/Library/Publications/2020/A-75-274-SG-report-EVAWG-Infographic-and-recommendations-en.pdf, 15.09.2023.
2. Ibid.
3. United Nations Department of Economic and Social Affairs, *The World's Women 2010: Trends and Statistics*, United Nations, New York, 2010, 19.
4. Kelly, L., *VIP Guide - Vision, Innovation and Professionalism in Police Activities Related to Violence Against Women*, Beograd: Savet Evrope, Kancelarija u Beogradu, 2003, quoted according to: T. Ignjatović, *Violence Against Women in Intimate Partner Relationships: A Model of Coordinated Community Response*, RŽC, Beograd, 2011, 21.
5. C. English, *Confronting Gender Inequality*, Gender Institute, London, 2018, 3.
6. https://www.publicpolicyexchange.co.uk/?ss=em&tg=1b; Public Policy Exchange Ltd Registered in England & Wales, № 7350384, Registered Office: 253 Grays Inn Road, London, WC1X 8QT, "Domestic Violence: Building on the Domestic Abuse Act to Better Protect and Support Victims and Survivors," *Webinar*, 20.10.2022.
7. Ibid., 05. 02. 2023.
8. C. English, *Confronting Gender Inequality*, 2.
9. https://unstats.un.org/sdgs/report/2022/Goal-05/, 05.02.2023.

Chapter 1

Concept of Law

Whoever knows only the words of the law, that law doesn't know yet, until he understands his reason and meaning.

Valtazar Bogišić (1834–1908)[1]

BINDING LAW AND SOFT LAW

Since ancient times, many jurists and philosophers have tried to define the concept of law, but they were not completely successful. There is no generally accepted answer to the question of what is law, despite a large number of various definitions.[2] Defining law is a very complex process. Therefore, law can be viewed from different angles. Some definitions of law are more general, some are narrower, some give priority to one element, considering it key to the definition of law, and some to another element. Exactly because of the existence of a large number of different definitions of law, it is optimal to start from the broadest definition of law being rules that govern human behavior and action.[3]

Law is a set of rules that are created and are enforceable by social or governmental institutions to regulate behavior.[4] Of course, legal rules on human behavior and actions are not the only ones that exist in each society. In addition to legal rules, there are many other rules, among which can be recognized customary rules, moral, religious, and so on. The main difference between legal rules on human behavior and action and other rules, such as customary, moral, or religious, is in the sanctions that threaten those who violate the rules of conduct. The coercive character of legal norms is a fundamental feature that distinguishes them from other rules of human behavior and action. *Pacta sunt servanda*[5] is a fundamental principle of law. According to Hans Wehberg, a professor of international law, "few rules for the ordering of Society have such a deep moral and religious influence" as this principle.[6] In its most common sense, this principle refers to private contracts and prescribes that the provisions, that is, clauses of a contract are law between the parties to the contract, and therefore implies that neglect of their respective obligations is a violation of the contract. Under international law, every treaty in force is binding upon the parties to it and must be performed by them in good faith.[7] Basis of good faith for treaties implies that a party to a treaty cannot invoke provisions of its domestic law as justification for negligence of its obligations pursuant to the treaty in question. The only limits to the application of the *Pacta sunt servanda* principle are the peremptory norms of general international law, which are denominated *jus cogens* that is, compelling law. A peremptory norm is a fundamental principle of international law that is accepted by the international community of states as a norm from which no derogation is permitted. There is no universal agreement regarding precisely which norms are *jus cogens* nor how a norm reaches that status, but it is generally accepted that *jus cogens* bans genocide, maritime piracy, enslaving in general (i.e., slavery as well as slave trade), wars of aggression and territorial aggrandizement, torture, and refoulement.[8] Under Article 53 of the Vienna Convention on the Law of Treaties, any treaty that conflicts with a peremptory norm is void. However, the legal principle of *clausula rebus sic stantibus* in customary international law permits non-satisfaction of obligations pursuant to a treaty, because of a compelling change of circumstances.

Law has been described as a science[9] and as the art of justice.[10] State-enforced laws can be made by a group legislature or by a single legislator, resulting in statutes; by the executive through decrees and regulations; or established by judges through precedent, usually in common law jurisdictions. Private individuals may create legally binding contracts, including arbitration agreements that adopt alternative ways of resolving disputes to standard court litigation. The creation of laws themselves may be influenced by a constitution, written or tacit, and the rights encoded therein.

The task of law in all societies is, first of all, to regulate relations in a society with the aim of increasing the level of social stability and security, and in this way, it enables the continuous progress of the whole society. In order to achieve that goal, it is necessary that there is a threat to the disobedient ones that they will be driven to apply legal rules by force.[11] Since law regulates the social relations in which common interests or a conflict of interest occurs, legal rules are to be defined in advance in order to achieve the desirable behavior of legal subjects. Social relations regulated by law include property relations, organization of government and society, economic relations, family relations, and numerous other relations for which the law must establish precise authorizations and obligations of legal subjects, so that they are in advance known, clear, and understandable. The legal order has a pretension to regulate almost all social relations.[12]

In the essence of law lies a certain system of values accepted in one society, the state, and the international community. Those values are justice, fairness, freedom, human dignity, tolerance, security, equality, order, and peace.[13] The highest value that stands above all those mentioned is certainly the freedom of individuals. The law must regulate individual freedom in order to achieve the highest possible level of individual freedom. Since legal entities constantly and in different ways threaten the freedom of individuals, it is necessary to establish a system of rules and sanctions aimed at the protection of the highest possible level of individual freedoms. In order to protect the basic values of society, the law, that is, the legal system, must be based on certain technical values and principles such as expediency, effectiveness, clarity, precision, brevity, coherence, completeness, and definiteness.[14]

The law regulates relationships in which there is a conflict of interest, and often there are disputes between natural and legal entities, so it is necessary to have a neutral third party that will resolve those disputes, namely the court. The law regulates in detail the proceedings before the courts to enable disputing legal subjects to resolve their disputes and determine responsibility for conduct that is inconsistent with the conduct defined in legal norms. In this way, legal security and legal predictability are ensured. The notion of legal security in the context of human right context consists of human security, social security, and security of the legal system. According to some authors, the principle of legal security has a specific normative function: to justify and develop effective legislation.[15]

Sanction for illegal behavior is an essential feature of the law and must be provided by law, proportionate, precise, and measurable.[16] This is a legal principle that states that one cannot be punished for doing something that is not prohibited by law. This principle is accepted and codified in modern democratic states as a basic requirement of the rule of law. The execution of the sanction must also be precisely defined by law. The most severe sanctions are imposed for the violation of the most important legal norms, which protect human life and authority.

For the purposes of our book, we will define the term law as a set of rules that includes, on the one hand, positive (binding) law, that is, legal system of norms that regulates the behavior of natural and legal entities, their actions and inaction followed by threatened sanctions and an effective mechanism for their realization.

On the other hand, law encompasses a set of universal business, ethical and moral rules and standards that most often do not have effective sanctioning mechanisms (natural law, soft law), but they are of great importance precisely for the regulation of an area such as violence against women, in which there are not enough norms of positive law at the international level. The term soft law is primarily related to international law because it proved in many cases that soft law norms are the only instruments that represent a solution that could be applied globally or at the regional level. In a relatively short period of time, soft law instruments began to apply in various legal fields, such as banking and finance, trade, arbitration law, insurance law, human rights protection, environmental protection, and other.

Lord McNair is credited with launching the term soft law in the middle of the 1970s of the twentieth century, although he did not offer an explicit definition of it. Regarding this term, two basic approaches have been present: on the one hand, the terms hard (binding) law and soft law should be interpreted as synonyms for *lex lata* and *lex ferenda*, and on the other hand, Lord McNair meant the principles of international public law under the term soft law. However, regardless of the initial idea regarding the meaning of this term, the fact is that it is widely accepted today, both in the academic milieu and in legal practice. Francis Snyder defined the notion of soft law as: "a set of rules of conduct which, in principle, are not legally binding, but which can nevertheless produce certain legal consequences in a practical sense."[17]

The usual is that the term soft law refers to non-binding acts such as strategies, opinions, recommendations, guidelines, and declarations[18] of the international organizations or states or the EU (being a *sui generis* entity in international relations). The instruments of soft law are mostly present in the sphere of international public law, and examples in that context are the resolutions and recommendations of the United Nations General Assembly (UNGA) at the global level. Soft law is also very important within other international organizations, such as the Council of Europe and others.

Soft law includes norms, the application of which depends solely on the will of the addressee, and which, therefore, does not rest on the regime of legal sanctions, but which, regardless of the lack of legally binding power, produce *de facto* certain legal effects. Precisely in the area of the inappropriate action of sanctions, soft law appeared in response to the growing complexity of modern societies and to the contemporary unstoppable process of globalization. Sanctions due to non-compliance with the norms of soft law may, in some cases be more drastic than the sanctions provided for by binding law, when they result in serious economic losses. Addressees of soft norms have a wide range of discretion in terms of their application. Soft law instruments take the form of legal acts, which distinguishes them from political statements.

Common features of soft law instruments are non-binding character and written form. These instruments actually consist of all kinds of soft provisions in international agreements and other legal documents, which do not create obligations in the traditional sense. Soft law refers to international norms that are created with the intention of being non-binding, but they still have legal significance.[19] In the literature, there is a division into binding and non-binding international agreements. In this context, when states want to undertake certain obligations, they conclude legally binding agreements. When this is not the case, the states will conclude a non-binding agreement based on the so-called soft law. Binding agreements often do not contain coercive mechanisms, while non-binding agreements can nevertheless impose some kind of obligations on their signatories.[20] In other words, the differences are as follows: the violation of binding engagements is "more costly" for the violator than for violator of non-binding arrangements, who may nevertheless bear certain consequences.

Soft law, in certain cases, can be just as effective as hard law. Norms from the arsenal of soft law can, given their flexibility, provide adequate and quick answers in order to solve problems. Soft law has another specific advantage. Namely, it is oriented *pro futuro*, because its instruments pave the way for hard law, which often *post factum* only defines the legal framework for a specific situation, which has already been brought under control and / or directed in the desired direction by applying soft law instruments. Soft law emerged spontaneously as a consequence of the need to simplify and speed up the process of creating law in order to more efficiently regulate problems, which, due to their nature, require a quick response. A. Peters and I. Pagotto pointed out three functions of soft law related to the hard, binding law: a pre-law function (*lex ferenda*), a law-plus function (post-law function: filling legal gaps and interpreting hard law provisions), and a para-law function (when used instead of hard law).[21]

Three theoretical approaches to the concept of soft law are likewise developed, all three aimed at explaining the legal profile of soft law:

- legal positivism (H. Kelsen)—they consider that soft law is inferior in relation to hard law, but that it should not be rejected because of that, as it potentially represents a step toward hard law;
- legal constructivism[22]—soft law represents a complement to hard law, because it facilitates dialogue and puts to the test transnational and internal processes, which transform norms, but also perceptions of state interests—they emphasize the social context; and
- legal realism (C. Lipson)[23]—soft law instruments are significant in generating information that leads to better mutual understanding in situations characterized by uncertainty.

However, the prevailing opinion in legal theory is that the relationship between hard and soft law can have an alternative, complementary or antagonistic character. Understanding these different interactions of hard and soft law is essential for the comprehension of the development of contemporary international law, as well as national legal orders.

Benefits of soft law are:

- enabling the conclusion of agreements that would not be otherwise concluded;
- preservation of sovereignty;
- harmonization of different interests;
- flexibility;
- simplicity and speed;
- participatory features and
- gradualism in a sense to pave the way to binding law.

Soft law can serve as a communication mechanism through which actors signal to each other about their intentions to take certain regulatory activity or to accept a specific regulatory approach.

POSITIVE LAW AND NATURAL LAW

Positive law (*ius cogens*) is the norms whose application is ultimately guaranteed by the state with its monopoly of physical force and a spectrum of different sanctions. Positive law encompasses legal rules enacted by people in a political community and enforced by its courts and the police,[24] as a legal system of norms that represents an organized entirety, composed of a series of parts and elements. Positivists believe that what distinguishes law from non-legal norms is the requirement that the addressee's obligations are legally regulated and provide for sanctions for non-fulfillment of assumed obligations. "Laws have no power without punishment, and punishments are absolutely inappropriate in this case because they are not a convenient way to convince someone's spirit" (J. Locke, XVII century).

Legal norms, which are the basic elements of the legal system, are divided according to their strength into higher and lower, and according to their width into general and individual. Grouping of legal norms is furthermore possible according to their content, that is, the area of social life that they regulate. In this way, they are grouped into certain branches of law such as constitutional law, civil law, criminal law, family law, administrative law, labor law, and so on.

Back in the 1930s, Hans Kelsen noted that "law no longer represents an eternal and absolute category; it is realized that its content is subject to historical change and that it is as positive law, a real phenomenon that is conditioned by the circumstances of time and space."[25]

Positivists point out that it is the state that should formalize the norms, which is why we actually live in an era of post-positivism. Legal systems of norms can be divided into national, supranational, and international ones. However, this division is relative because the norms of supranational systems and international legal systems are largely implemented in national legal systems. Their importance is absolute, especially bearing in mind the example of the influence of the supranational system of norms of the European Union (EU), which is so great that even non-member countries adapt to that system, while others are studying it as a model of unification of different national interests in the regulation of many economic and social domains.[26]

An example of the influence of EU legal norms is the adoption of the General Regulation on Data Protection (GDPR) by the EU in 2016, which had the goal of ensuring respect for all fundamental rights and freedoms, and in particular respect for private and family life, communication, personal data protection, freedom of opinion, religion, freedom of expression and information, freedom of entrepreneurship, the right to an effective legal remedy and fair trial, as well as rights to cultural, religious, and linguistic diversity.[27] A large number of countries around the world have harmonized their legal regulations in the field of data protection with the EU General Regulation on Data Protection (GDPR). Consequences of the application of EU legal norms in the field of data protection of data since 2018 to present, are a large number of monetary fines and high reputational risk.[28] This was the reason that the largest number of countries and companies around the world harmonized their regulations with the General Regulation on Data Protection (GDPR) of the EU.

In addition to positive law, great importance for the protection of human rights have and will have universal business, ethical and moral rules and standards embodied in natural law[29]—a philosophical theory claiming to derive moral and legal principles from a set of universal truths about people and justice,[30] that is, the unwritten body of universal moral principles that underlie the ethical and legal norms by which human conduct is sometimes evaluated and governed,[31] and in various international conventions and declarations (soft law). This is particularly valid for the area of preventing and combating the global phenomenon of violence against women.

Morality, as a system of social norms that shows and determines what is good and what is bad in the existence of a man, as a social being of nature, is guided by the principle of Good from the point of view of a certain space and time. It judges many individual and social contrasts, such as love and hate, truth and lies, conscience and temptation, freedom and non-freedom, the beauty of good and the ghost of evil, the culture of peace and the non-culture of war and violence, dogmatic recklessness, and tolerance as the pivot of the virtue of enlightened reason.[32]

Natural law serves justice as a moral disposition of equal treatment of equal things. The realization of natural law is an expression of a democratic culture that accepts tolerance as an act of spiritual freedom and a culture of reason. Natural law represents the totality of rights that are confirmed in the being of every human being, in their nature, human innate rights. Every human being has equal natural rights to the same extent (e.g., the right to life and physical inviolability or personal freedom), regardless of their gender, age, position in society, regardless of the time, place, or the state system in which they live. Natural rights are supranational and therefore inalienable, "eternal" rights. These rights differ from laws and other state-imposed legal norms that change over time, so they differ from positive law and require a higher legal quality than positive law.

The roots of the idea of natural law go back to Greek antiquity. Natural law is contained to a certain extent in the philosophy of some Sophists (fifth and fourth centuries BC), in the philosophy of Plato (427–347 BC) and Aristotle (384–322 BC), it was especially shaped by the philosopher Zeno (from the third century BC) and by his Greek and Roman followers, and further developed by Cicero (106–43 BC), Seneca (ca. 4 BC–65 AD), and Epictetus (ca. 50–138). In the Christian philosophy and theology of the Middle Ages, and especially in the philosophy of Thomas Aquinas (1225–74) and other scholastics, natural rights are considered as the confluence of divine rights that act in a man.

Natural rights gained political significance exactly in the Age of Enlightenment (seventeenth to eighteenth century). The theory of natural law, developed by J. Althusius (1557–1638) and H. Grotius (1583–1645), and further processed and developed by S. Pufendorf (1632–1694), Chr. Thomasius (1655–1728), Chr. Wolff (1679–1754), J. J. Rousseau (1712–1778), I. Kant (1724–1804), and others, according to which natural rights are the rights confirmed in the rational nature of man (reasonable rights), were used as the philosophical basis of the French Revolution (1789) and other "civil" revolutions of the eighteenth and nineteenth centuries. In this way, natural rights became a means for citizens in their struggle against the feudalistic state system (feudalism) and the absolutist state (absolutism), and for the rule of law. In the basic human and civil rights on which the legal state of the modern age rests, natural rights take on a concrete form.[33]

It is clear that human rights derive from this tradition. The rationalist and Enlightenment science of natural law reached its peak during the seventeenth and eighteenth centuries. Contrary to natural law, law in the system of positive law can be just or unjust, precisely according to the criterion of the degree of proclamation and realization of justice as moral categories.[34]

Non omne quod licet honestum est (D. 50, 17, 144 pr)—Latin proverb says: Not everything that is permitted is honest. Dignity as the absolute purpose of humanity is the presupposition of all rational freedom and the equality of men regardless of their differences by birth or any legitimate belief. Freedom and dignity form a unique whole of humanity. There is no dignity without freedom, as there is no freedom without dignity. A man who is restrained by the shackles of violence of any kind simultaneously loses both freedom and dignity. Tolerance is a way of overcoming differences. Tolerance is, above all, an active attitude inspired by the recognition and protection of human rights and the fundamental freedoms of others. It has to be practiced by individuals, groups, and states. According to the principle of tolerance, no one has the right to put himself above another and, by force, to turn the pluralism of life into a monism of his power and supremacy. Natural law is based on these ethical postulates that are to be universally applied irrespective of positive norms. When it comes to the influence of tolerance principle on positive law, the right to tolerance should be used to constitute a special subjective right provided for by the constitution and other laws. This is the subjective right that would consist of a certain authority or a set of authorities of a physical or legal entity, as well as requests, that is, lawsuits in the material sense of the word, which is the possibility of an authorized person to request a certain behavior from a certain person. The right to tolerance should work *erga omnes* or *inter partes*, depending on the nature of the specific right.[35]

During the nineteenth century, the opposite movement dominated, the movement against the theory of natural law—legal positivism, which starts from the fact that positive (legal) law is the only valid one, regardless of what it contains. Politics decides the content of law. "Even the smallest legal right, even though it is only formally enacted, we are obliged to consider binding."[36] "It is an indisputable truth that the legal authority (power) can establish any legal content."[37] On the other side, natural law starts from the thesis that there is a superior and always valid natural law, which is a template and a basis of positive norms. "Therefore, there are legal principles that are stronger than any legal form, so that any law that contradicts these principles simply does not apply. These principles are called natural or common law. These rights are certainly surrounded by some doubts, but they have developed from centuries of work some parts of which have been collected in the Charter of Human and Civil Rights with universal approval throughout the world."[38] It follows that the judge has the right to give priority to his common sense and reasoning before the letter of the law. However, the result can be a danger of uncertain rights and arbitrariness. In a positive law system, the judge is strictly bound by the laws passed by the state, but there is a danger of the implementation of unjust laws enacted by some dictator. The legal positivism of the nineteenth century considered the extreme case of establishing unjust law as only a hypothetical case. But this is exactly what happened in the totalitarian and fascist dictatorships of the twentieth century. That is why after the

Second World War, there was a turning point, a return to natural law. Within the framework of the United Nations, natural law is being tried to be made positive in the form of human rights. This means that the idea that there is a superior law is maintained, but that superior law is tried to be prescribed as binding for all people. It is, therefore, a compromise between the two extreme positions described above. Of course, the prescribed laws apply first, but if laws violate justice, then man has an obligation not to follow them. What is meant by the notion of justice can be seen from documents recognized around the world, especially from the UN Universal Charter of Human Rights.

Consequently, relevant international conventions and declarations contain the highest moral and ethical standards and principles aimed at the combating violence against women at a global level and serve as a valuable resource and model for national legal regulations in the field of violence against women. One of the reasons for the increasing application of soft law instruments is reflected in the fact that states, as well as other actors, are more willing to accept certain requests voluntarily than in the case when those same requests are conditioned by a formal obligation to enforce them.

Soft law has specific advantage. Namely, it is oriented *pro futuro*, because its instruments pave the way for binding (positive, hard) law, which often *post factum* only defines the legal framework for a specific situation, which has already been brought under control and / or directed in the desired direction by applying soft law instruments. Exactly in this point the legal importance and effectiveness of international declarations and conventions regulating women's human rights and combating violence against women are mirroring the real degree of human rights protection, together with the prevention of violence against women, in each country.

Soft law has the role of a facilitator in the successful implementation of mandatory legal regulations in a particular area. This is especially applicable to national rules that follow internationally set up legal standards by international conventions. Soft law furthermore has the position of creating a consensus among member states of a concrete international organization on minimum common principles of future legislation. This was the case with Recommendation Rec (2002)5 of the Committee of Ministers of the Council of Europe (CoE) to member states on the protection of women against violence (2002), which was the predecessor of the CoE Istanbul Convention (2014) on preventing and combating violence against women and domestic violence. For assessing the effectiveness of soft law, its transparency is important, and monitoring and appropriate supervision of its implementation are especially valuable. The GREVIO monitoring body of the CoE Istanbul Convention is composed of fifteen independent experts with the task of closely report on the implementation of the Istanbul Convention at the national level in countries that are signatories to the Convention. Since these GREVIO experts have produced relevant reports on the state of play in several countries, it is a good example of achieving the effectiveness of soft law in the field of prevention and combating violence against women.

NOTES

1. Famous Montenegrin jurist, the author of the Montenegrin civil code of 1888. In 1902 Bogišić was elected president of the International Institute of Sociology in Paris, France.
2. R. Vasić, M. Jovanović, and G. Dajović, *Introduction to Law*, Law Faculty of the University Belgrade, Serbia, 2015, 4.
3. K. Čavoški, R. Vasić, *Introduction to Law*, Law Faculty of the University Belgrade, Serbia, Službeni glasnik, Belgrade, 2006, 21.
4. W. H. Evander, "A Definition of Law," *Virginia Law Review,* 12/1926, 203–214.
5. Latin formula *Pacta sunt servanda* "Agreements must be kept" is arguably the oldest principle of international law. Without such a rule, no international agreement would be binding or enforceable. *Pacta sunt servanda* is directly referred to in many international agreements governing treaties, including the Vienna Convention on the Law of Treaties (1969, entered into force in 1980, United Nations, Treaty Series, vol. 1155, 331).
6. H. Wehberg, "Pacta Sunt Servanda," *The American Journal of International Law*, 4/1959, 775–786.
7. Vienna Convention on the Law of Treaties (1969, entered into force in 1980, United Nations, Treaty Series, vol. 1155, 331), Article 26.
8. M. C. Bassiouni, "International Crimes: '*Jus Cogens*' and '*Obligatio Erga* Omnes,'" *Law and Contemporary Problems*, 4/1996, 68.
9. N. V. Álvaro, "Five Models of Legal Science," *Revus. Journal for Constitutional Theory and Philosophy of Law,* 19/2013, 53–81.
10. C. Morris, "Law: The Art of Justice," *Beaux Arts Editions*, 1992; Adolf Berger, "Encyclopedic Dictionary of Roman Law," (vol. 43, part 2). American Philosophical Society, 1953, 525.
11. R. Vasić, M. Jovanović, G. Dajović, "Introduction to Law," 18.
12. Ibid., 16.
13. D. Mitrović, *On Law: Selected Essays*, Law Faculty of the University of Belgrade, Dosije Studio, Belgrade, 2017, 87.
14. Ibid., 95–98.
15. C. B. Ivaylova, "Legal Security as a Principle in Lawmaking," *Globalization, the State and the Individual*, 2/2017, 24.
16. *Nulla poena sine lege, a* Latin proverb for "No penalty without law."
17. F. Snyder, "Soft Law and Institutional Practice in the European Community," *The Construction of Europe* (ed. S. Martin), Kluwer Academic Publishers, 1993.
18. D. Djurdjev, "Soft law u evropskom komunitarnom pravu," *Zbornik radova Pravnog fakulteta u Novom Sadu*, 1/2013, 101–116.

19. J. B. Skjærseth, O. S. Stokke, J. Wettestad, "Soft Law, Hard Law, and Effective Implementation of International Environmental Norms," *Global Environmental Politics,* 3/2006, 104.

20. A. T. Guzman, "The Design of International Agreements," *European Journal of International Law,* 4/2005, 583, 610.

21. A. Peters, I. Pagotto, "Soft Law as a New Mode of Governance: A Legal Perspective," NEWGOV: New Modes of Governance, Ref. No. 04/D11, University of Basel, 2006, 22–24.

22. G. Shaffer, M. A. Pollack, "Hard and Soft Law, Interdisciplinary Perspectives on International Law and International Relations," *The State of the Art* (eds. Jeffrey D. Lunoff, M. A. Pollack), Cambridge University Press, Cambridge, 2013, 198–199.

23. C. Lipson, "Why are Some International Agreements Informal?," *International Law and International Relations* (eds. B. A. Simmons, Richard H. Steinberg), Cambridge University Press, Cambridge, 2006, 305–306.

24. https://www.law.cornell.edu/wex/positive_law, 26.02.2024.

25. H. Kelsen, *The Pure Theory of Law*, Faculty of Law, University of Belgrade, 2007, 22.

26. In more detail: G. Gasmi, "Quo Vadis *EU—Relevant Legal and Institutional Factors"* Institute of Comparative Law, Belgrade, 2016, 95–97.

27. A. Diligenski, D. Prlja, D. Cerović, *The Right to Data Protection GDPR*, Institute of Comparative Law, Belgrade, 2018, 11.

28. S. Andonović, D. Prlja, "Basics of the Right to Protection of Personal Data" Institute of Comparative Law, Belgrade, 2020, 198.

29. The term natural law is derived from the Roman term *ius naturale.*

30. https://www.law.cornell.edu/wex/natural_law, 26.02.2024.

31. https://legal-dictionary.thefreedictionary.com/natural+law, 29.02.2024.

32. S. Perović, *Speeches from Kopaonik*, Belgrade, 2018, 895–930.

33. B. Reinhard, *Professional Dictionary of Politics*, Kröner, Stuttgart, 1986, 637.

34. S. Perović, *Speeches from Kopaonik,* 910.

35. Ibid., 931–959.

36. K. Bergbohm, *Jurisprudence and the Philosophy of Law*, 1892, 53.

37. Somló, Felix, *Juristische Grundlehre* (2nd edn), Meiner, 1927, 23.

38. G. Radbruch, *Philosophy of Law*, Harvard University Press, 1950, 18.

Chapter 2

Notion of Human Rights

Hominem causa omne ius constitutum est.[1]

Hermogenianus

THE ESSENCE AND EVOLUTION OF HUMAN RIGHTS

The origin of human rights stems from the theory of natural law. Human rights as natural rights are acquired by every human being by birth. Human rights apply equally to all people, regardless of race, sex, language, religion, economic condition, education, political, and other opinion, in any circumstances. Regardless of the diversity among societies and people, human rights form the thread that connects them. They represent universal values, which are common to all.[2]

The rights that every human being has, by virtue of being a human being, independent of the state and without the state, are human rights.[3] They belong to all human beings without any distinction and are based on values which modern humanity acknowledges to all human beings.[4] Consequently, human rights are a set of inalienable rights and freedoms of individuals.[5] Namely, human rights are not merits or rewards, so they are not given away or taken away but belong to all persons based on the fact of their existence. At the core of the concept of human rights is the aspiration for the protection of human dignity. It puts the personality of the man at the center of attention and is based on a shared general value system.[6]

Certain groups of people such as women, children, foreigners, stateless persons, and refugees are protected by special international acts (e.g., the UN Convention on the Rights of the Child, the UN Convention on the Elimination of All Forms of Discrimination against Women, the UN Convention on the Rights of Persons with Disabilities). However, this does not jeopardize the principle of universality of human rights, but rather provides more efficient and precise protection of particularly sensitive groups, which represents an affirmative approach to the human rights of vulnerable populations.

Holistic approach assumes that human rights are indivisible and interdependent, which means that groups of human rights have equal importance. Furthermore, individual rights cannot be realized without the simultaneous realization of some other rights (e.g., without the right to freedom of movement, it will be difficult to realize the right to participate in cultural life of the community; without the right to freedom of opinion, it will be difficult to realize the right to freedom of religion).

The idea of human rights has its roots in ancient Greek philosophy and religion: all people are equal before God. The development of this idea can be divided into three steps:

Step 1: Philosophical roots (universal law);
Step 2: Political realization within nation-states;
Step 3: Political realization within universal law in the United Nations (UN).

In ancient Greek philosophy, therefore, more than 2000 years ago, the idea of the equality of all people, the idea of natural rights that belong to every person, was developed. However, slaves did not enjoy human rights but were considered as "belongings that can speak." Afterwards, in Roman law, the idea of protection against tyranny was taken, but only for free people, which was the seed of further theories in the seventeenth century. H. Grotius (1583–1645) and Thomas Hobbes (1588–1679) developed ideas about natural rights for human beings. The tradition of natural law saw its further development in early Christianity and other religions: God created all men equal in his own image. These two threads: Greek philosophy and the natural law concept, form the root of the idea of human rights. Therefore, many authors define human rights as being the specific form of natural rights. The essence of human rights is not positivism, but moral origin.[7] It was about philosophical observations that required universal law but which were transferred to the world of politics and law gradually.

The central importance of this belongs to the modern philosophy of natural law, and above all, to the English philosopher John Locke. His work marked a decisive spiritual breakthrough of the idea of inalienable human rights: "The State of Nature has a Law of Nature to govern it, which obliges everyone: and Reason, which is that Law, teaches all Mankind, who will but consult it, that being all equal and independent, no one ought to harm another in his Life, Health, Liberty and Possessions." Life, health, liberty, and private property are, for John Locke, the unchangeable innate rights of man. The purpose of every state is to protect these natural human rights. Therefore, with his political philosophy, he obliges the state to protect human rights and thereby takes a decisive step from the abstract idea of human rights to its concrete realization within the state. These ideas were accepted by the constitutional makers in England and the United States of America and have been incorporated into their constitutions.

Political realization of human rights was within nation-states where England played a leading role in this development. Already in 1215, with the *Magna Carta Libertatum*, certain rights were extorted from the king, the "Petition of Right" document from 1628 guaranteed the inviolability of the citizen, and the *Habeas Corpus Act* from 1679 was a decisive turning point for establishing the idea of human rights in concrete state law. With that act, the citizen was protected from arbitrary arrest. The arrested person had to be brought before a judge within twenty days.

These rights were also valid in the English colonies, therefore, also in the United States of America. In the midst of the struggle for independence, the Catalog of Human Rights was formulated there for the first time in history, referring directly to the ideas of John Locke, that is, "Virginia Bill of Rights" from 1776, a document that, along with the American Declaration of Independence from the same year, is one of the most important documents in the history of human rights.

The "Virginia Bill of Rights" (1776) declared the following rights as inalienable human rights, and since then they have formed the core of human rights:

- Right to life, liberty, and private property,
- Freedom of assembly and freedom of the press,
- Freedom of movement and the right to petition,
- The right to legal protection,
- The right to vote.

The constitutional legal realization of the idea of human rights started with a great rush from France to continental Europe. The French Revolution of 1789, with its slogan: *liberté, égalité, fraternité* had an extraordinary impact, and on August 26, 1789, the "Charter of Human and Civil Rights" was accepted. The Charter marked an attempt to ensure the meaning of fundamental rights in individual national constitutions for human rights, which happened in almost all European countries during the nineteenth century. The political and legal realization of the philosophical idea of human rights was largely successful until the middle of the twentieth century. Nonetheless, during the eighteenth century and later, human rights were requested only for men with property and against the aristocracy, but women, poor people, and black population also started to fight for an equal level of human rights protection.[8]

Subsequently, the following problem arose: human rights require universal validity; however, the binding guarantee for them as fundamental rights was limited to the narrow framework of nation-states. This contradiction was resolved by an attempt at universal political and legal realization of human rights within the United Nations (UN). First of all, the terrible war crimes during the Second World War encouraged people to think about how to ensure the validity of human rights around the world. What happened in wars should not happen again. All people in the world should have basic rights and freedoms. It was one of the most important drivers for the establishment of the United Nations. By the conclusion of all states, human rights were no longer a matter of individual states but became a matter of the international community of states. This is contained in a contract between the states, in the so-called Charter of the UN, which was adopted on June 26, 1945. The UN Charter states that all member states undertake to cooperate with the Organization together and individually in terms of implementing the Organization's goals (Article 56), and these goals include the protection of human rights. By virtue of this article, every member state of the United Nations, which today are almost all the countries of the world, undertakes to respect human rights.

In order to make it clear what exactly human rights are, the Universal Declaration of Human Rights was drafted, which was adopted on December 10, 1948. Therefore, each 10th December is the International Day of Human Rights. The Universal Declaration presents a list of human rights, which can be divided into several groups. The UN Universal Declaration of Human Rights marks the beginning of attempts at universal political and legal implementation of human rights. It aims to abolish the contradiction between the universal scope and demand on the one side, and the national meaning and implementation of human rights on the other.

The UN Universal Declaration was followed on November 4, 1950, by the European Convention on Human Rights drafted within the Council of Europe (CoE) at the regional level. The Convention for the Protection of Human Rights and Fundamental Freedoms, better known as the European Convention on Human Rights, was signed in Rome (Italy) on November 4, 1950, by twelve member states of the Council of Europe and entered into force on September 3, 1953.[9] European Convention was the first instrument to give effect and binding force to certain of the rights stated in the Universal Declaration of Human Rights. It was also the first treaty to establish a supranational organ to ensure that the States Parties fulfilled their undertakings. The Convention was a milestone in the development of international law. Once states had accepted that a supranational court could challenge decisions taken by their own courts, human rights *de facto* and *de iure* gained precedence over national legislation and practice. Any individual, group of individuals, company, or non-governmental organization can apply to the Strasbourg Court (European Court for Human Rights), provided that they have exhausted all domestic remedies. Furthermore, in order to join the Council of Europe, a State must first sign and ratify the European Convention on Human Rights, thus confirming its commitments to the aims of the Organization, namely the achievement of greater unity between its members based on human rights and fundamental freedoms, peace, and respect for democracy and the rule of law.[10]

Europe is not the only continent to have a court protecting human rights. There are two other regional courts: the Inter-American Court of Human Rights and the African Court on Human and Peoples' Rights. In 2008, to mark the sixtieth anniversary of the Universal Declaration of Human Rights, the three regional courts met together at a seminar in Strasbourg. On that occasion, in his address, Jean-Paul Costa, President of the European Court of Human Rights, said: "Is there a better way to show the universal scope of human rights?"[11]

At global level, the principles from the UN Universal Declaration of Human Rights became legally binding only in 1966, that is 1976, when the International Covenant on Civil and Political Rights and the International Covenant on Economic, Social and Cultural Rights entered into force, which took over and elaborated the human rights standards from the Universal Declaration.

Further chronology of relevant documents on human rights:

- November 22, 1969, American Convention on Human Rights;
- August 1, 1975, Final Act from Helsinki;
- June 27, 1981, Banjul Charter on Human and Peoples' Rights (Africa);
- September 19, 1981, General Declaration on Human Rights in Islam;
- June 14, 1992, Rio Declaration on Development and Environmental Protection; and
- June 1993, World Conference on Human Rights (Vienna).

Human rights change and adapt. The scientific researcher of the preconditions of war and peace, Johan Galtung, found a beautiful metaphor for this process:

> "Perhaps a metaphor is helpful here." On December 10, 1948, the Universal Declaration of Human Rights, born by the full United Nations Assembly, saw the light of day. The result reflects the Jewish-Christian culture, including the tendency of that culture to see itself as universal. Let's take this as one stop on a long and possibly endless bus ride. There are other such stops. New passengers get on. There is a dialogue on the bus. Maybe some passengers get off. There

> are even more such stops and new charters (declaration), where these each time reflect a deeper and wider dialogue of civilizations. Each culture gives something. Each culture is grateful because others have contributed something. Each culture feels: "If you take something from me, I will behave accordingly." And as the journey continues, we all achieve success composed of sincere universality. Of one universality as one process that will never stop, and that encompasses all cultures.[12]

Human rights, on their dynamic development path, have ceased to exist as an internal matter of a state. The state has, to some extent, renounced its absolute sovereignty in favor of international obligations of human rights protection. The dynamism of human rights is also reflected in their constant expansion. In recent times, there is an accelerated tendency to increase their number, and the recognition of new rights is furthermore requested at the global level.

CATEGORIES AND TYPES OF HUMAN RIGHTS

Before categorization of human rights, it is necessary to make difference between objective and subjective rights. The set of all legal norms created by the legislative power in a state represents objective law. Subjective rights are the rights of legal subjects, both natural and legal persons. Human rights are subjective rights that are independent of the will of the state—they are above the state. Human rights are of moral origin, original, universal, and inalienable. They belong to all people without distinction. An essential characteristic of human rights is equality. All persons are equal in law. Every man has the right to human rights and freedoms only on the basis of their "being as a human being," regardless of his individual belonging to a nation, regardless of what he believes in and regardless of his gender. For this reason, human rights are inalienable, which means they are always valid and cannot be taken away from anyone. Their most important function is to protect the citizen from the state.

Human rights cover many different areas of human life. Therefore, it is necessary to divide them into several groups according to the chronology. The moment of their international recognition is taken as the criterion here:

- Group 1: Civil and political rights (first-generation rights)
- Group 2: Social, economic, and cultural rights (second generation rights),
- Group 3: Third-generation rights—collective solidarity rights.

First group of civil and political rights are based on the principle of liberty, proclaimed in the French revolution of 1789 (*liberté*) with the aim of protection of human dignity. Consequently, the basic human right is the right to life, which is the foundation for all other human rights and freedoms. Civil rights are the core of human rights that are contained in all human rights conventions and related documents, primarily in the International Covenant on Civil and Political Rights (1966). Political rights are to guarantee to all people unhindered participation in political life within their community, without fear of being unduly punished for it. For example, freedom of thought and freedom of the press play an important rôle here, because they reflect people's attitudes toward their government and their satisfaction with it. However, if these views can no longer be expressed without censorship, then the government loses its right to democratically represent the interests of its citizens. Within political rights, the right to vote and to be voted for is important too, but it was applied very late for women in different parts of the world.[13]

Civil and political rights encompass:

- The right to life;
- Prohibition of torture, cruel and inhumane treatment, and punishments;
- The right to freedom and personal security;
- The right to a fair trial;
- The right to privacy;
- Freedom of thought, conscience, and religion;
- Freedom of speech;
- The right to peaceful assembly;
- Freedom of association;
- The right to vote and to be elected;
- The right to participate in the management of public affairs and equal access to public services;
- The right to marriage and the equality of spouses in marriage; and
- Child rights.

Second-generation rights are contained in the International Covenant on Economic, Social and Cultural Rights (1966), which obliges each state to provide for its citizens the right to work and fair compensation for work, the right to education, the right to social protection, and the right to realize cultural needs. Those human rights are highly dependent on economic conditions and the level of development of each state. The basic principle of those rights is solidarity.[14]

Social, economic, and cultural rights are:

- The right to work, limited working hours, fair compensation for work, and protection at work;
- The right to property;
- The right to social security;
- The right to strike;

- The right to health;
- The right to education; and
- The right to participate in cultural life.

Third-generation rights—collective solidarity rights, were defined in the twentieth century. The 1972 United Nations (UN) Conference on the Human Environment declared that "man's environment, the natural and the man-made, are essential to his well-being and to the enjoyment of basic human rights—even the right to life itself."[15] This UN Declaration was the first international document on the issue of a clean environment. The first principle of the Stockholm Declaration clearly set the scene by recognizing that "man has the fundamental right to freedom, equality and adequate conditions of life, in an environment of a quality that permits a life of dignity and well-being, and he bears a solemn responsibility to protect and improve the environment for present and future generations."[16] UN Framework Convention on Climate Change (Framework Convention, May 9, 1992) and international agreements concluded in connection with it: the Kyoto Protocol (December 11, 1997) and the Paris Agreement (December 12, 2015) contain international standards for guarantees that the natural living spaces of man will not be too damaged or even completely destroyed.

The right to sustainable development should help reduce the gap between poverty and wealth in the world. Collective solidarity rights indicate permanent evolution of human rights categories due to new problems of contemporary human life that are to be addressed through the human rights protection system. Nonetheless, third-generation rights have been severely questioned from the point of view of the essence of human rights.

> Since the collapse of the communist regimes and the discrediting of the ideas of organization that they carried, the ideologically too harsh human rights controversies have also decreased. The idea of human rights in view of the diversity of world cultures. In the area of the first discussion, representatives of the southern hemisphere, as well as 'progressive' supporters of human rights from the north, try to insert so-called solidarity rights into the concept of human rights. This includes, first of all: the right to peace, the right to development and the right to a clean environment. Although these are honorable and important political goals, it remains debatable whether these collective goals can be considered an equally valuable category of legal requirements as individual political rights. Rights are, without exception, a reflection of collective conditions and condition political action, in which failure must also be taken into account. But for the philosophy of the idea of human rights, it has always been central the fact that human rights must be moral and legally sustainable rights of every individual, which must be fulfilled or maintained in every state.[17]

Collective human rights are:

- The right to peace;
- Rights of national, religious, or ethnic minorities;
- The right to sustainable development; and
- The right to a clean environment.

Challenging the universality of all categories of human rights is permanently present. One of the reasons is the fact that human rights arose from the philosophy of the Christian world. Another reason is the fact that since the signing of the Universal Declaration of Human Rights, dozens of new states have emerged as a result of liberation from the colonial yoke. Since 1946, approximately 120 new states have been created that did not participate in the formulation of the UN Charter. These countries did not participate in the creation of the UN Universal Declaration of Human Rights. Consequently, some of those states raised their voice. With a human rights controversy between the United States of America (USA) and Europe on one side and China and South Asia on the other, the 1997 Conference of the Association of South Asian Nations (ASEAN) in the capital of Malaysia, Kuala Lumpur, ended. The conflict developed after Malaysian minister President Mahathir's proposal to rewrite the United Nations Human Rights Declaration in favor of poor countries. The USA and the European Union decisively rejected Mahathir's request as unacceptable at the closing press conference. In contrast, the foreign ministers of Malaysia, Indonesia, and the Philippines have declared themselves in favor of an inspection. "Given the time that has passed, we should not be so categorical," said Indonesian foreign minister Altas. Malaysia's foreign minister said emphasizing individual rights to freedom is not appropriate in a multiracial and multi-religious third-world nation like Malaysia. "Too much freedom can destroy democracy"(. . .).[18]

Permanent discussions on the question of whether the claim of human rights to universal importance is justified because they originated in Christian Europe led to a movement that, in dialogue with all religions and cultures, elaborated common basic values for all people, one world ethos. The foundation of these efforts for values that would be recognized by all people is the comprehension that everywhere in the world, in all cultures and religions of all times, one maxim should be found that forms the core of all ethics, one so-called golden rule of human rights. All known ethics are based on it and it creates the basis for the legitimate action of individuals, groups, states, and communities of states. The golden rule says that we should treat others as we would like others to treat us. Therefore, human rights are universal and are to be implemented *erga omnes*.

WOMEN HUMAN RIGHTS

The General Assembly of the UN designated the Universal Declaration of Human Rights from 1948 as an ideal to which all peoples and nations should strive together (Preamble), which in the future (time after the Second World War) should become something self-evident. Today we must say that the world has clearly not come close to this ideal of 1948: the gap between the rich and the poor is growing; no universal right to education has been established; we are still fighting for women's equality; the number of unemployed and poor is growing even in prosperous societies; every day people die of hunger or of some other diseases, and among them are thousands of children; the right to asylum is still a big unresolved issue; wars still exist. All this is not happening anywhere, but in this "one world," in front of our own doors, in our countries. We are not observers, but—directly or indirectly—participants. In other words: the ideal set by the UN Universal Declaration of Human Rights remains one thing, but the reality is another.

Toward vulnerable groups of the population, the principle of affirmative measures is applied, that is, positive discrimination, with the aim of equalizing those persons in the exercise of their rights and providing additional guarantees for achieving their equality—affirmative approach. These are permitted exceptions to the application of the principle of absolute equality.

The concept of gender equality has evolved over the years. In the modern moment, the concept of equality includes equality before the law, in the form of formal equality (*de iure*), which is a means of achieving equality of rights, obligations, and responsibilities, that is, real, factual equality (*de facto*). The purpose of real equality is to go beyond the formal—legal, demanding social changes and the transformation of cultural and social norms. Hence, the mere existence of legal regulations is not enough, but it is a necessary tool, as it serves as a catalyst for social change and provides a legal basis for women's aspirations toward equality.

International principles of women's equality protection include legal regulation of the position of women on a double track.

1. Women's rights as part of basic human rights—general protection guaranteed by the following international legal documents:
   - UN Charter (1945),
   - UN Universal Declaration of Human Rights (1948),
   - International Covenant on Civil and Political Rights (1966), and
   - International Covenant on Economic, Social and Cultural Rights (1966).
2. Special rights of women. Special protection of women's rights is based on:

- development of general standards through specific obligations of states;
- includes areas in which discrimination against women is particularly pronounced (economic sphere, participation in public life, education, etc.);
- refers to situations in which special rights are provided to women compared to men.

Many international documents—conventions, recommendations, and declarations are dealing with the human rights of sensitive groups, *inter alia*, women's human rights. These are (by chronology):

- Convention on the Suppression of Trafficking in Human Beings and Exploitation of the Prostitution of Others (1949);
- Convention on Equal Remuneration of Male and Female Workforce for Work of Equal Value (1951);
- Convention on the Political Rights of Women (1952);
- Convention on the Citizenship of Married Woman (1957);
- Convention on Consent to Marriage, Minimum Age for Marriage and Registration of Marriages (1962);
- UN Declaration on the Abolition of Discrimination against Women (1967);
- UN Declaration on the Protection of Women and Children in Emergency Situations and Armed Conflicts (1974);
- UN Convention on the Elimination of All Forms of Discrimination Against Women (CEDAW, 1979) with its Optional Protocol (1999), and General Recommendations No. 12 (1989), No. 19 (1992) and No. 35 (2017) of the Committee on the Elimination of Discrimination against Women;
- United Nations General Assembly Declaration on the Elimination of Violence against Women (Resolution 48/104 of 1993);
- The Beijing Declaration and Platform for Action, the most progressive blueprint for advancing women's rights (1995); and
- UN Security Council Resolution 1325 on women, peace, and security.

There are furthermore regional legal documents on women's human rights:

- Inter-American Convention on the Prevention, Punishment, and eradication of Violence against Women (1994), adopted by the Organization of American States;
- Revised European Social Charter (Art. 8 on the right of working women to maternity protection, 1996);
- The Protocol to the African Charter on Human and Peoples' Rights on the Rights of Women in Africa (2003), adopted by the African Union;
- The CoE Recommendation Rec (2002) 5 of the Committee of Ministers to member states on the protection of women against violence (2002);

- The Council of Europe Convention on Action against Trafficking in Human Beings (CETS No. 197, 2005);
- The Council of Europe Convention on the Protection of Children against Sexual Exploitation and Sexual Abuse (CETS No. 201, 2007);
- The Council of Europe (CoE) Convention on preventing and combating violence against women and domestic violence (Istanbul Convention, 2014).

Many international organizations, agencies, and international non-governmental organizations deal with enhancing women's positions, such as: the Commission of the UN Economic and Social Council for the Legal Status of Women, UN Women, International Labor Organization (ILO), UNICEF, UNESCO, the World Health Organization (WHO), the UN Committee on the Elimination of Discrimination against Women, the Council of Europe, the European Union, Amnesty International, Human Rights Watch, and so on.

Throughout history, women's rights have survived the complete negation of their existence and then came the limitation of their rights to exclusively "female" roles, stemming from the "natural division" of work in the archival community, which arose from the biological features of women who were exclusively responsible for the expansion of the genus and tribe. In some ancient societies, this was reflected in the legal position of a woman, where her husband could send her away if she did not bear him children, with the obligation to return her dowry (sherikta, Hammurabi's Code, art. 138). Historical epochs record some positive examples. This is evidenced, for example, by the state of women's rights in the Mesopotamian states of Sumer and Babylon, where women enjoyed several legally guaranteed rights. Thus, they could own property, inherit, and work.[19] Furthermore, in ancient Rome, women were born as free citizens (*cives*), but they did not have the right to vote or perform political functions. Such a situation existed since the time of early Rome, which was a military democracy in which the most important decisions were made exclusively by adult men in curiat commissions—assemblies (*comitia curiata*).[20]

In recent times, the emergence of capitalism has brought new economic and political relations in society, but not a change in the subordinate position of women. The general socio-cultural milieu of a patriarchal-oriented society contributed to this. While the pre-capitalist subjugation of women was associated with socially insurmountable natural roles, with the advent of capitalism, these limitations of women's human rights were articulated through socially prescribed roles.[21] In a contemporary moment, women enjoy legally established equality in terms of formal equality, but not at a global level nor in practice.

Besides legal frameworks, the theoretical foundation for women's human rights was laid down by thoughts of the enlightenment philosophies of Montesquieu and Rousseau. However, although the concept of human rights was first mentioned in 1689 in the Bill of Rights in Great Britain, in 1776 in the Virginia Declaration of Rights, and then in the French revolutionary Declaration of Rights of man and citizen (*Déclaration des droits de l'homme et du citoyen*) in 1789, none of these documents regulate the basic legal position of women. The attempt of the French woman Olympe de Gouges to influence the direction of the French Revolution with her Declaration on the Rights of Women and Citizens (*Déclaration des droits de la femme et de la citoyenne*) in 1791, with the idea that women and men are equal in society and should have the same civil rights, ended with her arrest and execution of the death sentence, although not only because of the aforementioned reasons but also because of her overall political advocacy.[22] In modern theory, it is emphasized that the traditional division of labor by gender has remained unchanged and that this is the cause of distorted emancipation as its essential opposite.[23] In addition, conservative political populism also leads to stagnation or regression of achieved standards of gender equality and non-discrimination and the violation of women's rights.

Apart from the traditional understanding of the role of women, their position in society can further deteriorate during major social and economic changes. Women can be disproportionately more affected than men by the negative consequences of the structural adjustment of the economy and the operation of market laws: the loss of a job, loss of acquired rights and benefits from the previous period, an increase in the cost of living, unemployment and poverty, a decrease in wages and difficult access to health services, social protection, education, and resources.[24]

Female non-equality and discrimination at a global level remains despite positive developments in certain regions and states. Therefore, the UN General Assembly declared 1975 as the International Year of Women. Besides, the period 1976–1985 was proclaimed as the UN Decade devoted to women. In 1985, the World Conference was held in Nairobi to evaluate the achievements of the decade dedicated to women, when the Strategy for improving the position of women until the year 2000 was adopted. Despite this, the position of women in many parts of the world is still very unfavorable. International legal documents and national laws intended to guarantee gender equality are incomplete. They do not address the issue of women's discrimination at home. Tasks and duties' division within home, which puts almost exclusive responsibility on women's shoulders, brings a huge burden for women. That is why women are limited in full and free participation in social, economic, and political life. Without a solution to this problem, improvement of women's life conditions will be delayed in a long-term, despite significant legal reforms.

Within the Council of Europe, a turning point in its work began in 1988, when gender equality was no longer seen as a legal or social issue, but as a human rights principle and a fundamental criterion of democracy.[25]

In the context of women's human rights, special attention has been dedicated to the protection of maternity, ever since 1919, when the Convention No. 3 on the protection of maternity was adopted within the International Labor Organization. In more recent periods, this protection is provided in the International Covenant on Economic, Social and Cultural Rights (Art.10, par. 2, 1966): "Special protection should be accorded to mothers during a reasonable period before and after childbirth. During such period working mothers should be accorded paid leave or leave with adequate social security benefits."[26] Additionally, the Revised European Social Charter (1996) provides for the rights of employed women to protect maternity (Art.8).

NOTES

1. "All legislation was created for the sake of a man." Hermogenianus, the author of the Codex Hermogenianus.
2. M. M. Grahovac, *Human Rights*, Faculty of Law for Economy and Justice, Novi Sad, 2020, 11.
3. V. Dimitrijević, M. Paunović, *Human Rights*, Belgrade Center for Human Rights, Belgrade, 1997, 26.
4. M. Paunović, B. Krivokapić, I. Krstić, *International Human Rights*, University in Belgrade, Law Faculty, Belgrade, 2021, 23.
5. D. Prlja, G. Gasmi, V. Korać, *Human Rights and Artificial Intelligence*, Institute of Comparative Law, Belgrade, 2022, 19, S. Gajin, *Human Rights: Legal—Systemic Framework*, Law Faculty, University Union, Belgrade, 2011, 15.
6. W. Benedek, M. Nikolova, *Understanding Human Rights*, European Center for Training and Research on Human Rights and Democracy, Graz, 2003, 18.
7. M. Paunović, B. Krivokapić, I. Krstić, *International Human Rights*, 22.
8. Ibid., 25.
9. Founded in 1949 by 10 states, the Council of Europe (CoE) is an international organization with its headquarters in Strasbourg (France). Today it has 46 member states, representing 700 million people. Official website: https://www.coe.int/en/web/portal/.
10. https://www.coe.int/en/web/human-rights-convention/the-convention-in-1950, 04.03.2023.
11. Council of Europe, *Rights and Freedoms in Practice*, July 2013.
12. J. Galtung, *Human Rights—Viewed Differently*, Frankfurt/Main, 1994, 230.
13. For example, in Switzerland, women are afforded with the right to vote in 1971.

14. M. Paunović, B. Krivokapić, I. Krstić, *International Human Rights,* 27.

15. Declaration of the United Nations Conference on the Human Environment, June 16, 1972, Stockholm (A/CONF.48/14/Rev.1).

16. Ibid.

17. L. Kühnhardt, "Human Rights, Protection of Minorities and the Nation-state in the KSZE Process" *From Politics and Recent History*, 47/1994, 13.

18. Frankfurter Allgemeine Zeitung, published on July 30, 1997.

19. S. N. Kramer, *The Sumerians: Their History, Culture, and Character*, University of Chicago Press, Chicago, 1963, Hammurabi's Code, art. 39, 78.

20. N. A. Maškin, *Istorija starog Rima (The history of ancient Rome)*, Belgrade, Naučna knjiga, 1987, 79., D. Stojčević, *Rimsko privatno pravo (Roman Private Law)*, Belgrade, Naučna knjiga, 1985, 19.

21. A. Y. Davis, "Women and Capitalism: Dialectics of Oppresion and Liberation," *The Black Feminist Reader* (eds. J. James and D. Sharpley-Whiting), Oxford, John Wiley and Sons Ltd., 2000, 157.

22. M. Beauchamps, "Olympe de Gouges's Trial and the Affective Politics of Denaturalization in France," *Citizenship Studies*, 8/2016, 943–956.

23. Z. Uhde, "From Women's Struggles to Distorted Emancipation," *International Feminist Journal of Politics*, 3/2016, 401.

24. M. Dokmanović, "Women and Economic Changes 2000–2005," *Journal for Political Theory and Research on Globalization, Development and Gender Issues*, 2006, https://cdn.atria.nl/ezines/web/Globalizacija.com/2006/November.pdf, 15.09.2023.

25. Council of Europe, "Make Equality in Law a Reality in Fact—Compilation of Recommendations of the Committee of Ministers in the Field of Equality Between Women and Men," Directorate of Communication (F-67075 Strasbourg Cedex), 2011, 5.

26. https://www.ohchr.org/en/instruments-mechanisms/instruments/international-covenant-economic-social-and-cultural-rights, 28.03.2024.

Chapter 3

Relevant Universal International Legal Documents on Violence to Women

Male nostro iure uti non debemus.

(*Gai 1,53*)[1]

IN MEDIAS RES[2]

Violence against women and girls persists as a global pandemic—one in three women is subjected to physical and/or sexual violence at least once in their lifetime.[3] It is exacerbated by COVID-19: 45 percent of women reported that they or a woman they know experienced violence since COVID-19, and six in ten women said sexual harassment in public worsened. Gender inequality and social tolerance toward violence against women are root causes of violence against women, as well as weak legal sanctions and unreported cases.

Online violence against women and girls occurs on a continuum and can take many forms, including sexual harassment, cyberstalking, zoom bombing, intimate image abuse, and misogynistic hate speech, among others. Online and ICT-facilitated violence against women and girls also escalated in the shadows of the pandemic as women and girls' lives shifted online for work, school, access to services, and social activities.[4] Findings of one global research show that 38 percent of women have personal experiences of online violence and 85 percent of women who are online have witnessed digital violence against other women.[5] Online violence against women and girls can be as harmful as offline violence, with serious impacts on health and well-being, as well as with serious economic, social, and political impacts as it affects women's professional lives.[6] Groups of women that are at greater risk of violence are:

- women in public life,
- women human rights defenders,
- young women and girls,
- indigenous women,
- migrant and ethnic minority women,
- lesbian, bisexual, and transgender women and
- women with disabilities.

International organizations with mandate to combat violence against women, besides The Committee on the Elimination of Discrimination against Women—CEDAW and the Commission on the Status of Women, include UN Women.[7] UN Women, as a global champion for gender equality, works with UN Member States on the harmonization of international standards for gender equality and assists them in their application. One of the scopes of work that this organization deals with is a question of eliminating discrimination and violence against women and girls. The creation of UN Women came about as part of the UN reform agenda, bringing together resources and mandates for greater impact. It merges and builds on the important work of four previously distinct parts of the UN system, which focused exclusively on gender equality and women's empowerment:

- Division for the Advancement of Women (DAW);
- International Research and Training Institute for the Advancement of Women (INSTRAW);
- Office of the Special Adviser on Gender Issues and Advancement of Women (OSAGI); and
- United Nations Development Fund for Women (UNIFEM).[8]

The United Nations Population Fund—UNFPA[9] is the UN sexual and reproductive health agency with the mission to deliver a world where every pregnancy is wanted, every childbirth is safe, and every young person's potential is fulfilled. In addition to promoting the rights of women and girls to live free of violence, its programs offer psychosocial support, medical treatment, and assistance to survivors of rape, as well as elimination of female genital mutilation. UNFPA, jointly with UNICEF, leads the Joint Programme on the Elimination of Female Genital Mutilation (FGM), the largest global program to accelerate the abandonment of this harmful practice. The program currently focuses on seventeen countries and also supports regional and global initiatives. An estimated 68 million girls are at risk of being mutilated by 2030.[10]

The World Health Organization (WHO), as a special entity within the UN system that works as a coordination body of international public health, is also an important actor since it has been involved in the monitoring of, providing information and programs on the health aspects of violence against women. Violence against women is preventable. The health sector has an important role to play in providing comprehensive health care to women subjected to violence and as an entry point for referring women to other support services they may need. Over a quarter of women aged fifteen to forty-nine years who have been in a relationship have been subjected to physical and/or sexual violence by their intimate partner at least once in their lifetime (since age fifteen). The prevalence estimates of lifetime intimate partner violence range from 20 percent in the Western Pacific, 22 percent in high-income countries and Europe, and 25 percent in the WHO Regions of the Americas to 33 percent in the WHO African region, 31 percent in the WHO Eastern Mediterranean region, and 33 percent in the WHO South-East Asia region. Globally, as many as 38 percent of all murders of women are committed by intimate partners. In addition to intimate partner violence, globally 6 percent of women report having been sexually assaulted by someone other than a partner, although data for non-partner sexual violence are more limited. Intimate partner and sexual violence are mostly perpetrated by men against women. Lockdowns during the COVID-19 pandemic and its social and economic impacts have increased the exposure of women to abusive partners and known risk factors while limiting their access to services.[11]

Report of the UN Secretary General of 2022 on "Intensification of Efforts to Eliminate all Forms of Violence against Women and Girls" recommends to States to:

- "Recognize violence against women and girls (VAWG) in digital contexts as a human rights violation and to introduce effective laws, policies and regulatory frameworks in line with existing international human rights instruments to criminalize and prohibit all forms of violence in digital contexts and strengthen capacities of law enforcement agencies to investigate and prosecute crimes effectively.
- Continue to intensify efforts to eliminate all forms of VAWG (including in digital contexts) through the implementation and enforcement of comprehensive laws and budgeted national action plans; evidence-based, whole-of-government prevention strategies; increase access to high-quality, specialized multisector services including access to justice and reparations and greater accountability of perpetrators.

- Address the impacts of COVID on violence against women and girls including the economic fallout as well as the impact of climate change and environmental degradation, conflict and crises.
- Increase cooperation with the technology sector, women's rights organizations, civil society and national human rights institutions to ensure that technology companies and intermediaries strengthen policies and measures to prevent and respond to violence against women and girls in digital contexts; to provide fast and effective responses and remedies to violence when it occurs; as well as to ensure transparency reporting from technology intermediaries on the nature and extent of the problem, and the actions taken in response.
- Ensure flexible funding is available for civil society and women's rights organizations so that they can inform decisiondecision-making and policy on VAWG and play a lead role in implementing effective prevention and response measures.
- Continue to address data gaps and regularly collect data on VAWG as well as to invest in evidence and knowledge of what works in eliminating VAWG including in digital contexts."[12]

Furthermore, this report defines that UN agencies will:

- Ensure VAWG in digital contexts is addressed under the Common Agenda and Global Digital Compact to be agreed at the Summit of the Future in September 2023.
- Strengthen cooperation between states, the technology sector and CSOs to effectively address VAWG through key partnerships such as the Action Coalition on GBV, Action Coalition on Technology and Innovation and the US led Global Partnership for Action on Gender-Based Online Harassment and Abuse.
- Convene partners to develop international standards and framework for preventing and responding to VAWG in digital contexts, including standardized definitions, legal standards, roles and responsibilities, standards of accountability for internet intermediaries and technology sector; internationally agreed standards and methodologies for measuring VAWG to address data and evidence gaps.[13]

Many cases of violence remain unreported[14] and that is the reason for the high level of impunity. When it comes to criminal proceedings, the impunity rate is rather high in most countries. The UN established the International Day for the Elimination of Violence against Women on November 25, and more than 1,700 organizations in more than 100 countries around the world start the "16 Days of Activism" campaign on this day.[15] This fact speaks for itself on the global character of gender-based violence against women. Women often suffer violence out of fear of abusers or condemnation of the surroundings in which they live, and often because they are economically dependent on the person who abuses them.[16] Harmful social norms and stereotypes across cultures and social classes are the root of gender-based violence that affects all societies with enormous cost for victims, their families, and economies.[17]

DISCRIMINATION HAS WOMAN'S FACE—UN CONVENTION ON THE ELIMINATION OF ALL FORMS OF DISCRIMINATION AGAINST WOMEN (CEDAW)

CEDAW Convention and CEDAW Committee

UN Convention on the Elimination of All Forms of Discrimination Against Women (CEDAW Convention, 1979) with its Optional Protocol (1999), and General Recommendations No. 12 (1989), No. 19 (1992), and No. 35 (2017) of the Committee on the Elimination of Discrimination against Women mark a starting point in the international legal regulation of combating discrimination against women. The CEDAW Convention is the result of work of the Commission of the UN Economic and Social Council for the Status of Women (established in 1946) and decades of efforts by feminist organizations at the international level. These are the reasons to consider the CEDAW Convention as the Charter of women's human rights, because it proclaims the equality of women *de jure* and *de facto*. The CEDAW Convention legally binds signatory countries to end all forms of discrimination against women in public and private life, including within the family, and aims to achieve substantive equality between women and men—not just in laws but also in reality. In 2010, UN Women became the first UN agency to advocate exclusively for women's rights.

The basis of the Convention was the Declaration on the Elimination of Discrimination against Women, adopted by the UN General Assembly in 1967. The CEDAW Convention was adopted at the session of the UN General Assembly on December 18, 1979, and opened for the ratification process. The UN Convention on the Elimination of All Forms of Discrimination Against Women (CEDAW) entered into force on September 3, 1981, after it had been ratified by 20 member states and has 198 signatory countries (90 percent of the members of the United Nations, UN).

> As a matter of fact, the effort to secure the US Senate's support has been stalled at the committee level: the issue of American ratification of CEDAW has never made it pass the Senate Foreign Relations Committee, where it has been stuck since 1980. One core argument by conservatives and Republicans in opposing CEDAW ratification has been the fear that America's exceptionalism was threatened by an international treaty such as CEDAW superseding American federal and state laws and thus relinquishing US sovereignty to the international community.[18]

U.S. president Jimmy Carter signed the Convention on July 17, 1980, but the United States has never ratified it. The U.S. president has the power to make treaties, but the "advice and consent" of the United States Senate is needed before a treaty can be ratified. In the U.S. Senate a two-thirds supermajority is needed, meaning 67 Senators in favor. This has been a huge obstacle to overcome in the U.S. legislative body for the past four decades.

CEDAW Convention is enforced through two mechanisms:

(1) Reporting, including state reports to the CEDAW Committee every four years and the CEDAW Committee's Concluding Observations with recommendations to concrete countries on the basis of national reports (official reports by the government and shadow reports by relevant NGOs).
(2) the Optional Protocol (1999), which is an avenue for individuals, groups, and the CEDAW Committee to arbitrate state compliance with the Convention provisions. Many signatory countries, however, have made reservations on certain provisions of this Convention, thereby partially limiting its mandatory application in their countries. Sixty-one states have made reservations to CEDAW, which have included Article 2, which condemns all forms of discrimination; Article 9 on equal nationality rights; Article 15 on equality before the law; and Article 16 on equality in family life. The high number of reservations demonstrate that States Parties have varying levels of commitment to the principles of CEDAW, undermining its ability to push progress in key areas, including violence against women. [19]

The guiding idea of the CEDAW Convention is the legal embodiment of affirmative measures, that is, affirmative actions of the state toward women as a category of the vulnerable population subjected very often to various forms of discrimination. Affirmative actions or preferential treatment are to be implemented in order to eliminate discrimination and thus bring women into equality with other categories of the population in their enjoyment of civil, political, economic, and cultural rights. Consequently, without those specific positive measures, women will be in an unfavorable and unequal position. These are the arguments that legitimize and justify affirmative actions toward women. Article 4 of the Convention is formulated in that spirit:

"1. Adoption by States Parties of temporary special measures aimed at accelerating *de facto* equality between men and women shall not be considered discrimination as defined in the present Convention, but shall in no way entail as a consequence the maintenance of unequal or separate standards; these measures shall be discontinued when the objectives of equality of opportunity and treatment have been achieved.
2. Adoption by States Parties of special measures, including those measures contained in the present Convention, aimed at protecting maternity shall not be considered discriminatory."[20]

The definition of discrimination in the Convention is widened; besides direct discrimination, it encompassed furthermore indirect discrimination. Consisting of a Preamble and thirty articles, the Convention defines discrimination against women as:

> any distinction, exclusion or restriction made on the basis of sex which has the effect or purpose of impairing or nullifying the recognition, enjoyment or exercise by women, irrespective of their marital status, on a basis of equality of men and women, of human rights and fundamental freedoms in the political, economic, social, cultural, civil or any other field. (Art. 1)[21]

The CEDAW Convention establishes a Committee to monitor the implementation of the Convention—"the CEDAW Committee (Art. 17)," consisting of twenty-three experts of high moral standing and competence in the field covered by the Convention. Elected by State Parties, experts serve in their personal capacity, while consideration is given to equitable geographical distribution and to the representation of the different forms of civilization as well as the principal legal systems. A total of 151 experts have served as members of the Committee since 1982. The persons elected to the Committee are those nominees who obtained the largest number of votes and an absolute majority of the votes of the representatives of States Parties present and voting. The members of the CEDAW Committee (on the Elimination of Discrimination against Women) are elected for a term of four years.[22]

The Convention establishes not only an international bill of rights for women, but it is also an agenda for action by countries to guarantee the enjoyment of those rights.[23] The female half of humanity is prevented from the equal enjoyment of their civil rights, such as the right to vote and to be elected, to hold public office, and to exercise public functions, including the right for women to represent their countries at the international level. Therefore, the Convention requires from the State Parties to eliminate discrimination toward women in those areas (Art.7, 8). Women's rights to non-discrimination in education, employment, and economic and social activities are elaborated in articles 10, 11, and 13, respectively.

The full equality of women in civil and business matters, demanding that all instruments directed at restricting women's legal capacity "shall be deemed null and void," is guaranteed in Article 15. The Convention asserts the equal rights and obligations of women and men with regard to choice of spouse, parenthood, personal rights, and command over property (Art. 16). Special attention is devoted to women's reproductive rights, proclaiming in the Preamble that "the role of women in procreation should not be a basis for discrimination but that the upbringing of children requires a sharing of responsibility between men and women and society as a whole."[24]

The extraordinary civilizational achievement of the Convention lies in the fact that it recognizes the negative influence of culture and some outdated patterns of tradition resulting in restricting women's enjoyment of their fundamental rights. Countries signatories are therefore obliged to eliminate negative gender stereotypes, customs, and norms that give rise to a multitude of legal, political, and economic constraints on the advancement of women, in order to eliminate "prejudices and customary and all other practices which are based on the idea of the inferiority or the superiority of either of the sexes or on stereotyped roles for men and women" (Art. 5). The Convention (Art. 10, par. c) asks for the revision of textbooks, school programs, and teaching methods with a view to eliminating stereotyped concepts in the field of education.

Each country that is a signatory to the Convention decides how best to achieve its implementation. The CEDAW Committee—the body that monitors States Parties' compliance with the CEDAW Convention—does not have direct jurisdiction over the implementation of the Convention but can only make recommendations to States Parties on the basis of periodical state reports. The recommendations of the CEDAW Committee highlight areas where the situation in a particular country needs to be improved. Countries that ratify the Convention agree to take all appropriate measures to implement its provisions. Countries that ratify the Convention submit a national report on its implementation one year after ratification, and then every four years. The CEDAW Committee reviews each report and comments on the progress of the specific country in the form of recommendations.

The CEDAW Convention requires States signatories (Art. 2, 3) to undertake obligations and appropriate measures to eliminate discrimination against women in all areas of life, both public and private. Article 2 defines the measures that states should take to eliminate discrimination against women, including reforms at the constitutional, political, and legal levels, as well as monitoring and sanctioning to eliminate discrimination against women by any person, organization, or company. Along with laws and regulations, states must change practices and customs that place women in discriminatory positions. Not only to adopt laws, but the state should also promote equality, launch campaigns in the media and change educational programs. The obligations of the states are as follows:

- Abolition of discriminatory regulations;
- Harmonization of the legislation with the provisions of the Convention;
- The adoption of new laws and the undertaking of specific public policy measures to promote the equality of women.

The CEDAW Committee indicated that the existing international mechanisms for the implementation of the CEDAW Convention are insufficient and weak. The UN system did not contain procedures that would allow individuals or groups to complain about violations of women's human rights. Therefore, the recommendation of the CEDAW Committee was sent to the UN Commission for the Advancement of the Status of Women to prepare an Optional Protocol to the Convention (1999), which would enable an appeal procedure before the Committee. The Optional Protocol entered into force on December 22, 2000. It has been adopted by over ninety countries.[25] By ratifying the Optional Protocol, a State Party recognizes the competence of the CEDAW Committee to receive and consider complaints from individuals or groups within its jurisdiction. Communications may be submitted by or on behalf of individuals or groups of individuals, under the jurisdiction of a State Party, claiming to be victims of a violation of any of the rights set forth in the Convention by that State Party (Art. 2). However, it is necessary for a State Party to the Convention to be a party to the Optional protocol too (Art. 3). Within six months, the receiving State Party shall submit to the CEDAW Committee written explanations or statements clarifying the matter and the remedy, if any, that may have been provided by that State Party (Art. 6).

Main features of an appeal procedure:

- Communication procedure is initiated by or on behalf of individuals or groups of individuals, in written form;
- It contains the claim that there has been a violation of rights set forth in the Convention;
- All internal legal remedies have been exhausted, unless the deadlines have been extended without reason or it is unlikely that the judgment will bring an effective resolution;

- The possibility of interim measures under urgent procedure to avoid possible irreparable damage to the victim (Art. 5).
- Investigative (inquiry) procedure: when there is a gross and systematic violation of the UN CEDAW Convention. Where warranted and with the consent of the State Party, the inquiry may include a visit to its territory (Art. 8). This procedure enables widespread violations to be investigated, where individuals or groups may be unable to make communications (for practical reasons or because of fear of reprisals). The inquiry procedure allows the Committee an opportunity to make recommendations regarding the structural causes of violations in a particular country.[26]

Relevant example of the inquiry procedure in practice represents the Report of the CEDAW Committee related to Mexico. At its thirty-first session in July 2004, the Committee on the Elimination of Discrimination against Women concluded an inquiry under Article 8 of the Optional Protocol to the Convention on the Elimination of All Forms of Discrimination against Women in regard to Mexico, which included a visit to the State Party's territory. The Committee included a procedural summary of the inquiry in its annual report (A/59/38, Part II, Chapter V.B). It decided to make public at a later date its findings and recommendations regarding the abduction, rape, and murder of women in the Ciudad Juarez area of Chihuahua, Mexico, as well as the observations received from the Government of Mexico thereon (2005).[27]

CEDAW Committee in this case made a general recommendation:

> Noting that the efforts recently made, although they represent a belated response to a problem that is ten years old, might put an end to the murders of women and to impunity, and help to prevent and eradicate all forms of violence and discrimination against women, the Committee is nevertheless concerned that not all actions and programs have clearly incorporated a gender perspective, that is, that consideration has not been given to the impact of such policies on women and men, bearing in mind their socially constructed roles and the power relations between them. Such a perspective is essential to the attainment of these objectives.[28]

Recommendations concerning the investigation of the crimes and punishment of the perpetrators in this case included, *inter alia*, the following:

> The Committee is alarmed at the fact that the murders of women are spreading to the capital of the state of Chihuahua and other cities of the Mexican Republic, and therefore makes the following recommendation: 286. Sensitize all state and municipal authorities to the need for violence against women to be regarded as a violation of fundamental rights, in order to conduct a substantial revision of the laws from that standpoint, for a diligent and effective investigation of

> such cases, punishment of the guilty, provision of support to the families of the victims, and for combating the structural causes of such violence as reflected in these crimes, in domestic violence, and at the level of society as a whole.[29]

With regard to the case in Mexico and in the context of violence toward women prevention, the CEDAW Committee emphasized the need to organize, with the active participation of civil society organizations, at each stage of the process, including men and boys, massive, immediate, and ongoing campaigns to eradicate discrimination against women, promote equality between women and men, and contribute to women's empowerment. Far-reaching recommendations, both medium and long-term, include the following actions:

> Monitor such campaigns systematically with a view to achieving concrete and positive results. Include in educational and training programs at various levels, including in the labor sector, information and sensitization modules on respect for others, human dignity and gender violence as a violation of human rights. Promote training and capacity-building for public officials in general, and judges and judicial personnel in particular, in the area of gender violence and human rights and the need to take the gender dimension into account in their actions and procedures and in judgements and judicial decisions. Heighten the mass media's awareness of gender violence and challenge them to take a positive and pedagogical approach to the issue, bearing in mind their social responsibility, which stems from the power they wield in an information society.[30]

CEDAW Committee furthermore pointed out that prevention requires stepping up violence prevention programs and policies, including early warning mechanisms, the reinforcement of security in dangerous or isolated areas, monitoring programs, and systematic information on security measures.

CEDAW Convention and Violence against Women—Legal Evolution

Violence against women was not explicitly mentioned in the CEDAW Convention. Nonetheless, in its interpretation, the CEDAW Committee has made it clear that violence against women is a human rights violation and a severe form of discrimination against women, which is prohibited under international law. The provisions of Article 2, 5, and 16 of the CEDAW Convention are relevant for application in cases of gender-based violence against women, because the Convention does not explicitly regulate gender-based violence in its provisions, but this was done by General Recommendation No. 19 of 1992 by the CEDAW Committee. This recommendation has fulfilled the legal gap in the Convention, by interpretation of its norms, through extension of the notion of discrimination to cases of violence against women. The CEDAW Committee acted on the basis of Article 21 of the Convention, which enables the Committee to make suggestions and general recommendations based on the examination of reports and information received from the States Parties. The Committee has stated that gender-based violence is a form of discrimination that seriously inhibits women's ability to enjoy rights and freedoms on a basis of equality with men.

CEDAW General Recommendation No. 12: Violence against women, 1989[31] was the first Committee's recommendation on the issue, arising from the consideration of reports submitted by States Parties on the implementation of the CEDAW Convention. "Considering that articles 2, 5, 11, 12 and 16 of the Convention require the States Parties to act to protect women against violence of any kind occurring within the family, at the work place or in any other area of social life, Committee recommends to the States Parties that they should include in their periodic reports to the Committee information about the following:

1. The legislation in force to protect women against the incidence of all kinds of violence in everyday life (including sexual violence, abuses in the family, sexual harassment at the work place etc.);
2. Other measures adopted to eradicate this violence;
3. The existence of support services for women who are the victims of aggression or abuses; and
4. Statistical data on the incidence of violence of all kinds against women and on women who are the victims of violence."[32]

CEDAW General Recommendation No. 19 of 1992, determines that the Convention in Article 1 defines discrimination against women. *The definition of discrimination includes gender-based violence, i.e., violence against a woman because she is a woman or violence that disproportionately affects women. It includes acts that inflict physical, mental or sexual harm or suffering, threats of such acts, coercion and other deprivations of liberty. Gender-based violence may breach specific provisions of the Convention, regardless of whether those provisions expressly mention violence.*[33]

Gender-based violence, which impairs or nullifies the enjoyment by women of human rights and fundamental freedoms under general international law or under human rights conventions, is discrimination within the meaning of Article 1 of the Convention. These rights and freedoms include:

(a) The right to life;
(b) The right not to be subject to torture or to cruel, inhuman, or degrading treatment or punishment;

(c) The right to equal protection according to humanitarian norms in time of international or internal armed conflict;
(d) The right to liberty and security of person;
(e) The right to equal protection under the law;
(f) The right to equality in the family;
(g) The right to the highest standard attainable of physical and mental health; and
(h) The right to just and favorable conditions of work.[34]

Furthermore, the Committee had, for the first time, established the duty of the State Parties to prevent and/or to investigate and punish effectively acts of violence against women with due diligence.

> Under general international law and specific human rights covenants, States may also be responsible for private acts if they fail to act with due diligence to prevent violations of rights or to investigate and punish acts of violence, and for providing compensation.[35]

General recommendation No. 19, with its wording and comments, paved the way for the later legally based principle of due diligence by the state in suppressing gender-based and family violence ("due diligence"), which became legally binding in the provisions of Article 5 of the Convention on preventing and combating violence against women and domestic violence (Istanbul Convention) of the Council of Europe (2014).

General recommendation No. 19. states that the CEDAW Convention applies to violence committed by the authorities. Such acts of violence may violate a state's obligations under general international law and other conventions, in addition to breaching the CEDAW Convention. General recommendation No. 19, however, indicates that discrimination under the CEDAW Convention does not only include acts of violence committed by or on behalf of the authorities. Consequently, in Article 2 (e), the CEDAW Convention calls on States Parties to take all appropriate measures to combat violence against women, performed by any person, organization, or enterprise. Gender-based violence is a form of discrimination against women and can be carried out in different forms (physical, mental, sexual, economic). It is related to negative gender stereotypes and discriminatory traditions, followed by social acceptance of violence against women, such as: "She deserved to be beaten, she annoyed him so much . . .?" Therefore, General Recommendation No. 19 clearly points out to the following: "Traditional attitudes by which women are regarded as subordinate to men or as having stereotyped roles perpetuate widespread practices involving violence or coercion, such as family violence and abuse, forced marriage, dowry deaths, acid attacks and female circumcision. Such prejudices and practices may justify gender-based violence as a form of protection or control of women. The effect of such violence on the physical and mental integrity of women is to deprive them of the equal enjoyment, exercise and knowledge of human rights and fundamental freedoms."[36] General recommendation No. 35 on gender-based violence against women, updating General recommendation No. 19, dates from 2017.[37] In this General recommendation, the CEDAW Committee declared that "the *opinio juris* and State practice suggest that the prohibition of gender-based violence against women has evolved into a principle of customary international law. General recommendation No. 19 has been a key catalyst for that process."[38]

During the period of twenty-five years, women's non-governmental organizations insisted in their social and political activities on the elimination of violence against women and thus contributed to the adoption of national laws and policies to combat it. Despite those positive developments, violence against women continues to be pervasive and entrenched in all societies, with high levels of impunity. In addition, violence against women manifests itself in multiple forms, including cyber violence.[39] The fact that national legislation on violence against women in many States Parties does not exist, or if exists, it is poorly implemented, contributed to the updating of General recommendation No. 19 in the form of General recommendation No. 35. In this recommendation, the term "gender-based violence against women" is used as a more precise term that makes explicit the gendered causes and impacts of the violence.

> The term further strengthens the understanding of the violence as a social rather than an individual problem, requiring comprehensive responses, beyond those to specific events, individual perpetrators and victims / survivors. The Committee has made clear that such violence is a critical obstacle to the achievement of substantive equality between women and men and to the enjoyment by women of their human rights and fundamental freedoms, as enshrined in the Convention.[40]

Women's right to a life free from gender-based violence is indivisible from and interdependent on other human rights, including the rights to life, health, liberty and security of the person, equality and equal protection within the family, freedom from torture, cruel, inhumane, or degrading treatment, and freedom of expression, movement, participation, assembly, and association. Violations of women's sexual and reproductive health and rights, such as forced sterilization, forced abortion, forced pregnancy, criminalization of abortion, denial or delay of safe abortion and/or post-abortion care, forced continuation of pregnancy, and abuse and mistreatment of women and girls seeking sexual and reproductive health information, goods, and services, are forms of gender-based violence that, depending on the circumstances, may amount to torture or cruel, inhuman, or degrading treatment.[41] Gender-based violence against women occurs in all spaces and spheres of human interaction, whether public or private, including in the contexts of the family, the community, public spaces, the workplace, leisure, politics, sport, health services and educational settings, and the redefinition of public and private through technology—mediated environments.[42] Negative stereotypes on gender roles, with social norms in relation to masculinity and the need to assert male control or power over women, all result in social tolerance of violence against women followed by high impunity rates.

Legal importance of the General Recommendation No. 35 lies in the fact that it introduced general legislative measures to be performed by States Parties, in the form of legal sanctions commensurate with the gravity of the offense, as well as civil remedies. Furthermore, victims/survivors of gender-based violence against women should have access to justice and to an effective remedy. States Parties are to repeal all legal provisions that are discriminatory against women and thereby encourage, justify, or tolerate any form of gender-based violence.[43]

The definition of sexual crimes, including marital and acquaintance or date rape, is to be based on the lack of freely given consent while taking into account coercive circumstances. Despite this recommendation, in a prevalent number of countries, this legal definition is not applied. Based on arguments of culture, tradition, and religion, many states furthermore avoid creating a legal framework for equality and the elimination of violence against women. This is a situation noted in General Recommendation 35, paragraph 7, which states:

> In many States, legislation addressing gender-based violence against women is non-existent, inadequate or poorly implemented. An erosion of the legal and policy frameworks that aim to eliminate gender-based discrimination or violence, often justified in the name of tradition, culture, religion or fundamentalist ideology . . . weaken States responses.

National legal reforms to come will indicate to what extent this recommendation bears transformative legal incentives.

Additionally, General recommendation No. 35 developed preventive measures to be applied by States Parties: "to address the underlying causes of gender-based violence against women, including patriarchal attitudes and stereotypes, inequality in the family and the neglect or denial of women's civil, political, economic, social and cultural rights, and to promote the empowerment, agency and voices of women."[44] States Parties are to implement effective measures to make public spaces safe and accessible to all women and girls.

The media are to eliminate discrimination against women, including the harmful and stereotypical portrayal of women or specific groups of women. Mandatory and effective capacity-building, education, and training for members of the judiciary, lawyers, and law enforcement officers, including forensic medical personnel, legislators, and health care professionals, are aimed at preventing gender-based violence against women. This recommendation calls for the engagement of the private sector, businesses, and transnational corporations in efforts to eradicate all forms of gender-based violence against women and in enhancing their responsibility for such violence within the scope of their actions.

Besides general legislative and preventive measures, Recommendation No. 35 foresees protection for women complainants and witnesses to gender-based violence before, during, and after legal proceedings, in order to prevent further or potential violence, without the precondition that victims/survivors initiate legal action. In the context of protective measures, Recommendation No. 35 requires States Parties to tackle factors that heighten the risk to women of exposure to serious forms of gender-based violence, such as the availability of firearms and situations of armed conflict or heightened insecurity. For women, especially those affected by intersecting forms of discrimination, such as those with disabilities, those who are illiterate, or those who have no or limited knowledge of the official languages of a country, it is recommended that a state provide accessible information on the legal and social resources available to victims/survivors, including reparations. As for reparations, the CEDAW Committee recommends that States Parties ensure effective reparations to victims/survivors of gender-based violence against women. Reparations should include different measures, such as monetary compensation and the provision of legal, social, and health services.[45] States Parties should establish specific funds for reparations or include allocations in the budgets of existing funds, including under transitional justice mechanisms, for reparations to victims of gender-based violence against women.

Finally, Recommendation No. 35 envisages prosecution and punishment in order to enable efficient access for victims to courts and tribunals and ensure that the authorities adequately respond to all cases of gender-based violence against women, including by applying criminal law and, as appropriate, *ex officio* prosecution. Gender-based violence against women is not to be referred to alternative dispute resolution procedures, including mediation and conciliation, in a mandatory manner. Alternative dispute resolution procedures should not constitute an obstacle to women's access to formal justice.[46]

CEDAW Committee furthermore recommends coordination, monitoring, and data collection to be performed by States Parties. International cooperation is also recommended to States Parties, aimed at combating gender-based violence against women. Implementation of the relevant Sustainable Development Goals, in particular Goal 5, to achieve gender equality and empowerment of all women and girls, and Goal 16, to promote peaceful and inclusive societies for sustainable development, provide access to justice, and build effective, accountable, and inclusive institutions at all levels, is particularly emphasized.[47]

It can be assessed that General Recommendation No. 35 fully upgraded the previous Recommendation No. 19 regarding violence against women by developing a holistic and multifaceted approach to the issue. This Recommendation (2017), although is part of a soft law, mirrored at the global level many norms from the most comprehensive regional legally binding Convention on Preventing and Combating Violence against Women and Domestic Violence (Istanbul Convention) of the Council of Europe (2014).

VIENNA DECLARATION AND PROGRAM OF ACTION, 1993, AND UN DECLARATION ON THE ELIMINATION OF VIOLENCE AGAINST WOMEN, 1993

Vienna Declaration and Program of Action, 1993

The United Nations World Conference on Human Rights, held in 1993 in Vienna, and Vienna Declaration and Program of Action[48] presented gender-based violence as structural and universal. The Vienna Declaration also sought the appointment of a UN Special Rapporteur on violence against women and contributed to the adoption of the Declaration on the Elimination of All Forms of Discrimination against Women, adopted by the UN General Assembly in December 1993.

"The human rights of women and of the girl-child are an inalienable, integral and indivisible part of universal human rights. The full and equal participation of women in political, civil, economic, social and cultural life, at the national, regional and international levels, and the eradication of all forms of discrimination on grounds of sex are priority objectives of the international community." Gender-based violence and all forms of sexual harassment and exploitation, including those resulting from cultural prejudice and international trafficking, are incompatible with the dignity and worth of the human person and must be eliminated. This can be achieved by legal measures and through national action and international cooperation in such fields as economic and social development, education, safe maternity and health care, and social support. Intimate partner violence stems from patriarchal structures in the majority of states that perpetuate male dominance, power, and control over women.

The human rights of women should form an integral part of the United Nations human rights activities, including the promotion of all human rights instruments relating to women.

The World Conference on Human Rights urges Governments, institutions, intergovernmental and non-governmental organizations to intensify their efforts for the protection and promotion of the human rights of women and the girl-child.[49]

The World Conference on Human Rights particularly emphasizes the importance of working on the elimination of violence against women in public and private life, the elimination of all forms of sexual harassment, exploitation, and trafficking of women, the elimination of gender bias in the administration of justice, and the eradication of any conflicts that may arise between women's rights and the harmful effects of certain traditional or customary practices, cultural prejudices, and religious extremism. The World Conference on Human Rights calls on the General Assembly to adopt the draft declaration on violence against women and urges states to combat violence against women in accordance with its provisions. Violations of women's human rights in situations of armed conflict represent a violation of the basic principles of international human rights and humanitarian law. All violations of this kind, including specifically murder, systematic rape, sexual slavery, and forced pregnancy, require a particularly effective response.

UN Declaration on the Elimination of Violence against Women, 1993

In the UN Declaration on the Elimination of Violence Against Women (December 20, 1993), the term "violence against women" is explicitly defined. The 1993 Declaration on the Elimination of Violence against Women became the first international legal instrument explicitly addressing violence against women, providing a framework for national and international action. It defines violence against women as any act of gender-based violence that results in, or is likely to result in, physical, sexual or psychological harm or suffering to women, including threats of such acts, coercion or arbitrary deprivation of liberty, whether occurring in public or in private life.

For the purposes of this Declaration, the term "violence against women" means any act of gender-based violence that results in, or is likely to result in, physical, sexual, or psychological harm or suffering to women, including threats of such acts, coercion or arbitrary deprivation of liberty, whether occurring in public or in private life."[50]

The Declaration included different forms of violence, such as female genital mutilation, rape and torture, dowry-related violence, marital rape, domestic beating, and female sexual slavery (Art. 2), all of which had previously been tolerated in some parts of the world as acceptable. The inclusion of such practices within the realm of international law was an important step by the UN in putting individual rights to physical integrity as a priority and above claims of negative tradition.

State Parties to the Declaration recognized that "violence against women is a manifestation of historically unequal power relations between men and women, which have led to domination over and discrimination against women by men and to the prevention of the full advancement of women."[51]

UN Declaration states that some groups of women, such as women belonging to minority groups, indigenous women, refugee women, migrant women, women living in rural or remote communities, destitute women, women in institutions or in detention, female children, women with disabilities, elderly women and women in situations of armed conflict, are especially vulnerable to violence.

Women are entitled to the equal enjoyment and protection of all human rights and fundamental freedoms in the political, economic, social, cultural, civil, or any other field. These rights include, *inter alia*:

(a) The right to life;
(b) The right to equality;
(c) The right to liberty and security of person; (d) The right to equal protection under the law;
(e) The right to be free from all forms of discrimination;
(f) The right to the highest standard attainable of physical and mental health; (g) The right to just and favorable conditions of work;
(h) The right not to be subjected to torture, or other cruel, inhuman, or degrading treatment or punishment.[52]

UN Declaration emphasizes duties of States to condemn and eliminate violence against women and to exercise due diligence to prevent, investigate and, in accordance with national legislation, punish acts of violence against women, whether those acts are perpetrated by the State or by private persons (Art. 4, c). Women victims of violence and their children should have specialized assistance, such as rehabilitation, assistance in child care, counseling, health and social services, facilities, and support programs (Art. 4, g).

Declaration asks from the UN system and specialized agencies (Art. 5, a) to foster international and regional cooperation with a view to defining regional strategies for combating violence, exchanging experiences, and financing programs relating to the elimination of violence against women. Furthermore, it is necessary to encourage coordination between organizations and bodies of the UN system to incorporate the issue of violence against women into ongoing programs, especially with reference to groups of women particularly vulnerable to violence (Art. 5, e). Cooperation with non-governmental organizations in addressing the issue of violence against women is also the task of UN organs and agencies.

Special importance of the Declaration lies in the fact that it prohibits not only state violence against women, but also private violence in all forms. Therefore, the Declaration requires the States to "develop, in a comprehensive way, preventive approaches and all those measures of a legal, political, administrative and cultural nature that promote the protection of women against any form of violence, and ensure that the re-victimization of women does not occur because of laws insensitive to gender considerations, enforcement practices or other interventions" (Art. 4, f).

Although it is not a binding document, but belongs to the soft law instruments, the UN Declaration made a significant turning point for the explicit recognition of violence against women as an international human rights violation.

THE BEIJING DECLARATION AND PLATFORM FOR ACTION, 1995

The Beijing Declaration and Platform for Action on Violence against Women

The Beijing Declaration and Platform for Action is the most progressive blueprint for advancing women's rights (1995). It belongs to the soft law international instruments. However, its significance lies in the fact that 189 UN member states have adopted it as a framework for achieving gender equality. "This pivotal document continues to guide the global struggle against constraints and obstacles to the empowerment of women around the world. When we empower women and girls, we will realize a better future for all. Where women are educated and empowered, economies are more productive and strong. Where women are fully represented, societies are more peaceful and stable." (Ban Ki-Moon UN Secretary-General, 2015).

The Beijing Declaration and Platform for Action of 1995, the most comprehensive global policy framework and blueprint for action, was the outcome of the Fourth World Conference on Women, held in Beijing, China, in September 1995. This landmark Declaration consists of twelve relevant areas that are still applicable for empowerment of women:

- poverty;
- education and training;
- health;

- violence;
- armed conflict;
- economy;
- power and decision-making;
- institutional mechanisms;
- human rights;
- media;
- environment and
- the girl child.

Strategic objectives are identified for each of those areas, as well as a detailed catalogue of related actions to be taken by governments and other stakeholders, at national, regional and international levels. "Violence against women is a manifestation of the historically unequal power relations between men and women, which have led to domination over and discrimination against women by men and to the prevention of women's full advancement." (UN-United Nations: The Beijing Declaration and the Platform for Action, Fourth World Conference on Women, Beijing, China, September 4-September 15, 1995).[53]

At the twenty-third special session of the General Assembly in June 2000, held to review the implementation of the Beijing Declaration and Platform for Action, governments agreed on further actions to accelerate the implementation of the Platform for Action and to ensure that commitments for gender equality, development and peace were fully realized.[54] As a result, positive gains indicated that discriminatory legislation is being removed and violence against women and girls and harmful practices had been addressed in a prevalent number of UN member countries, that is, at a global level. Despite this, progress has been unacceptably slow and uneven, particularly for the most marginalized women and girls who experience multiple and intersecting forms of discrimination. Since the adoption of the Platform for Action, no country has achieved equality for women and girls, and significant levels of inequality between women and men persist. It is important to stress that gender equality is not only a goal in itself, but a means for achieving all other goals on the global agenda.[55]

In relation to violence against women, the Beijing Declaration and Platform for Action follows definitions of the UN CEDAW Committee in its General Recommendations Nos 19 and 35. The declaration proclaims that violence against women is an obstacle to equality, development and peace and that it impairs or nullifies the enjoyment by women of their human rights and fundamental freedoms.

> Violence against women is a manifestation of the historically unequal power relations between men and women, which have led to domination over and

> discrimination against women by men and to the prevention of women's full advancement. Violence against women throughout the life cycle derives essentially from cultural patterns, in particular the harmful effects of certain traditional or customary practices and all acts of extremism linked to race, sex, language or religion that perpetuate the lower status accorded to women in the family, the workplace, the community and society.[56]

At the same time, it is evident that there is a lack of relevant data and statistical analysis of different forms of violence against women, which hampers the formulation of targeted strategies with a list of optimal actions. Therefore, to address the issue of violence against women, the Beijing Declaration requires countries to implement the following strategic objectives:

1. Integrated measures to prevent and eliminate violence against women, which encompass a plethora of actions to be taken by governments, local governments, employers, trade unions, community and youth organizations, non-governmental organizations, educational institutions, the public and private sectors, particularly enterprises, the mass media, and international organizations. The UN Secretary-General is to provide the Special Rapporteur of the Commission on Human Rights on violence against women with all necessary assistance, in particular the staff and resources required to perform all mandated functions.
2. Studying the causes and consequences of violence against women and the effectiveness of preventive measures, with adequate actions of governments, regional organizations, the United Nations, other international organizations, research institutions, women's and youth organizations, and non-governmental organizations.
3. Elimination of trafficking in women and aid to victims of violence due to prostitution and trafficking, which assumes the ratification and enforcement of international conventions on trafficking in persons and on slavery; appropriate measures to address the root factors that encourage trafficking in women and girls for prostitution; advancing concerted action by all relevant law enforcement authorities and institutions with a view to dismantling national, regional and international networks in trafficking; allocation of resources for comprehensive programs designed to heal and rehabilitate into society the victims of trafficking; development of educational and training programs and policies, and enacting legislation aimed at preventing sex tourism and trafficking.

Strategic objectives of all twelve relevant areas, with lists of actions to be taken, are intertwined, which derives from the complexity of the issue of violence against women. In June 2000, a special session of the UN General

Assembly assessed the achievements in the implementation of the Beijing Declaration and Platform for Action. The assessment indicated that violence against women, whether perpetrated or condoned by the State or its agents, constitutes a human rights violation. "It is also accepted that States have an obligation to exercise due diligence to prevent, investigate and punish acts of violence, whether those acts are perpetrated by the State or by private persons, and provide protection to victims. Governments have initiated policy reforms and mechanisms, such as interdepartmental committees, guidelines and protocols, national, multidisciplinary and coordinated programs to address violence. Some Governments have introduced or reformed laws to protect women and girls from all forms of violence and laws to prosecute the perpetrators."[57]

On the other side, it was estimated that there is a lack of comprehensive programs dealing with the perpetrators and that women's inferior position in society continues due to discriminatory norms and negative social attitudes. A coordinated multidisciplinary response to violence (health system, the workplace, the media, the education system, and the justice system) is lacking in many states. Measures in criminal justice are weak to eliminate different forms of violence against women and children (physical, sexual, and psychological violence occurring in the family, including battering, sexual abuse of female children in the household, dowry-related violence, marital rape, female genital mutilation, and other traditional practices harmful to women, non-spousal violence and violence related to exploitation).[58] In addition, sexual violence in marriage is still treated as a private matter in some countries. Strategies for violence prevention are fragmented and insufficient. It is registered that the use of new information and communication technologies for trafficking in women and children poses new problems.

Implementation of the Beijing Declaration and Platform for Action in the Area of Combating Violence against Women

Appraisal of the implementation of the Beijing Declaration and Platform for Action was made in a rapidly changing global context, when new challenges have arisen. The globalization process has, in some countries, caused policy paths toward more open trade and financial flows, privatization of state-owned enterprises, and lower public spending, particularly on social services, which resulted in an increase in gender inequality and the feminization of poverty. Women continue to be employed in low-paid part-time and contract jobs marked by insecurity and by safety and health hazards in many countries. Full implementation of the Beijing Platform for Action was severely hampered by the increasing debt burden of developing countries and countries in transition because women bear the biggest cost induced by economic restructuring and are the first to lose jobs in a recession. Therefore, women should have equal access to and adequate training in new technologies, aimed at job creation.

Aging of the population in some countries showed the gap between male and female life expectancy, and the number of widows and older single women has increased considerably, often leading to their social isolation and other social challenges. One of the challenges to the proper implementation of the Beijing Platform for Action is, furthermore, the HIV/AIDS pandemic, particularly in the developing world, which has had a devastating impact on women. Gender roles are thoroughly discussed in many states, and in that context, the need for changing stereotypical and traditional roles that limit women's full potential is present. "As long as there is insufficient sharing of tasks and responsibilities with men, the combination of remunerated work and caregiving will lead to the continued disproportionate burden for women in comparison to men."[59] Violence against women and girls is a major obstacle to the achievement of the objectives of gender equality; it nullifies the enjoyment by women of their human rights and fundamental freedoms. Consequently, further actions and initiatives to implement the Beijing Declaration and Platform for Action are focused on the elimination of violence against women. States are to treat all forms of violence against women and girls of all ages as a criminal offense punishable by law. Additionally, governments, the private sector, non-governmental organizations, and other actors of civil society are to secure gender-sensitive training for all actors, including police, prosecutors, and the judiciary, in dealing with victims of violence, particularly women and girls, including sexual violence.

Further actions for the application of the Beijing Platform for Action (2000) consider launching an international "zero tolerance" campaign on violence against women and developing, with the full participation of all countries, an international consensus on indicators and ways to measure violence against women. It considers establishing a readily accessible database on statistics, legislation, training models, good practices, lessons learned, and other resources with regard to all forms of violence against women, including women migrant workers.

Actions to be taken at the national and international levels in the area of combating violence against women include the need to increase cooperation, policy responses, and effective implementation of national legislation, as well as other protective and preventive measures aimed at the elimination of violence against women and girls. This is especially of all forms of commercial sexual exploitation, as well as economic exploitation, including trafficking in women and children, female infanticide, crimes committed in the name of honor, crimes committed in the name of passion, racially motivated crimes, abduction and sale of children, dowry-related violence and deaths, acid attacks, and harmful traditional or customary practices such as female genital mutilation and early and forced marriages. Subsequently, it is necessary to provide support to non-governmental organizations, in collaboration with the UN system, in addressing all forms of violence against women and girls, including programs to combat race- and ethnic-based violence against women and girls. Furthermore, it is important to encourage and support public campaigns to enhance public awareness of the unacceptability and social costs of violence against women and to undertake prevention activities that promote balanced relationships based on gender equality. In order to eliminate impunity, it is necessary to strengthen existing mechanisms for prosecuting perpetrators of violations of the human rights of women.

European Institute for Gender Equality (EIGE) of the European Union[60] (EU) prepared the Review of the Implementation of the Beijing Platform for Action in the EU Member States: Violence against Women—Victim Support.[61] In this report from 2012, the findings show that specialized services for victims are insufficient and unequally distributed in and among the Member States (27 Member States). Funding to ensure access to services is similarly inconsistent. "However, there is evidence of some progress in the Member States. The vast majority of the Member States have developed and implemented national action plans to combat domestic violence and to criminalize intimate partner violence, as well as adopted protection orders."[62] The provision of specialized support services for women victims of domestic violence is one of the three strategic objectives of the Beijing Platform for Action on violence against women, requiring states to take integrated measures to prevent and eliminate violence against women. EU Member States have defined violence against women as an issue of human rights and gender equality in their national action plans. This approach is important from the point of addressing the root causes of men's violence against women. On the contrary, the gender-neutral approach in criminal codes in some EU Member States does not tackle the fundamental causes of men's violence against women.

EIGE Review notes positive trends in using protection orders for the safety of victims: "A police ban, expelling the perpetrator from the residence and forbidding him to approach or contact the victim for a set period of time, clearly offers the highest level of immediate safety and protection if police are appropriately trained to recognize when a perpetrator poses a danger. The majority of Member States have introduced legal protection orders that are either explicitly designed for cases of domestic violence against women or have been modified to be used against an intimate partner or ex-partner."[63]

Perpetrators' programs are legally foreseen in many EU Member States (15), but they are not offered in all of these cases and their effectiveness is difficult to evaluate. Training of professionals in EU Member States is often not systematic, nor included in basic training, and is neither mandatory nor well-funded, says Review. Specialized immediate and long-term services are vital to support women survivors of domestic violence and their children, such as:

- 24-hour hotlines,
- women's shelters,
- specialized advice and counselling centers,
- specialized police and prosecution units/staff,
- health care,
- specialized psychological counseling,
- safe and affordable housing,
- support for labor market re-entry and other services.

Those services for victims should be free of charge and accessible to all women, especially to multiple-discriminated women: migrant, minority, and asylum-seeking women regardless of their legal status, older women, LBT women and women with disabilities. Women's NGOs across the EU play a crucial role in the delivery of specialist services. However, the lack of reliable and comparable data in the EU Member States severely limits the measuring of performed actions and implemented measures for the eradication of violence against women. Data collection should be disaggregated by the sex and age of both the victim and the perpetrator, and should also include the type of violence and the relationship of the perpetrator to the victim.[64] The European Parliament adopted the Resolution on priorities and the outline of the EU policy framework to fight violence against women. This Resolution calls on the European Commission to develop and provide annual statistics on violence against women.[65] EIGE recommended the establishment of observatories in each Member State to collect unified data, aimed at improving policy and strategy development and measures to eliminate violence against women.

At the global level, the lack of data seriously hampers efforts to end violence against women. Therefore, under the auspices of the UNECE[66] regional review meetings are held every five years, focused on ending violence against women and girls, as it is a crucial part of both the Beijing Platform for Action and the 2030 Agenda for Sustainable Development.[67] Recent Regional review meeting, "Beijing +25 Regional Review Meeting," was held in October 2019, where key trends on gender equality across the ECE region were discussed.[68] Resolution 2018/8 of the Economic and Social Council encouraged the United Nations Regional Commissions to undertake a regional review of the implementation of the Beijing Declaration and Platform for Action, so that the outcomes of intergovernmental processes at the regional level can feed into the 2020 review undertaken by the Commission on the Status of Women at its sixty-fourth session. The presented report addressed trends in gender equality in selected areas over the last twenty-five years, focusing on the last five years, using data from the United Nations Economic Commission for Europe (ECE) Statistical Database. It examines life expectancy, education, employment, pay, power and decision-making, time use, and violence against women.

Notwithstanding considerable improvements in most countries, important gender gaps remain. There is also great variation among ECE countries in all the areas examined.[69] In relation to ending violence against women and girls, reliable and comparable data are rare, but data on recorded homicides provide the best means of gauging trends. The Report of the UN ECE stated that although two-thirds of the ECE countries analyzed show low and unchanging levels of homicide of women, there are exceptions where high levels and/or large increases are seen in the past five years (2014–2019). Current or former partners or relatives perform a prevalent number of homicides of women.[70] The most serious manifestation of violence, murders of women, are less likely than other forms of violence to go unreported, and therefore are more reliably compared than other forms of violence against women.

UN PROTOCOL TO PREVENT, SUPPRESS, AND PUNISH TRAFFICKING IN PERSONS, ESPECIALLY WOMEN AND CHILDREN, SUPPLEMENTING THE UN CONVENTION AGAINST TRANS-NATIONAL ORGANIZED CRIME, NOVEMBER 15, 2000

UN Protocol to Prevent, Suppress and Punish Trafficking in Persons Especially Women and Children, supplementing the United Nations Convention against Transnational Organized Crime, was adopted and opened for signature, ratification, and accession by General Assembly resolution 55/25 of November 15, 2000.[71] Protocol is open for signature by all States and by regional economic integration organizations, provided that at least one Member State of such an organization has signed the protocol, from December 12 to December 15, 2000, at the Palazzi di Giustizia in Palermo, Italy, and thereafter at United Nations Headquarters in New York until December 12, 2002.[72] Brief title is the Palermo Protocol, and it has 117 signatories (at the moment of writing this book). The protocol entered into force on December 25, 2003 (Article 17).

United States of America has signed Protocol on December 13, 2000, and has ratified it on November 3, 2005, but with reservations in relation to Article 15 of the Protocol concerning the settlement of disputes in relation to the interpretation or application of this Protocol through negotiation. Reservations:

(1) The United States of America reserves the right not to apply in part the obligation set forth in Article 15, paragraph 1 (b), of the United Nations Convention Against Transnational Organized Crime with respect to the offenses established in the Trafficking Protocol. The United States does not provide for plenary jurisdiction over offenses that are committed on board ships flying its flag or aircraft registered under its laws. However, in a number of circumstances, U.S. law provides for jurisdiction over such offenses committed on board U.S.-flagged ships or aircraft registered under U.S. law. Accordingly, the United States will implement paragraph 1 (b) of the Convention to the extent provided for under its federal law.

(2) The United States of America reserves the right to assume obligations under this Protocol in a manner consistent with its fundamental principles of federalism, pursuant to which both federal and state criminal laws must be considered in relation to conduct addressed in the Protocol. U.S. federal criminal law, which regulates conduct based on its effect on interstate or foreign commerce, or another federal interest, such as the Thirteenth Amendment's prohibition of "slavery" and "involuntary servitude," serves as the principal legal regime within the United States for combating the conduct addressed in this Protocol and is broadly effective for this purpose. Federal criminal law does not apply in the rare case where such criminal conduct does not involve interstate or foreign commerce, or otherwise implicate another federal interest, such as the Thirteenth Amendment. There are a small number of conceivable situations involving rare offenses of a purely local character where U.S. federal and state criminal law may not be entirely adequate to satisfy an obligation under the Protocol. The United States of America therefore reserves to the obligations set forth in the Protocol to the extent they address conduct that would fall within this narrow category of highly localized activity. This reservation does not affect in any respect the ability of the United States to provide international cooperation to other Parties as contemplated in the Protocol.

(3) In accordance with Article 15, paragraph 3, the United States of America declares that it does not consider itself bound by the obligation set forth in Article 15, paragraph 2.[73]

The Protocol defines the first common international definition of "trafficking in persons" with the aim of preventing and combating such crime and facilitating international cooperation against it. The consent of the victim is irrelevant where illicit means are established. Inhuman, degrading, and dangerous exploitation of trafficked persons brought the attribute of this crime as being modern slavery. As is the case with the parent UN Convention against Trans-National Organized Crime (2000), the Protocol is expected to standardize terminology, laws, and practices of countries, parties of the Protocol. The Protocol contains general protection and support measures for victims. These include a list of social support benefits such as counseling, housing, education, medical and psychological assistance, and an opportunity for victims to obtain legal status allowing them to remain in the country of the receiving Party, either temporarily or permanently.[74] States Parties are required to implement security and border controls to detect and prevent trafficking.

The Protocol emphasizes the gender component already in its name, and the preamble is focused on women and children as victims of human trafficking. It is a fact that according to recent data from the United Nations Office on Drugs and Crime published in 2022, women and girls make up 60 percent of the total number of victims of trafficking in persons.[75] Since 91 percent of trafficked women and girls are subjected to sexual exploitation,[76] human trafficking is characterized by a strong gender dimension.

Numerous factors contribute to the pronounced gender dimension of human trafficking.[77] The patriarchal relations that still characterize many societies traditionally make the position of women in society less favorable in relation to the position of men. There is furthermore a certain phenomenon that existed in earlier times and has gained new outlines, which specifically encourages the gender aspects of human trafficking, such as the feminization of poverty.[78] This phenomenon is closely linked with limited access to education for women and the consequent impossibility of employment for women. According to UNICEF data, as many as 129 million girls do not attend school. In only 49 percent of countries is gender parity is achieved in terms of primary education, while the percentage declines when it comes to lower (42 percent) and higher (24 percent) secondary education.[79]

Especially important is that gender-based violence is considered to be an essential factor of human trafficking in terms that it significantly encourages disproportionate exposure of women and men at risk of human trafficking, because research has shown that earlier exposure to some form of violence "contributes to the cycle of violence against women and makes them more vulnerable when it comes to trafficking."[80] Additionally, different types of crises, situations of armed conflicts, and the post-conflict environment are also among the factors that influence the manifestation of the gender dimension of human trafficking, affecting mostly women and girls.[81] Finally, among the risk factors for human trafficking, migrations are counted, primarily due to the fact that migrant women and girls are at particular risk of becoming victims of trafficking.[82]

The pronounced gender dimension of human trafficking requires an effectiveness of protection to be provided to women victims of human trafficking at the international legal level. The Palermo Protocol to Prevent, Suppress and Punish Trafficking in Persons, Especially Women and Children, supplementing the United Nations Convention against Transnational Organized Crime (the Palermo Protocol) requires, *inter alia*, States Parties to:[83]

- Adopt necessary legislative and other measures to establish trafficking in persons as a criminal offense when committed intentionally (Article 5);
- Secure that their domestic legal or administrative system contains measures that provide victims information on court and administrative proceedings and assistance to enable their views and concerns to be presented and considered during criminal proceedings against offenders (Article 6).

The analysis showed that the gender dimension is included in international legal regimes in this area. The American Convention on Human Rights goes one step further in this regard and, in the first paragraph of Article 6, except for slavery, servitude, and slave trade, explicitly prohibits trafficking in women.[84] Various international instruments influence each other when it comes to the recognition and inclusion of gender dimensions in the obligations of states in connection with the suppression of the aforementioned crimes and protecting victims from them.

UN SECURITY COUNCIL RESOLUTION 1325 ON WOMEN, PEACE AND SECURITY, 2000

The first resolution on women, peace and security, Security Council Resolution 1325 (SCR 1325), was unanimously adopted by the United Nations Security Council on October 31, 2000. For the first time, the UN Security Council addressed the disproportionate and unique impact of armed conflict on women and recognized the under-valued and under-utilized contributions women make to conflict prevention, peace-keeping, conflict resolution, and peace-building. This resolution pointed to the importance of women's equal and full participation as active agents in peace and security.

SCR 1325 is binding upon all UN Member States, and the adoption of the Resolution marked an important international political recognition that women and gender are relevant to international peace and security. While SCR 1325 is recognized as a historic and unprecedented document, it does not exist in a vacuum; many resolutions, treaties, conventions, statements, and reports preceded it and thus, form its foundation and an integral part of the women, peace, and security policy framework.

Key provisions of SCR 1325 are the following:

- Increased participation and representation of women at all levels of decision-making;
- attention to specific protection needs of women and girls in conflict;
- gender perspective in post-conflict processes;
- gender perspective in UN programming, reporting, and in the Security Council Missions;
- gender perspective and training in UN peace support operations.

Key actors addressed in SCR 1325 are: the Security Council; UN Member States; all actors (including parties to armed conflict); and the UN Secretary General.

However, in practice, this UN Resolution did not bring improvements to the women's role in peace negotiations, as it was measured at a measly 19 percent in UN-led processes.[85] Due to the intertwining negative effects of rising conflicts, the COVID-19 pandemic, and climate change, which all together hamper global well-being, recent progress on gender equality has decreased significantly. These trends are followed by heightened violence against women to human rights defenders—including those involved in UN peace and security processes. Since 2018, more than a third of briefers at the Security Council assisted by the NGO Working Group on Women, Peace, and Security have been subjected to reprisals and intimidation. In addition, funding for women's organizations in conflict-affected countries is diminishing drastically.[86] Therefore, the UN secretary-general, in his 2022 Report on women, peace, and security, places the unconditional defense of women's rights and the protection of women human rights defenders as central pillars of the UN's peace and security work.

UN RESOLUTION ON INTENSIFICATION OF EFFORTS TO PREVENT AND ELIMINATE ALL FORMS OF VIOLENCE AGAINST WOMEN AND GIRLS, 2020

UN Resolution on intensification of efforts to prevent and eliminate all forms of violence against women and girls was adopted by the General Assembly on December 16, 2020.[87] This Resolution No. 75/161 reaffirms all previous resolutions on the elimination of violence against women and the Declaration on the Elimination of Violence against Women (1993),[88] as well as the Beijing Declaration and Platform for Action (1995). Thus, it represents the continuation of the UN's work on the prevention and elimination of all forms of violence against women. The general UN framework is the 2030 Agenda for Sustainable Development, which recognizes that women play a vital role as agents of development. Furthermore, states realizing gender equality and the empowerment of all women and girls are crucial to making progress across all Sustainable Development Goals.

Year 2020 marked the twenty-fifth anniversary of the Fourth World Conference on Women and the adoption of the Beijing Declaration and Platform for Action, which have contributed greatly to the progress made toward achieving gender equality. Besides, 2020 was the twentieth anniversary of the adoption of the UN Security Council Resolution 1325 (2000) of October 31, 2000, and the establishment of the women, peace, and security agenda at a global level.

The Resolution of 2020 was brought during the COVID-19 pandemic and consequently it underlines deep concern in relation to "the increased violence against women and girls around the world, including domestic violence, as well as harmful practices, such as female genital mutilation and child early and forced marriage, including in conflict-affected areas, particularly in the context of confinement measures and school closures adopted in response to the coronavirus disease."[89]

Furthermore, the Resolution underscores that "a lack of information and awareness, fear of reprisals, persisting impunity, all forms of discrimination, including structural discrimination, insufficient recourse for victims of violence against women and girls, gender stereotypes and negative social norms, including when leading to shame or stigma, as well as negative economic consequences, such as loss of livelihood or reduced income, prevent many women and girls, as applicable, from reporting or acting as witnesses and from seeking redress and justice for these crimes."[90] Consequently, the Resolution urges the States to address structural and underlying causes and risk factors, by appropriate domestic policies that are aimed at transforming discriminatory social attitudes and social and cultural patterns of conduct that condone violence against women and girls.

The lack of research and data on violence against women and girls, its prevalence, patterns, and drivers, impedes efforts to design and implement policies and legislation to prevent and eliminate all forms of violence against women and girls. The Resolution repeats that the States are to act with due diligence to prevent, investigate, and prosecute the perpetrators of all forms of violence against women and girls, to eliminate impunity, and provide for effective access to adequate remedies for victims. In addition, the States are to provide shelters, psychosocial services, counseling, health care, and other types of support services, in order to avoid re-victimization and to promote an empowering environment for victims.

States are furthermore invited to enable relevant, comprehensive, and victim-centered legal protection to support and assist victims of violence, including sexual harassment, in a gender-sensitive manner, including victim and witness protection from reprisals for bringing complaints or giving evidence, within the framework of their national legal systems. States should establish "coordinated, interdisciplinary, accessible and sustained multisector services, by relevant stakeholders, such as the police and the justice sector, as well as providers of legal aid services, health services, shelters, medical and psychological assistance, counselling services and protection, and, in cases of girl victims, ensuring that such services, programs and responses take into account the best interests of the child."[91]

In armed conflict and post-conflict situations, and in natural disaster situations, the prevention of and combating all forms of violence against women and girls, including sexual and gender-based violence, is prioritized. The resolution fosters the importance of partnership with the private sector and civil society, including women's organizations.

Protection of the human rights of all women, including their sexual and reproductive health and reproductive rights, in accordance with the Program of Action of the International Conference on Population and Development and the Beijing Platform for Action, has been placed in the arms of States by the strengthening of health systems and legislation.

UN system and regional and sub-regional organizations are to support national efforts to promote the empowerment of women and girls and gender equality in order to enhance international efforts to eliminate violence against women and girls through, *inter alia*, official development assistance. The UN Resolution strongly encourages States to provide updated information for the Secretary-General's Global Database on Violence against Women, on their national policies and legal frameworks aimed at eliminating violence against women and girls. Additionally, the Special Rapporteur of the Human Rights Council on violence against women, its causes and consequences, has to submit annual reports to the UN General Assembly.

It can be assessed that this Resolution, although belonging to the soft law, represents firm commitments within the UN system to continue alarming States to eliminate violence against women, especially in newly born negative conditions such as COVID-19 pandemic and digital violence, as well as to reaffirm existing obligations of the States.

NOTES

1. We ought not to abuse our legal rights.
2. Latin saying: To the heart of things. A figure of speech in which a phrase is applied to explain the essence of the situation.
3. https://www.unwomen.org/sites/default/files/Headquarters/Attachments/Sections/Library/Publications/2020/A-75-274-SG-report-EVAWG-Infographic-and-recommendations-en.pdf, 15.05.2024.
4. Ibid.

5. Ibid.

6. Ibid.

7. The UN Women, with the official title: UN Entity for Gender Equality and the Empowerment of Women, was established as a result of the agreement of the UN Member States with the strong support of the global women's movement, with the main idea to do more so that women can demand for equal rights and possibilities. It was established by the UN General Assembly resolution in July 2010, and its work started at the beginning of 2011. http://www.unwomen.org/en/about-us.

8. http://www.unwomen.org/en/about-us, 28.09.2023.

9. UNFPA, United Nations Population Fund, founded in 1969, works to improve gender equality and women's empowerment. The goal of UNFPA is to ensure sexual and reproductive rights and choices for all, especially women and young people, so that they can access high-quality sexual and reproductive health services, including voluntary family planning, maternal health care, and comprehensive sexuality education. http://www.unfpa.org/about-us, 28.09.2023.

10. See more at: https://www.unfpa.org/female-genital-mutilation.

11. See more at: http://www.who.int, 30.09.2023.

12. Source: A/77/302)—Intensification of efforts to eliminate all forms of violence against women and girls.

13. Ibid.

14. E. Gracia, "Unreported Cases of Domestic Violence against Women: Towards an Epidemiology of Social Silence, Tolerance, and Inhibition," *Epidemiol Community Health*, 58/2004, 536.

15. G. Gasmi, Ž. Nikač, "Sexual and Gender-Based Violence in Serbia: After the Istanbul Convention," *Global Problems in Sexual Offenses* (ed. Erbaş, Rahime), Lexington Books, London, 2022, 128.

16. Ibid.

17. OSCE, *Welfare and Safety of Women*, 2019, https://www.osce.org/files/f/documents/7/5/419756_1.pdf, 09.02.2023.

18. L. Schalatek, "CEDAW and the USA: When Belief in Exceptionalism Becomes Exemptionalism," December 10, 2019, https://www.boell.de/en/2019/12/10/cedaw-and-usa-when-belief-exceptionalism-becomes- xemptionalism#:~:text=While%20US%20President%20Jimmy%20Carter,States%20has%20never%20ratified%20it . 29.01.2024.

19. H. Rubenstein et al., "Time for a Change, the Need for a Binding International Treaty on Violence Against Women," *Global Rights for Women*, 4, https:// globalrightsforwomen.org/treaty-paper-final-112618-1/, 07.09.2023.

20. https://www.un.org/womenwatch/daw/cedaw/text/econvention.htm#article1, 26.10.2023.

21. Ibid.

22. https://www.ohchr.org/en/treaty-bodies/cedaw/membership, 26.10.2023.

23. Ibid.

24. Ibid.

25. The original text of the Optional Protocol is available on the website: http://www.ohchr.org/EN/ProfessionalInterest/Pages/OPCEDAW.aspx, 09.10.2023.

26. https://www.un.org/womenwatch/daw/cedaw/protocol/whatis.htm, 11.10.2023.

27. CEDAW/C/2005/OP.8/MEXICO, 27.01.2005.

28. Ibid., 42.

29. Ibid., 45, 46.

30. Ibid., 46.

31. https://www.refworld.org/docid/52d927444.html, 22.11.2023.

32. Ibid.

33. The original text of the General Recommendation No. 19 is available on the website: http://www.ohchr.org/EN/HRBodies/CEDAW/Pages/Recommendations .aspx.

34. Ibid.

35. Ibid.

36. Ibid.

37. CEDAW/C/GC/35, 26.07.2017.

38. Ibid.

39. Report of the Working Group for Broadband and Gender of the Broadband Commission for Sustainable Development, co-chaired by the United Nations Development Program—United Nations Entity for Gender Equality and the Empowerment of Women (UN Women), entitled: "Cyber violence against women and girls: a worldwide wake-up call," October 2015; and agreed conclusions of the fifty-seventh session of the Commission on the Status of Women (E/2013/27, chap. I, sect. A).

40. CEDAW/C/GC/35, 26.07.2017.

41. Ibid.

42. See the report of the Secretary-General entitled: "In-depth study on all forms of violence against women" (A/61/122/Add.1 and Corr.1).

43. CEDAW/C/GC/35, 26.07.2017, 12.

44. Ibid.

45. Ibid.

46. Ibid.

47. Ibid.

48. Vienna Declaration and Program of Action: https://www.ohchr.org/en/instruments-mechanisms/instruments/vienna-declaration-and-program-action, 05.02.2024.

49. Ibid.

50. Article 1, UN Declaration on the Elimination of Violence against Women, 1993, (A/RES/48/104).

51. Preamble to the Declaration on the Elimination of Violence against Women (A/RES/48/104), https://www.un.org/documents/ga/res/48/a48r104.htm, 23.10.2023.

52. Article 3, UN Declaration on the Elimination of Violence against Women (A/RES/48/104).

53. UN Women, *The Beijing Declaration and Platform for Action—Beijing+5 Political Declaration and Outcome*, United Nations Entity for Gender Equality and the Empowerment of Women (UN Women), 2014, 5.

54. Ibid.

55. Ibid.

56. Ibid.
57. Ibid.
58. Ibid.
59. Ibid.
60. G. Gasmi, Quo Vadis *EU? Relevant Legal and Institutional Factors*, Institute of Comparative Law, Belgrade, 2016, 111.
61. EIGE, *Review of the Implementation of the Beijing Platform for Action in the EU Member States: Violence against Women—Victim Support*, Luxembourg, 2012. The European Institute for Gender Equality is an autonomous body of the European Union, established to contribute to and strengthen the promotion of gender equality, including gender mainstreaming in all Community policies and the resulting national policies, and the fight against discrimination based on sex, and to raise EU citizens' awareness of gender equality. Further information can be found online at http://www.eige.europa.eu.
62. Ibid.
63. Ibid.
64. Ibid.
65. European Parliament, European Parliament Resolution of April 5, 2011, on priorities and outline of a new EU policy framework to fight violence against women (2010/2209(INI), http://www.europarl.europa.eu/sides/getDoc.do?type=TA&language=EN&reference=P7-TA-2011-0127, 29.09.2023.
66. The United Nations Economic Commission for Europe (UNECE) was set up in 1947 by the UN Economic and Social Council (ECOSOC). It is one of five regional commissions of the United Nations. UNECE includes fifty-six member States in Europe, North America, and Asia. However, all interested UN member States may participate in the work of UNECE. Over seventy international professional organizations and other non-governmental organizations take part in the UNECE activities.
67. https://unece.org/statistics/news/why-we-must-urgently-close-data-gap-end-violence-against-women, 24.11.2023.
68. UN Economic Commission for Europe, ECE/AC.28/2019/6, Geneva. Item four of the provisional agenda: Key trends on gender equality across the ECE region, 29 and 30.10.2019.
69. Ibid.
70. Ibid.
71. https://www.ohchr.org/sites/default/files/ProtocolonTrafficking.pdf, 22.12.2023.
72. https://treaties.un.org, 22.12.2023.
73. Ibid.
74. www.unodc.org/documents/treaties/Special/2000_Protocol_to_Prevent_2C_Suppress_and_Punish_Trafficking_in_Persons.pdf, 11.01.2024.
75. United Nations Office on Drugs and Crime, Global Report on Trafficking in Persons 2022, United Nations, New York, 2022, 25. The report noted an 11 percent decline in the ratio to the data published in 2017 by the International Labor Organization in its Global Estimates of Modern Slavery: Forced Labor and Forced Marriage, International Labor Office, Geneva, 2017, 5. This decline is explained by

the reduction in the number of cases of human trafficking for the purpose of sexual exploitation, which mostly affects women and girls, which is a consequence of the more difficult detection of cases due to the use of less visible and less secure locations during the COVID-19 pandemic. Global Report on Trafficking in Persons 2022, 32.

76. Ibid.

77. M. Evola, J. Jungfleisch, T. Marinković, "Human Rights Law Through the Lens of the Gender Perspective," *Gender-Competent Legal Education* (eds. D. Vujadinović, M. Frohlich, T. Giegerich), Springer, London, 2022, 224.

78. K. A. Doung, "Human Trafficking in a Globalized World: Gender Aspects of the Issue and Anti-Trafficking Politics," *Journal of Research in Gender Studies*, 2(1)/2012, 57.

79. https://www.unicef.org/supply/stories/inclusive-construction-keeps-girls-school-and-learning, 17.11.2023.

80. The Inter-Agency Coordination Group against Trafficking in Persons, *The Gender Dimensions of Human Trafficking*, Issue Brief No. 4, 09/2017, 1.

81. C. Kenny, N. Malik, "Trafficking Terror and Sexual Violence: Accountability for Human Trafficking and Sexual and Gender-Based Violence by Terrorist Groups under the Rome Statute," *Vanderbilt Journal of Transnational Law*, 52(1)/January 2019, 43.

82. CEDAW, General Recommendation No. 38 on Trafficking in Women and Girls in the Context of Global Migration, CEDAW/C/GC/38, November 2020, 20.

83. UN Handbook for Legislation on Violence Against Women, 2010, http://www.un.org/womenwatch/daw/vaw/handbook/Handbook%20for%20legislation%20on%20violence%20again t%20women.pdf, 11.10.2023.

84. Organization of American States (OAS), American Convention on Human Rights, "Pact of San Jose," *Costa Rica*, November 22, 1969.

85. According to the official estimate by UNWOMEN, https://www.unwomen.org/en/news-stories/in- focus/2022/10/in-focus-women-peace-and-security?gclid=CjwKCAiAheacBhB8EiwAItVO2- ibNHlyDEZ7wWp962YxFZOri0HR1aTgLBPiEed7HVlh3sb2VMwf_xoCyowQAvD_BwE, 18.11.2023.

86. Ibid.

87. UN Resolution adopted by the General Assembly on December 16, 2020 [on the report of the Third Committee (A/75/471, para. 80)] 75/161, Intensification of efforts to prevent and eliminate all forms of violence against women and girls, A/RES/75/161.

88. UN Resolution No 48/104.

89. UN Resolution on intensification of efforts to prevent and eliminate all forms of violence against women and girls, A/RES/75/161.

90. Ibid.

91. Ibid.

Chapter 4

Regionally the Most Comprehensive International Legal Norms on Violence to Women

Ius est ars boni et aequi.[1]

CHRONOLOGY OF REGIONAL LEGAL FIGHTS AGAINST VIOLENCE TO WOMEN—SPECIAL INSIGHT INTO THE CONVENTION OF BELÉM DO PARÁ, BRAZIL, 1994, AND MAPUTO PROTOCOL, 2003

UN CEDAW's standard-setting has been strengthened by many additional regional human rights instruments for the protection of women and girls against violence. Several of them have gone beyond CEDAW's standards. The 1994 Inter-American Convention on the Prevention, Punishment, and Eradication of Violence against Women (Convention of Belém do Pará) recognized women's human right to live free from violence, which includes the right to live free from all forms of discrimination. The Convention of Belém do Pará also established the state duty to apply due diligence in order to prevent, punish, and eradicate violence against women. This regional Convention and the 2003 Protocol to the African Charter on Human and People's Rights on the Human Rights of Women (Maputo Protocol) have both included economic violence as a form of violence against women.

Relevant regional international instruments are:

Inter-American Convention on the prevention, punishment and eradication of violence against women (Convention of Belém do Pará, Brazil, 1994) adopted by the Organization of American States (OAS);

- Protocol to the African Charter on Human and People's Rights on the Human Rights of Women (Maputo Protocol, 2003);
- Declaration on the Elimination of Violence against Children in the Association of Southeast Asian Nations (ASEAN, 2013);
- Convention on Preventing and Combating Violence against Women and Domestic Violence (Istanbul Convention, 2014), adopted by the Council of Europe;
- ASEAN Regional Plan of Action on the Elimination of Violence Against Women (2015);
- ASEAN Regional Plan of Action on the Elimination of Violence Against Children (2016);
- ASEAN Convention Against Trafficking in Persons, Especially Women and Children (Association of Southeast Asian Nations [ASEAN], 2017);
- Arab Strategy for Combating Violence against Women, 2011–2020[2] and
- Regional Strategy for the Protection of Arab Women (2012).

ASEAN countries have established (2010) the ASEAN Commission on The Promotion and Protection of the Rights of Women and Children (ACWC), which is responsible for promoting and protecting the rights of women and children in the Southeast Asian region.[3]

Inter-American Convention on the Prevention, Punishment, and Eradication of Violence against Women, Convention of Belém do Pará, Brazil, 1994

The Inter-American Convention on the Prevention, Punishment, and Eradication of Violence against Women, known as the Convention of Belém do Pará (where it was adopted in 1994), defines violence against women, establishes that women have the right to live a life free of violence, and that violence against women constitutes a violation of human rights and fundamental freedoms. It was adopted by the Organization of American States (OAS).

Belém do Pará was the first treaty in the world to focus solely on ending violence against women. It was created in response to the gap in the legal framework on the issue, as an analysis of the Inter-American Human Rights System notes: "the jurisprudence of the Inter-American Commission and Court has made clear general human rights treaties do not address with sufficient specificity the particular complexities and nuances that arise in cases of violence against women."[4]

This Convention consists of five main sections and twenty-five articles and calls for the first time for the establishment of mechanisms for protecting and defending women's rights as essential to combating the phenomenon of violence against women's physical, sexual, and psychological integrity, whether in the public or private sphere.[5] Besides, this Convention fosters asserting those rights within society. A key strength is the specific mention of marginalized communities, including women with disabilities, refugees and displaced women, and women from minority ethnic groups.

Parameter of due diligence by the State to prevent, investigate, and impose penalties for violence against women was formulated for the first time in the international convention in Article 7 (b) of the Belém do Pará Convention. The due diligence standard is both a negative duty on the state and a positive obligation for the state to respond appropriately to prevent, analyze, execute appropriate sentencing, and provide redress. It was inspired by the UN CEDAW General Recommendation No. 19 (1992): "Under general international law and specific human rights covenants, States may also be responsible for private acts if they fail to act with due diligence to prevent violations of rights or to investigate and punish acts of violence, and for providing compensation."[6] In particular, States must prevent, investigate, and punish violations of human rights committed by private persons or entities, which are not State organs. The Inter-American Court of Human Rights, in the case *Velásquez Rodríguez v. Honduras*,[7] addressed for the first time the issue of State responsibility for acts committed by non-State actors.

Belém do Pará Convention has a positive impact, since it has led to the development of domestic legislation and public policy reforms that provide greater protection for women. A prime example is the "Maria da Penha Law" in Brazil, which acknowledged different types of domestic violence and outlined protective measures for victims and preventive arrest of offenders.[8]

Belém do Pará Convention requires States Parties to submit reports to the Inter-American Commission of Women. However, to improve enforcement, the Statute of the Follow-up Mechanism to the Belém do Pará (MESECVI) was created in 2004, as a follow-up mechanism to these reports, which represents a testament to the OAS's commitment to the eradication of violence against women and the challenge of monitoring implementation.[9] MESECVI is composed of two bodies:

(1) a Conference of States Parties, the political organ made up of state representatives that meet periodically to discuss best practices and issue guidelines and resolutions; and
(2) a Committee of Experts, a more independent group, which receives reports and issues recommendations with the technical assistance of the Inter-American Commission of Women.

MESECVI publishes hemispheric reports on the progress and challenges of the Convention. It has found that the lack of data on violence against women and the lack of resources inhibit the treaty's effectiveness. Furthermore, another limitation is that Belém do Pará limits justiciability to a single article of the Convention, which makes it unclear which governing body has jurisdiction to deal with individual communications.

Protocol to the African Charter on Human and Peoples' Rights on the Rights of Women in Africa, the Maputo Protocol, 2003

The Protocol to the African Charter on Human and Peoples' Rights on the Rights of Women in Africa, also known as the Maputo Protocol, was adopted in 2003 and entered into force in 2005. Its adoption was born out of concern that "despite the ratification of the African Charter on Human and Peoples' Rights and other international human rights instruments by the majority of States Parties . . . women in Africa still continue to be victims of discrimination and harmful practices."[10]

Indeed, provisions for areas of concern such as polygamy, harmful traditional practices, sexual orientation, and women's right to control fertility were debatable during drafting. The Maputo Protocol, includes thirty-two articles guaranteeing women's equal rights in the public sphere and their autonomy in reproductive health decisions and calls for an end to harmful practices, including female genital mutilation and cutting.

Adoption of the Protocol was driven largely by women's rights NGOs, a testament to the strength of the women's rights movement and organizations in Africa. The Maputo Protocol is a women's rights treaty and it has a strong definition of violence against women, which includes acts that are not often viewed as violence themselves, but acts that could lead to physical, sexual, psychological, or economic harm, such as restrictions of freedom. Consequently, the Maputo Protocol addresses the contextual elements of violence against women, and the elements of power and control that restrict women's human rights.

The Protocol was a move toward a more specific and comprehensive approach to addressing violence against women and girls. It includes a provision on abortion, which marked the first time such provisions were included in an international or regional human rights instrument. It expanded on the UN CEDAW Convention in a context-specific manner, in particular outlining the private sphere as a space for women's rights to be realized. It requires the criminalization of rape within marriage and sets the minimum age of marriage at eighteen years. It provides greater protection for women in armed conflict and spells out socio-economic rights in greater detail than seen in CEDAW.[11]

Notably, the Preamble states that African values are based on the principles of equality, freedom, dignity, justice, solidarity, and democracy, an important clarification, "as research indicates that violence, including wife beating, has been considered or perceived to be one of the values of African families in some societies."[12]

The Maputo Protocol outlines the responsibilities of the state for legal and non-legal measures in addressing violence against women, including the enactment of legislation, application of punishment or sanctions, provision of services, including public awareness raising, and prioritizing adequate budgets for these interventions. Drawbacks of the Protocol center on the narrow language that deters some states from ratifying the convention (forty-two of fifty-five nations have ratified the Protocol) and aspirational provisions that create legal obligations states cannot meet.[13] African NGOs' shadow reports are largely absent or underutilized in the African Human Rights system.

Current implementation of the Protocol to the African Charter on Human and Peoples' Rights on the Rights of Women in Africa (Maputo Protocol, 2005) remains slow and inconsistent, although progressive policy commitments and institutional frameworks exist. Accountability for and tracking of the implementation of these commitments remains a major challenge in Africa.[14] Lack of resources and absence of political will together hamper the Protocol's success. The African Charter Court on Human and Peoples' Rights has yet to issue a judgment on a single case related to violence against women.

Regional Strategy for the Protection of Arab Women, 2012

The Regional Strategy for the Protection of Arab Women builds on and refers to regional and international human rights instruments and the international policy framework on women, peace, and security. It was developed in 2012 by the secretariat of the League of Arab States and the Arab Women Organization. Its visions are

> to guarantee the right of Arab women to be protected from all forms of gender-based violence in times of war and peace, to attain their full rights without any form of discrimination, and to enhance their role in a society where justice and equality prevail.

The overall objective is to establish a general Arab framework that creates a gender-sensitive environment that will stimulate other Arab parties concerned and decision-makers at the Arab regional level and at national levels in the various Arab countries to pursue concrete steps to protect women against all forms of gender-based violence to which they are exposed, particularly in wartime, occupation, and armed conflicts.

In 2016, the League and UN Women organized the first ministerial conference on Women and Achieving Peace and Security in the Arab Region. Conference participants from eighteen Arab countries discussed the implementation of the Regional Strategy and the UN Security Council Resolution 1325 (2000), concluding with a number of recommendations, including the provision of technical assistance to Arab countries to develop their national action plans. Other recommendations focused on the importance of developing monitoring mechanisms to enhance accountability for the women, peace, and security agenda, and of ensuring at least 30 percent representation of women in legislative bodies, decision-making circles, and peace negotiation teams. The closing statement urged the international community to support the development of reliable reporting mechanisms on sexual violence, and better access to services and medical and psychological care for VAW survivors, refugees, and internally displaced women and girls.[15]

ISTANBUL CONVENTION OF THE COUNCIL OF EUROPE (COE)—REGIONAL TREATY WITH GLOBAL LEGAL IMPORTANCE

> Achieving equality between women and men is an integral part leading to true democracy. As a precondition, the participation of all members, women and men, in all social spheres, must be fully ensured. Democracy must become gender sensitive.[16]

The Council of Europe Convention on Preventing and Combating Violence against Women and Domestic Violence—CoE Istanbul Convention—Main Features

More than ten years have passed since signing of the Council of Europe (CoE) Convention on Preventing and Combating Violence against Women and Domestic Violence in Istanbul.[17] Precisely, in May 2011, the Istanbul conference of the CoE Committee of Ministers marked the signing of the new Convention and the start of the ratification process. The CAHVIO expert Committee, formed by a decision of the Committee of Ministers of the CoE in December 2008, started its work in April 2009 on the basis of the mandate entrusted by the CoE Committee of Ministers to formulate the text of the Convention. Its work at the expert level lasted from April 2009 till February 2011.

The Council of Europe Convention on Preventing and Combating Violence against Women and Domestic Violence (Istanbul Convention, 2014) established a far-reaching and the most comprehensive set of legal standards to ensure the prevention of violence against women in all its forms, the protection and support of victims, and the prosecution of perpetrators. The Istanbul Convention of the Council of Europe is open to accession by non-member countries. The Istanbul Convention aims at zero tolerance in each society for gender-based violence against women and domestic violence.

Since the Convention regulates the prevention, protection of victims and prosecution of the perpetrators in a holistic manner, the Convention has global legal significance. Its applicability to the growing digital dimension of violence against women has been confirmed through GREVIO's General Recommendation No. 1 of October 2021.[18] Together, these legal instruments increase the protection standards for women and girls. Their implementation is supported by international and regional independent monitoring mechanisms, united in the Platform of Independent Expert Mechanisms on the Elimination of Discrimination and Violence against Women (EDVAW Platform). On the basis of firm legal standards and in view of the ongoing epidemic of violence against women, particularly during times of conflict, the EDVAW Platform calls on the international community, first and foremost states, to reaffirm the existing legal frameworks and to allocate greater efforts toward their effective implementation in order not to erode the established rights that these frameworks protect.[19] The respective monitoring bodies and mechanisms, as well as regional human rights courts, have consistently given specific meaning to the existing legal standards, further developing their implementation and scope of application.

The Council of Europe (CoE) Recommendation Rec (2002)5 of the Committee of Ministers to member states on the protection of women against violence (2002)[20] is the direct legal predecessor of the Istanbul Convention. This Recommendation belongs to the soft law instruments, but it was the result of the thorough work of the Task Force of the Council of Europe and it paved the way for many standards established by the Istanbul Convention. The foundation of the Istanbul Convention is the European Convention on Human Rights (1950) and the case law of the European Court of Human Rights, which safeguards, *inter alia*, the right to life and the right not to be subjected to torture or to inhuman or degrading treatment or punishment, the right to liberty and security, and the right to a fair trial. The CoE Convention on Action against Trafficking in Human Beings (CETS No. 197, 2005) and the CoE Convention on the Protection of Children against Sexual Exploitation and Sexual Abuse (CETS No. 201, 2007) represent complementary regional instruments to the Istanbul Convention.

Furthermore, the European Social Charter (1961) and the revised European Social Charter (1996), in particular the provisions therein concerning equality between women and men with regard to employment, as well as the Additional Protocol to the European Social Charter providing for a system of collective complaints, are regional legal frameworks of the CoE

Recommendation Rec (2002)5 of the Committee of Ministers to member states on the protection of women against violence (2002). Recommendation Rec No (2002)5 proposes for the first time in Europe a comprehensive strategy for the prevention of violence against women and the protection of victims in all Council of Europe member states. This Recommendation was later elaborated in the articles of the Istanbul Convention (eighty-one articles divided into twelve chapters).

Turkey was the first CoE member state to ratify the Convention. At the time of writing, a total of 37 member states of the Council of Europe have ratified the Istanbul Convention, as well as the European Union, for which the Convention entered into force on October 1, 2023.[21186] Convention is titled as "Istanbul Convention" to express gratitude to Turkey for the support of Turkey in its ratification and to mark the place where the Convention was signed. However, it is a historical paradox that we are witnessing the withdrawal of Turkey from the Istanbul Convention, which was notified in March 2021 and took effect on July 1, 2021. This withdrawal has a huge negative impact on Turkey in terms of the effective prevention of violence against women and domestic violence, as well as for victims' protection and the prosecution of perpetrators.

Ten years passed since the entry into force of the Convention, in August 2014, after ten state signatories had deposited their ratification instruments. Consequently, it is the first international treaty that establishes a comprehensive set of legally binding obligations to ensure a holistic response to all forms of violence against women, including domestic violence.[22] By accepting the Istanbul Convention, governments are obliged to change their laws, introduce practical measures, and allocate resources to effectively prevent and combat violence against women and domestic violence.[23]

The Preamble of the Convention recalls, *inter alia*, the most important international legal instruments which directly deal with the scope of this Convention in the framework of the United Nations, such as: the Beijing Declaration and Platform for Action (1995), with successive political declarations (Beijing + 15 and Women 2000); the UN Convention on the Elimination of All Forms of Discrimination Against Women ("CEDAW," 1979) and its Optional Protocol (1999) as well as General Recommendation No. 19 of the CEDAW Committee on violence against women; the UN Convention on the Rights of the Child (1989) and its Optional Protocols (2000); and the UN Convention on the Rights of Persons with Disabilities (2006).

The Istanbul Convention is based on the principles of prevention, protection, punishment (the concept of three "P's") plus comprehensive and coordinated policies, which all represent four pillars of the Convention. Starting from empirical facts, the focus is primarily on violence against women, since nine out of ten victims of domestic violence are women and girls.[24]

Violence against women is one of the most common violations of women's human rights. According to the World Health Organization, at least one in three women worldwide experiences one or more serious physical and/or sexual violent incidents during their lifetime, often from an intimate partner or ex-partner. In Europe, according to recently conducted surveys, one-fifth to one-quarter of all women have experienced physical violence at least once during their adult lives, and more than one-tenth have suffered sexual violence involving the use of force. Figures for all forms of violence, including stalking, are as high as 45 percent.

Gender inequality and social norms legitimizing violence against women are underlying forces that feed into gender-based violence against women. At the same time, social protests are growing, with contemporary international campaigns such as #NotOkay, #MeToo, and #IHave. Until the 1960s, it was believed that domestic violence was very rare and unusual behavior.[25] However, in most European legal systems, in contemporary situations, violence against women (gender-based violence) and family (domestic) violence are criminalized and considered to be serious social dangers with parallel economic negative consequences for the whole society. Until the adoption of the Council of Europe (CoE) Convention on the Prevention and Combating Violence against Women and Domestic Violence (Istanbul Convention), there was no international legal instrument on this subject implemented in Europe, except for the UN CEDAW Convention on the elimination of all forms of discrimination against women, with its Optional Protocol and Recommendation no. 19, brought by the CEDAW Committee under this UN Convention.

It can be assessed that there is a time "after the Istanbul Convention," in contrast with the time "before the Istanbul Convention," seen from a global and regional perspective. The Istanbul Convention is the first European treaty specifically targeting violence against women and domestic violence in a legally binding manner. The legally binding character is also assured through its monitoring mechanism, which has been established (GREVIO),[26] as well as through the precise content of state duties in this area of women human rights protection, such as protection against all forms of violence. Furthermore, this CoE Convention is based on several fundamental legal standards, which derive from international law, such as due diligence. In this way, the Istanbul Convention is mirroring global legal principles, aiming at the same time to gain global implementation for itself.

Istanbul Convention: A Legal Breakthrough

The Istanbul Convention aims at zero tolerance for gender-based violence in each society. In the Council of Europe's (CoE) Istanbul Convention, violence against women, that is, gender-based violence has been recognized as a form of discrimination and a violation of women's human rights. According to the Convention, it is the duty of governments to protect women as citizens against this violence and, above all, to prevent it. This Convention is a historic legal milestone. Countries ratifying the Convention have to establish services such as hotlines, shelters, medical services, counseling, and legal aid. The aim of the Istanbul Convention is to ensure protection for victims of domestic violence, particularly women and girls, since they are the most prevalent majority of victims, but also for other victims of domestic violence, including children, elderly people, and men.

The notion of gender is for the first time officially included into an international document with a legally binding nature, such as the CoE Istanbul Convention (Art. 3, Definitions). The notion of gender in this context assumes socially constructed roles, behaviors, activities and attributes that society considers appropriate behavior for women and men. Contemporary practice has shown that gender roles and stereotypes result in harmful patterns and contribute to making violence against women socially acceptable. Globally seen, reaching equality among all population groups and the absence of discrimination in contemporary society are moral imperatives.

Violence against women in partnerships, although it represents a relationship of "formal equality," occurs in the context of total discrimination against women, unequal opportunities, the inaccessibility of personal, social, political, economic, and other resources, as well as gender stereotypes and the marginalization of this type of violence. Consequently, it is of vital importance that the prevention and fight against gender-based violence are put within wider context of gender equality in the CoE Istanbul Convention, through the notion of gender and by focusing the Convention on women and girls as the most prevalent victims of family violence. Notwithstanding these facts, discussion during the negotiations of the Istanbul Convention about definitions of gender-based and domestic violence lasted six months at the expert level in the CAHVIO Committee. The negotiation results were separate definitions, contained in article 3 of the Convention.

The definition of "violence against women" makes clear that, for the purpose of the Convention, violence against women shall be understood to constitute a violation of women's human rights and a form of discrimination against women. This is in line with the purpose of the Convention set out in Article 1 (b): to contribute to the elimination of all forms of discrimination against women and to promote substantive equality between women and men, including by empowering women.

The second part of the definition is the same as that contained in Council of Europe Recommendation Rec (2002) 5 of the Committee of Ministers to member states on the protection of women against violence, the CEDAW Committee General Recommendation No. 19 on violence against women

(1992), as well as in Article 1 of the United Nations Declaration on the Elimination of All Forms of Violence against Women. The drafters have, however, expanded the definition to include the notion of "economic harm," which is often linked to psychological violence against women.

Article 3—Definitions

For the purpose of this Convention:

(a) "Violence against women" is understood as a violation of human rights and a form of discrimination against women and shall mean all acts of gender-based violence that result in, or are likely to result in, physical, sexual, psychological, or economic harm or suffering to women, including threats of such acts, coercion, or arbitrary deprivation of liberty, whether occurring in public or in private life;
(b) "Domesti violence" shall mean all acts of physical, sexual, psychological or economic violence that occur within the family or domestic unit or between former or current spouses or partners, whether or not the perpetrator shares or has shared the same residence with the victim;
(c) "Gender" shall mean the socially constructed roles, behaviors, activities and attributes that a given society considers appropriate for women and men;
(d) "Gender-based violence against women" shall mean violence that is directed against a woman because she is a woman or that affects women disproportionately;
(e) "Victim" shall mean any natural person who is subject to the conduct specified in points a and b;
(f) "Women" includes girls under the age of 18.

Article 3 (b) provides a definition of "domestic violence" that covers acts of physical, sexual, psychological or economic violence between members of the family or domestic unit, irrespective of biological or legal family ties. Economic violence can be related to psychological violence.

Domestic violence includes mainly two types of violence:

- intimate partner violence between current or former spouses or partners and
- inter-generational violence, which typically occurs between parents and children. It is a gender-neutral definition that encompasses victims and perpetrators of both sexes.

The term "gender-based violence against women" is used throughout the Istanbul Convention and refers to violence that is directed against a woman because she is a woman or that affects women disproportionately. It differs from other types of violence in that the victim's gender is the primary motive for the acts of violence. Gender-based violence refers to any harm that is perpetrated against a woman and that is both the cause and the result of unequal power relations, based on perceived differences between women and men that lead to women's subordinate status in both the private and public spheres. This type of violence is deeply rooted in the social and cultural structures, norms, and values that govern society and is often perpetuated by a culture of denial and silence. The use of the expression "gender-based violence against women" in this Convention is understood as equivalent to the expression "gender-based violence" used in the CEDAW Committee General Recommendation No. 19 on violence against women (1992), the UN General Assembly

Declaration on the Elimination of Violence against Women (1993), and Recommendation Rec (2002)5 of the Committee of Ministers of the Council of Europe to member states on the protection of women against violence (2002). This expression is to be understood as aimed at protecting women from violence resulting from gender stereotypes and specifically encompasses women. However, some authors warn that in practice, the interpretation of gender-related violence is still "in progress," and the lack of relevant harmonization could eventually hinder fundamental human rights instead of helping the Istanbul Convention save lives.[27]

Notion of economic harm, which is linked with psychological violence, is included in the definition of "violence against women" in the Convention. Economic violence happens when a woman is forced to become dependent through the improper use of money by a partner in an intimate relationship. The abuser may also forbid employment or education to gain additional financial control.[28] Psychological violence includes verbal and non-verbal communication, which inflicts emotional or mental harm. Emotional or psychological violence may be subtle, followed by the isolation of a woman from friends, family, school, and work. It is often very harmful to the victim, resulting in depression and suicide.[29]

Violence usually begins with verbal threats, which aggravate into physical violence. Violent manifestations are often unpredictable, and the triggers are unclear to the victims. Therefore, the victims sense a constant fear of the next violent attack. Violence is performed in an endless cycle involving three phases that are constantly repeating: tension-building, explosive (direct violence), and honeymoon, with remorse of the perpetrator. In practice, certain social roles and negative stereotypes contribute to make violence against women acceptable. To overcome such gender roles, Article 12 (1) of the CoE Istanbul Convention formulates the eradication of prejudices, customs, traditions, and other practices, which are based on the idea of the inferiority of women or on stereotyped gender roles, as a general obligation of states to prevent violence. The Convention calls for a gendered understanding of violence against women and domestic violence, as a basis for all measures to protect and support victims. Complexity of the phenomenon of violence against women urges has to be addressed in the context of the prevailing inequality between women and men, existing stereotypes, gender roles, and discrimination against women. The term "gender" under this definition is not intended as a replacement for the terms "women" and "men" used in the Istanbul Convention.[30]

Violence against women seriously violates and impairs or nullifies the enjoyment by women of their human rights, in particular their fundamental rights to life, security, freedom, dignity, and physical and emotional integrity, and therefore it cannot be ignored by governments. Moreover, gender-based violence against women affects not only women adversely, but society as a whole. Therefore, urgent action is required. Some groups of women, such as women and girls with disabilities, are often at greater risk of experiencing violence, injury, abuse, neglect or negligent treatment, maltreatment, or exploitation, both within and outside the home. Since many of the forms of violence covered by the CoE Istanbul Convention are perpetrated against both women and girls, the drafters did not intend to limit the applicability of the Convention to adult victims only. Consequently, this Convention clearly states that the term "women" includes girls under the age of eighteen years.

Men and boys may also be victims of domestic violence, and this kind of violence should also be addressed by governments. Consequently, Article 2, par. 2 of the Convention encourages States Parties to apply the Convention to all victims of domestic violence, but the focus of the Convention is certainly on the women victims of gender-based violence, since women are the prevalent victims of violence. Where children are concerned, they do not need to be directly affected by the violence to be considered as victims, but witnessing domestic violence is also traumatizing and therefore sufficient to victimize them.

Furthermore, the Convention applies in times of peace and in situations of armed conflict. Applicability of the Convention during armed conflict is valid, as complementary to the principles of international humanitarian law and international criminal law. The Preamble to the Convention refers to the basic principles of international humanitarian law and the Rome Statute of the International Criminal Court, affirming that individual criminal responsibility exists under international law for violence that occurs primarily (but not exclusively) during armed conflict. Article 7 of the Rome Statute (crimes against humanity committed as part of a widespread or systematic attack directed against any civilian population, and Article 8 (war crimes) include crimes of violence committed largely against women, such as rape and sexual violence. The Rome Statute of the International Criminal Court provides the broadest statutory recognition of gender-based violence as a crime under international criminal law to date. In Article 7 (1)(g), the Rome Statute classifies "rape, sexual slavery, enforced prostitution, forced pregnancy, enforced sterilization, or any other form of sexual violence of comparable gravity" committed "as part of a widespread or systematic attack directed against any civilian population" as crimes against humanity. These same offenses are classified in Article 8 (2) (b)(xxii) as serious violations of the laws and customs applicable to international armed conflict and thereby classifiable as war crimes. Bearing in mind that the Convention refers to the Rome Statute, an estimate arises that the scope of the Convention is comprehensive.

Violence against women often continues after an intimate relationship has ended. Therefore, a joint residence of the victim and perpetrator is not required as a precondition for violence to be identified. Forms and manifestations of violence against women vary depending on the specific social, economic, cultural, and political context. Violence in intimate partner relationships, especially physical violence, implies a system of continuously present violent tactics—threats, intimidation, and coercion,[31] the aim of which is to maintain power and control over women by creating a real and constantly present fear for life and well-being, or through very rough behavior over a long time period (battering).

Istanbul Convention: Due Diligence, Equality, and Non-discrimination

A requirement of due diligence has been adopted in a number of international human rights instruments, interpretations, and judgments with respect to violence against women. These include CEDAW Committee General Recommendation No. 19 on violence against women (1992), Article 4 of the UN General Assembly Declaration on the Elimination of Violence against Women (1993), the Convention on the Prevention of Violence against Women (Convention of Belém do Pará, 1994) adopted by the Organization of American States, as well as the Council of Europe Recommendation Rec (2002)5 of the Committee of Ministers to member states on the protection of women against violence (2002).

The due diligence standard has been widely used in the reports and work of a range of UN bodies. These include the reports of the special rapporteurs of the UN Commission on Human Rights (now Human Rights Council), for example, those on torture, on extrajudicial, summary and arbitrary executions, and on the use of mercenaries as a means of violating human rights and impeding the exercise of the right of people to self-determination, and in reports by representatives of the Secretary-General, for example, the Representative on internally displaced persons. An especially significant and excellent analysis of the obligation of due diligence is that of the UN Human Rights Council's Special Rapporteur on violence against women in the Annual Report, 2006, Standard of Due Diligence E/CN.4/2006/61. The report examines the due diligence standard as a tool for the effective implementation of women's human rights, including the right to live a life free from violence. It explains the development of due diligence in human rights law, especially in the context of violence against women, and also provides:

(a) A focus on State obligation to transform the societal values and institutions that sustain gender inequality while at the same time effectively responding to violence against women when it occurs, and
(b) Examine the shared responsibilities of State and non-State actors with respect to preventing and responding to violence and other violations of women's human rights.

The duty of due diligence under international law evolved from the principles of diplomatic protection whereby a state incurs international responsibility for the commission of an international wrongful act against a non-national person. It has been applied in the context of human rights violations since the landmark case of *Velasquez Rodriguez v. Honduras* (1989). In this case (which concerned disappearances), the Inter-American Court of Human Rights held that a state must take action to prevent human rights violations and to investigate, prosecute, and punish them when they occur. The Court determined that the state's failure or omission to take preventive or protective action "itself represents a violation of basic rights on the State's part. This is because the state controls the means to verify acts occurring within its territory."[32]

Under international public law, a state is responsible for the commission of an internationally wrongful act that is attributable to it, through the conduct of its agents such as the police, immigration officials, and prison officers. This principle is set out in the International Law Commission's Articles on the Responsibility of States for Internationally Wrongful Acts (2001), which are widely accepted as customary international law. Under international human rights law, the state has both negative duties and positive duties: state officials must both respect the law and refrain from the commission of internationally wrongful acts and, furthermore, must protect individuals from forbidden acts of non-state actors.

The legal basis for the ultimate attribution of responsibility to a State for private acts relies on the State's failure to comply with the duty to ensure human rights protection, as set out in Article 1(1) of the American Convention on Human Rights (1969).

Article 1—Obligation to Respect Rights

1. The States Parties to this Convention undertake to respect the rights and freedoms recognized herein and to ensure to all persons subject to

> their jurisdiction the free and full exercise of those rights and freedoms, without any discrimination for reasons of race, color, sex, language, religion, political or other opinion, national or social origin, economic status, birth, or any other social condition."[33]

Istanbul Convention, in its Article 5 (Due Diligence), paragraph 1, addresses the state obligation to ensure that their authorities, officials, agents, institutions and other actors acting on behalf of the state refrain from acts of violence against women, whereas paragraph 2 sets out States Parties' obligation to exercise due diligence in relation to acts covered by the scope of this Convention perpetrated by non-state actors. In both cases, failure to do so will incur state responsibility.

Article 5—Due Diligence

1. *Parties shall refrain from engaging in any act of violence against women and ensure that state authorities, officials, agents, institutions and other actors acting on behalf of the state act in conformity with this obligation.*
2. *Parties shall take the necessary legislative and other measures to exercise due diligence to prevent, investigate, punish and provide reparation for acts of violence covered by the scope of this Convention that are perpetrated by non-state actors.*

The term "non-state actor" refers to natural persons, as previously explained in the CoE Recommendation (2002)5 on the protection of women against violence. Furthermore, the content of Article 5 reflects the case law of the European Court of Human Rights (ECtHR). In its case law on domestic violence, the Court has adopted the obligation of due diligence (the judgment of Opuz v. Turkey, 2009).[34] The European Court has established that the positive obligation to protect the right to life (Article 2 of the European Convention for the Protection of Human Rights and Fundamental Freedoms, ECHR)[35] requires state authorities to display due diligence, particularly by taking preventive operational measures, in protecting an individual whose life is at risk.

States Parties are required to organize their response to all forms of violence covered by the scope of this Convention in a way that allows relevant authorities to diligently prevent, investigate, punish and provide reparation for such acts of violence. Failure to do so incurs state responsibility for an act otherwise solely attributed to a non-state actor. As such, violence against women perpetrated by non-state actors crosses the threshold of constituting a violation of human rights as referred to in Article 2, to such an extent that *States Parties have the obligation to take the legislative and other measures necessary to exercise due diligence to prevent, investigate, punish and provide reparation for acts of violence covered by the scope of this Convention, as well as to provide protection to the victims. State failure to do so violates and impairs or nullifies the enjoyment of victim's human rights and fundamental freedoms.*

The term "reparation" may encompass different forms of reparation under international human rights law, such as restitution, compensation, rehabilitation, satisfaction, and guarantee of non-repetition. As regards compensation, this form of reparation shall only be provided by a State Party under the conditions set out in Article 30 (2) of the Istanbul Convention:

> *Adequate State compensation shall be awarded to those who have sustained serious bodily injury or impairment of health, to the extent that the damage is not covered by other sources such as the perpetrator, insurance or State-funded health and social provisions. This does not preclude Parties from claiming regress for compensation awarded from the perpetrator, as long as due regard is paid to the victim's safety.*

This norm (paragraph 2) establishes a subsidiary obligation for the state to compensate. The conditions regarding the application for compensation may be established by internal law, such as the requirement that the victim has first and foremost sought compensation from the perpetrator. Impairment of health encompasses serious psychological damages caused by acts of psychological violence, as referred to in Article 33 of the Convention. Although the scope of state compensation is limited to serious injury and impairment of health, this does not preclude Parties from providing for more generous compensation arrangements, nor from setting higher and/or lower limits for any or all elements of compensation to be paid by the state. However, paragraph 2 of this article is open to reservations, pursuant to Article 78 (2) of this Convention, and some States Parties have made reservations.[36] However, some States Parties of the Convention have established special budget items or funds for the purposes of reparations for victims.

According to Article 30 (par.1), it is primarily the perpetrator who is liable for damages and restitution. In the event that state compensation is paid to the victim, because the perpetrator is unwilling or unable, although the court ordered it, the state shall have recourse against the perpetrator.

The Istanbul Convention is a comprehensive and complex treaty—it is at the same time a human rights treaty, covering both civil and criminal laws, and a normative instrument for greater gender equality. Putting an end to *de jure* discrimination against women is a fundamental prerequisite for the achievement of true, *de facto* equality between women and men.[37] Article 1 of the Istanbul Convention therefore lists the contribution "to the elimination of all forms of discrimination against women" and the promotion of "substantive equality between women and men, including by empowering women" as the purposes of the Convention.

The Preamble contains the drafters' recognition that the "realization of *de jure* and *de facto* equality between women and men is a key element in the prevention of violence against women" and that violence against women is a manifestation of historically unequal power relations between women and men, which have led to domination over, and discrimination against, women by men and to the prevention of the full advancement of women. *It is important to stress that the Preamble thus firmly establishes the link between achieving gender equality and the eradication of violence against women.*

The Convention legally establishes the principle (Article 4) that every person has the right to live free from violence in the public and private spheres. Regarding the focus of the implementation of the Convention, it is particularly important that women predominate among the victims of gender-based violence, and a special obligation to promote and protect this right for women has been introduced and legally guaranteed.

During the negotiations, some delegations in the expert Committee of the Council of Europe (CAHVIO Committee) objected to the accentuation of primarily women as victims of violence and demanded that the right to live free from violence in the public and private spheres should be broadly defined for all persons. A compromise solution prevailed that this right will be proclaimed and protected for all, but that the signatory states are invited to undertake legislative and other public policy measures to promote and protect the rights of everyone, and especially of women, to live free from violence in both the public and private spheres. Discrimination against women is fertile ground for the tolerance of violence against women. All measures taken to prevent and combat violence against women should promote equality between women and men as the only essential equality, which will contribute to the prevention of such violence in the future.

The provisions of Article 4, paragraph 2, confirm the principle of essential equality between women and men,[38] requiring member states not only to condemn all forms of violence against women but also to include the principle of equality in legislation, ensure its realization in practice, as well as to prohibit discrimination by law, and abolish all discriminatory laws and practices.[39]

The principle of essential equality between women and men implies that the enjoyment of the right to freedom from violence is intertwined with the obligation of member states to ensure equality between women and men in the exercise and enjoyment of all civil, political, economic, social, and cultural rights in accordance with the Council of Europe instruments in the area of human rights, especially the European Convention on Human Rights (ECHR) and its protocols, the European Social Charter, and other international instruments of which they are members, especially the UN Convention on the Elimination of All Forms of Discrimination against Women (CEDAW).[40] States Parties have two options to meet the requirement of enshrining in law the principle of equality between women and men: a constitutional amendment or its embodiment in another legislative act. The obligation to ensure the practical realization of equality between women and men assumes that enshrining it in law is often insufficient and therefore practical measures are required to implement this principle in reality (*de facto*) through affirmative public policy measures.

Provisions of Article 4 (par 3) follow the notion of discrimination that already exists in Article 14 of the European Convention on Human Rights. Furthermore, in the case of *Opuz v. Turkey*, the European Court of Human Rights discussed the link between discrimination and violence against women. The Court concluded that gender-based violence constitutes a form of discrimination because it mainly affects women and women are not protected by the law on an equal footing with men. It is of great importance for the subject of the Convention not to discriminate on the basis of the following categories: sex, gender, sexual orientation, gender identity, age, state of health, disability, marital status, and migrant or refugee status or other status, which means that this list is not exhaustive.

Research on the behavior of victims of violence against women and domestic violence regarding seeking help, as well as the provision of services in Europe, shows that discrimination against certain groups of victims is still widespread. Women can still experience discrimination from the police or the judiciary when reporting acts of gender-based violence. Similarly, gay, lesbian, and bisexual victims of domestic violence are often excluded from support services because of their sexual orientation. *Certain groups of people may also experience discrimination based on their gender identity, which simply means that the gender they identify with does not necessarily correspond to the sex they were born with.* These include categories of persons such as transgender and transsexual persons, cross-dressers, transvestites, and other groups of persons who do not correspond to what society has determined as "male" or "female" categories. In addition, *migrant and refugee women may also be excluded from support services due to their residency status. It is important to point out that women sometimes experience multiple forms of discrimination and violence, as is the case with women with disabilities and/or women from national minorities, Roma women, or women with HIV/AIDS.*

The prohibition of discrimination from paragraph 3 (Art 4) is much more limited in scope than the prohibition of discrimination against women from paragraph 2 of this article. It requires States parties to refrain from discrimination in applying the provisions of the Convention, while paragraph 2 calls on States to condemn discrimination in areas outside the jurisdiction of the Convention.

Paragraph 4 (Art. 4) refers to special measures that a member of the Convention can take to increase the protection of women from gender-based violence—measures that would be used only for women. This provision does not repeal the general prohibition of discrimination. In accordance with Article 4 of the UN CEDAW Convention, this paragraph determines that special measures are aimed at preventing and protecting women from gender-based violence and that they do not apply to men and do not constitute a form of discrimination. Those special measures toward women represent the essence of an affirmative approach, which is legitimate by its purpose to prevent and protect women from gender-based violence.

This is in line with the concept of discrimination as interpreted by the European Court of Human Rights in its case law relating to Article 14 of the ECHR Convention of the Council of Europe (ban of discrimination).[41] This jurisprudence specifically clarifies that not every different behavior constitutes discrimination. As the European Court stated, for example, in the judgment *Abdulaziz, Cabales and Balkandali v. the United Kingdom*, different behavior is discriminatory if it has no reason or reasonable justification, that is, if it does not follow a legitimate goal, that is, if there is no reasonable connection or reciprocity between the means used and the expected goal. The fact that women experience gender-based violence, including domestic violence, to a significantly greater extent than men can be considered a reason and a reasonable justification for the use of resources and taking special measures exclusively for the benefit of women who have experienced various forms of violence.

Istanbul Convention: Legal Principles on Investigation, Prosecution, and Protection in the Area of Combating Violence to Women

European states have changed their views on domestic violence, and people are increasingly aware that it is a negative social factor and not only a personal problem. Family violence is classified as a criminal offense in most legal systems.[42] The Istanbul Convention is comprehensive international legally binding instrument at the regional level, with twelve chapters consisting of eighty-one articles. However, starting from the point of the efficiency of those norms, a special legal analysis is to be given to a separate chapter (Chapter VI) in the CoE Istanbul Convention, which contains a variety of provisions that cover a broad range of issues related to investigation, prosecution, procedural law, and protection against all forms of violence covered by the scope of the Istanbul Convention.

What is even more important, the general obligations for states signatories of the Convention are established in this context of combating gender-based and domestic violence (Article 49—General obligations). States signatories of the Convention are obliged to take all necessary legislative or other measures to make certain that *investigations and judicial proceedings regarding all forms of violence covered by the scope of the Convention are performed without undue delay with parallel taking into consideration the rights of the victim during all stages of the criminal proceedings.* States parties of the Convention have the duty to take the necessary legislative or other measures, in line with the essential principles of human rights, while having regard to the gendered understanding of violence in order to ensure the effective investigation and prosecution of offenses established and defined in the Convention.

The objective of those standards is to prevent incidents of violence against women and domestic violence being assigned low priority in investigations and judicial proceedings, which contributes significantly to the sense of impunity among perpetrators. This aim helps to secure vital evidence, enhance conviction rates, and put an end to impunity. It is important to note that while it is essential to ensure swift investigations and proceedings, it is equally important to respect the rights of victims during these stages.

Effective investigation and prosecution of offenses established in accordance with this Convention means establishing the relevant facts, interviewing all available witnesses, and conducting forensic examinations based on a multidisciplinary approach and using state-of-the-art criminal investigative methodology to ensure a comprehensive analysis of the case.

All investigations and procedures are to be carried out in conformity with fundamental principles of human rights and with regard to a gendered understanding of violence—measures taken in implementation of this provision are not prejudicial to the rights of the defense and the requirements of a fair and impartial trial, in conformity with Article 6 European Convention on Human Rights (ECHR).[43] Especially important is the notion of a gendered understanding of violence, bearing in mind the fact that women are prevalent victims in the public and in private spheres. Law enforcement agencies in states signatories and parties to the Convention, are to react promptly and appropriately by offering adequate and immediate protection to victims, while paragraph 2 of the Article 50 calls for their prompt and appropriate engagement in the prevention of and protection against all forms of violence covered by the scope of this Convention, including the employment of preventive operational measures and the collection of evidence.

Article 50—Immediate response, prevention and protection

1. *Parties shall take the necessary legislative or other measures to ensure that the responsible law enforcement agencies respond to all forms of*

violence covered by the scope of this Convention promptly and appropriately by offering adequate and immediate protection to victims.

2. *Parties shall take the necessary legislative or other measures to ensure that the responsible law enforcement agencies engage promptly and appropriately in the prevention and protection against all forms of violence covered by the scope of this Convention, including the employment of preventive operational measures and the collection of evidence. (CoE Istanbul Convention).*

Compliance with this provision includes, for example, the following:

- the right of the responsible law enforcement agencies to enter the place where a person at risk is present;
- the treatment and giving advice to victims by the responsible law enforcement agencies in an appropriate manner;
- hearing victims without delay by specially trained, where appropriate, female staff in premises that are designed to establish a relationship of trust between the victim and the law enforcement personnel; and
- provide for an adequate number of female law enforcement officers, including at high levels of responsibility.

Effective measures should be taken to prevent the most blatant forms of violence, such as murder or attempted murder. Each such case should be carefully analyzed in order to identify any possible failure of protection, with a view of improving and developing further preventive measures.

Parties of the Convention have the obligation to ensure that any assessment of the risks faced by a victim should systematically takes into consideration, at all stages of the investigation and application of protective measures, whether the perpetrator legally or illegally possesses or has access to firearms in order to guarantee the safety of victims (Par 2). This article therefore establishes the obligation to ensure that all relevant authorities, not limited to the police, effectively assess and devise a plan to manage the safety risks a particular victim faces on a case-by-case basis, according to standardized procedures and in cooperation and coordination with each other.

Essential is that any risk assessment and risk management is to consider the probability of repeated violence, notably deadly violence, and adequately assess the seriousness of the situation. Essential is that such measures shall not aggravate any damage experienced by victims. Very important is that investigations and judicial proceedings should not lead to secondary victimization.

Article 51—Risk assessment and risk management

1. Parties shall take the necessary legislative or other measures to ensure that an assessment of the lethality risk, the seriousness of the situation,

and the risk of repeated violence is carried out by all relevant authorities in order to manage the risk and, if necessary to provide coordinated safety and support.

2. Parties shall take the necessary legislative or other measures to ensure that the assessment referred to in paragraph 1 duly takes into account, at all stages of the investigation and application of protective measures, the fact that perpetrators of acts of violence covered by the scope of this Convention possess or have access to firearms. (CoE Istanbul Convention).

The possession of firearms by perpetrators not only constitutes a powerful means to exert control over victims, but also increases the risk of homicide—therefore, risk assessment duly takes it into account. Multi-agency risk assessment of the violence is much needed, since the current situation shows that the police does not deal with the risk assessment of the violence (as well as other agencies, such as the public prosecutor office, judges, etc.). The purpose of this rule is to ensure that an effective multi-agency network of professionals is set up to protect high-risk victims.

In case of immediate danger, it has been foreseen that competent authorities *ex officio* will order the perpetrator to vacate the residence for a sufficient period of time. The goal is to achieve more protection for the victim by taking away the perpetrator for a certain period of time and granting the victim to stay safe at home.[44]

Furthermore, the Convention has established the duty of equipping the competent authorities with the power to order a perpetrator of domestic violence to vacate the residence of the victim and to forbid him or her from returning or contacting the victim. The immediate danger must be assessed by the relevant authorities. This kind of mandatory eviction is temporary and is not linked to the ownership status. In this case, the urgent need to protect the victim (the most often a woman) is of higher priority than the protection of the ownership of the perpetrator. It refers to any situations of domestic violence in which harm is imminent or has already materialized and is very likely to happen again. Existing examples of such *emergency barring orders* in CoE member states range between ten days and four weeks, with or without the possibility of renewal.

Article 52—Emergency barring orders

> *Parties shall take the necessary legislative or other measures to ensure that the competent authorities are granted the power to order, in situations of immediate danger, a perpetrator of domestic violence to vacate the residence of the victim or person at risk for a sufficient period of time and to prohibit the perpetrator from entering the residence of or contacting the victim or person at risk.*

Measures taken pursuant to this article shall give priority to the safety of victims or persons at risk. (CoE Istanbul Convention).

There are also provisions on *protection orders*, which set out the obligation to make certain that national legislation provides for restraining and / or protection orders for victims of all forms of violence covered by the scope of this Convention. Furthermore, criteria are established for such orders to ensure that they serve their highly protective nature.

Article 53—Restraining or protection orders

1. Parties shall take the necessary legislative or other measures to ensure that appropriate restraining or protection orders are available to victims of all forms of violence covered by the scope of this Convention.
2. Parties shall take the necessary legislative or other measures to ensure that the restraining or protection orders referred to in paragraph 1 are:
   - *available for immediate protection and without undue financial or administrative burdens placed on the victim;*
   - *issued for a specified period or until modified or discharged;*
   - *where necessary, issued on an ex parte basis which has immediate effect;*
   - *available irrespective of, or in addition to, other legal proceedings;*
   - *allowed to be introduced in subsequent legal proceedings.*
3. Parties shall take the necessary legislative or other measures to ensure that breaches of restraining or protection orders issued pursuant to paragraph 1 shall be subject to effective, proportionate and dissuasive criminal or other legal sanctions." (CoE Istanbul Convention).

National legislation of certain countries Parties of the Istanbul Convention may provide for the combined use of restraining and protection orders. A restraining or protection order may be considered complementary to a short-term emergency barring order. Its purpose is to offer a fast legal remedy to protect persons at risk of any of the forms of violence covered by the scope of this Convention by prohibiting, restraining, or prescribing certain behavior by the perpetrator.[45] Whether restraining or protection orders are based in civil law, criminal procedure law, administrative law, or in all of them, will depend on the national legal system and above all on the necessity for effective protection of victims. This wide range of measures covered by such orders means that they exist under various names, such as restraining order, barring order, eviction order, protection order, or injunction. Despite these differences, they serve the same purpose: preventing the commission of violence and protecting the victim.

Any order should take effect immediately after it has been issued and shall be available without lengthy court proceedings at the national level. Order is to be issued for a specified or determined period or until modified or discharged. *It follows from the principle of legal certainty, which requires the duration of a legal measure to be spelt out clearly.* In certain cases, these orders may be issued, where necessary, on an *ex parte* basis with immediate effect. This means a judge or other competent official would have the authority to issue a temporary restraining or protection order based on the request of one party only.

Many victims who want to apply for a restraining or protection order may not be prepared to press criminal charges (which could lead to a criminal investigation and possibly criminal proceedings) against the perpetrator. Standing to apply for a restraining or protection order should therefore not be dependent on the institution of criminal proceedings against the same perpetrator. Similarly, those protection orders should not be dependent on the institution of divorce proceedings.

Paragraph 3 (Art. 53) aims to ensure respect for restraining and protection orders by requiring "effective, proportionate and dissuasive" *sanctions for any breach of such orders* (sanctions may be of a criminal law or other legal nature) and may include prison sentences, fines, or any other legal sanction.

Regarding court proceedings, the Convention provides for a gender-sensitive approach in requesting that a victim's past sexual behavior should not be considered as an excuse for acts of violence against women and/or domestic violence.[46]

Where judges admit previous sexual history evidence, it should only be presented in a way that does not lead to secondary victimization. Victims should have access to legal recourse without suffering additional trauma because of their sexual history and conduct. Nonetheless, in judicial proceedings, evidence relating to the sexual history and sexual conduct of a victim is sometimes exploited in order to discredit the evidence presented by the victim or in order to challenge the victim's respectability, credibility, and the lack of consent of the victim, which is especially problematic in the case of rape. This particularly regards cases of other forms of sexual violence, including rape.

In certain countries, members of the Convention, the admissibility and consideration of evidence lies within the discretion of the judge, while in others it is strictly prescribed in advance by the rules of criminal procedural law. This provision of the Convention limits the admissibility of such evidence relating to the sexual history and conduct of the victim, both in civil and criminal proceedings, to cases where it is relevant to the specific issue at trial and under the condition that it has significant probative value.

Istanbul Convention regulates *ex parte* and *ex officio* proceedings. Aim of those provisions is to ease the burden that lengthy criminal investigations and proceedings often place on the victims, while at the same time ensuring that perpetrators are brought to justice—to enable criminal investigations and proceedings to be carried out without placing the onus of initiating such proceedings and securing convictions on the victim.

Article 55—Ex parte and ex officio proceedings

1. Parties shall ensure that investigations into or prosecution of offenses established in accordance with Articles 35, 36, 37, 38 and 39 of this Convention shall not be wholly dependent upon a report or complaint filed by a victim if the offense was committed in whole or in part on its territory, and that the proceedings may continue even if the victim withdraws her or his statement or complaint.
2. Parties shall take the necessary legislative or other measures to ensure, in accordance *with the conditions provided for by their internal law, the possibility for governmental and non-governmental organizations and domestic violence counsellorscounselors to assist and/or support victims, at their request, during investigations and judicial proceedings concerning the offenses established in accordance with this Convention*

Crimes that are punishable within the scope of the Istanbul Convention are defined precisely (Chapter V on Substantive law):

- *Psychological violence (Art. 33),*
- *Stalking (Art. 34),*
- *Physical violence (Art. 35),*
- *Sexual violence, including rape (Art. 36),*
- *Forced marriage (Art. 37),*
- *Female genital mutilation (Art. 38),*
- *Forced abortion and forced sterilization (Art. 39),*
- *Sexual harassment (Art. 40).*

The Convention requires the States Parties to take the necessary legislative or other measures to criminalize those forms of violence. Parties are to ensure that investigations into or prosecution of offenses established in accordance with Articles 35, 36, 37, 38 and 39 of this Convention shall not be wholly dependent upon a report or complaint filed by a victim (*ex officio* proceedings), and that the proceedings may continue even if the victim withdraws her complaint. This norm establishes the priority of the public interest in the prosecution of those crimes over the protection of the victim's privacy[47] (physical violence (Art. 35), sexual violence, including rape (Art. 36), forced marriage (Art. 37), female genital mutilation (Art. 38), forced abortion and forced sterilization (Art. 39). National law enforcement authorities should investigate in a proactive way to make sure that the proceedings may be carried out even if the victim withdraws her statement or complaint. Proactive way of investigations assume gathering evidence, such as substantial evidence, testimonies of witnesses, medical expertise, and so on, in order to make sure that the proceedings may be carried out even if the victim withdraws her complaint, at least with regard to serious offenses, such as physical violence resulting in death or bodily harm. *Ex officio* proceedings have a worthy rationale: to establish the concept that violence against women and domestic violence must never be justified.[48]

Acts resulting in severe bodily harm or deprivation of life must be addressed promptly and directly by competent authorities. Many of the offenses covered by this Convention are perpetrated by family members, intimate partners, or persons in the immediate social environment of the victim, and the resulting feelings of shame, fear, and helplessness lead to low numbers of reporting and, subsequently, convictions.

Victims of domestic violence do not have an automatic right to free legal aid.[49] Istanbul Convention foresees that even in the absence of legislation granting free legal assistance in civil matters, it must be assessed whether, in the interest of justice, an applicant who is without financial means should be granted legal assistance if unable to afford a lawyer. The European Court of Human Rights in Strasbourg (ECtHR) has taken into account the complexity of procedures and the emotional character of a situation in deciding whether someone was in a position to present her or his own case effectively: European Court of Human Rights ECHR case law (*Airey v. Ireland* judgment, October 9, 1979). The Court's view is that effective access to a court may necessitate free legal assistance. Its position is that it must be ascertained whether appearance before a court without the assistance of a lawyer would be effective in the sense that the persons concerned would be able to present their case properly and satisfactorily.

Istanbul Convention includes a comprehensive set of protection measures for victims of gender-based and domestic violence (Art. 56).[50] Non-exhaustive list of procedures are established to protect victims of all forms of violence covered by the scope of this Convention during proceedings. These measures of protection apply at all stages of the proceedings. State Parties of the Convention must secure that victims are safe from intimidation, retaliation and repeat victimization. By virtue of this rule, the Convention affirms the obligation to inform victims when the perpetrator is released temporarily or definitively or escapes, at least in cases where the victim and the family might be in danger. This does not prevent States Parties to inform victims in other circumstances where this seems necessary (for instance, in cases where there is a risk of retaliation or intimidation).

In the case of child victims and child witnesses, paragraph 2 of the Article 56 determines that States Parties of the Convention must take special care of children's needs and ensure their rights to special protection measures because a child is more vulnerable than an adult and can be intimidated. Consequently, special protection measures must give due regard to the best interests of the child, which may include measures such as not obliging a child to testify in the presence of the perpetrator. Children witnesses include not only children who are present during the violence but also those who are exposed to screams and other sounds of violence while hiding close by or who are exposed to the long-term consequences of such violence. This rule (Art. 56) is inspired by Article 31, paragraph 1 of the Convention on the Protection of Children against Sexual Exploitation and Sexual Abuse (ETS No. 201).

The assessment is that the above-analyzed provisions on investigation, prosecution, and protection in the domain of fighting domestic violence and violence against women, besides their direct obligations for states signatories of the Istanbul Convention, furthermore have a specific deterrent effect through setting legal standards that are the general legal framework in Europe for achieving zero tolerance toward gender-based violence to women and domestic violence.

Istanbul Convention: States' Obligations, Prevention, Protection of Victims, and Coordinated Policies on Violence to Women and Domestic Violence

Convention requires States Parties to criminalize several behaviors which constitute violence against women and domestic violence if these conduct-sacts have not yet been included in their respective criminal codes. These behaviors include forced marriage, female genital mutilation, forced abortion and forced sterilization, stalking, sexual harassment, physical and psychological violence, and sexual violence, including rape. Article 35 on physical violence is open to reserving provisions regarding minor offenses regarding criminalization. Convention makes a clear distinction between serious offenses of physical violence, resulting in severe bodily harm or deprivation of life, which would be excluded from the possibility of reserve, and other, minor offenses of physical violence, which do not lead to such consequences. It is left to the States Parties of the Convention to define minor offenses.

Furthermore, the Convention requires States Parties to ensure that in criminal proceedings regarding the acts of violence covered by the Convention, "culture, custom, religion, tradition or so-called 'honor' are not regarded as justifications of such acts" (Article 42, par 1). In this context, an important message is proclaimed: that violence against women and domestic violence are not private matters nor can be justified through reasons of tradition or culture. In addition, by this norm, zero tolerance toward violence against women is affirmed.

The offenses established in accordance with this Convention shall apply irrespective of the nature of the relationship between victim and perpetrator (Art. 43). The most prominent example is rape within marriage, which for a long time had not been recognized as rape because of the relationship between victim and perpetrator. By virtue of this provision, the principle is established that the type of relationship between victim and perpetrator shall not preclude the application of any of the offenses identified in this Convention.

Istanbul Convention points out to the concept of interdiction of alternative resolving and mediation in marriage conflicts in case of gender-based violence and domestic violence (Art. 48)—in particular, if participation in such alternative dispute resolution methods is mandatory and replaces adversarial court proceedings. Victims of such violence can never enter the alternative dispute resolution processes on a level equal to that of the perpetrator. It is in the nature of such offenses that such victims are invariably left with a feeling of shame, helplessness, and vulnerability, while the perpetrator exudes a sense of power and dominance.

Statute of limitation is established in Article 58, defining it for offenses of sexual violence, including rape; forced marriage; female genital mutilation, forced abortion and forced sterilization, as a sufficient period of time to allow prosecutions to be effectively initiated after the victim has reached the age of majority. States' obligation, therefore, applies in relation to child victims only, who are often unable, for various reasons, to report the offenses perpetrated against them before reaching the age of majority.

In the prevention area, the Convention requires States Parties to take measures that are necessary to promote changes in mentality and attitudes:

- Change attitudes and stereotypes that make violence against women acceptable (Art. 12);
- Promote changes in the social and cultural patterns of behavior of women and men;[51]
- Train professionals working with victims or perpetrators to recognize and respond to violence and make appropriate referrals;
- Awareness-raising campaigns: raising awareness of the different forms of violence, their devastating nature, and negative impact that they have on women and children (Art. 13);
- Include teaching material on gender equality, gender-based violence against women, non-violent conflict resolution, and right to personal integrity in the formal curricula at all levels of education;
- Cooperate with NGOs, the media, and the private sector to reach out to the public;—Setting standards that enhance respectful gender roles and challenge attitudes that excuse violence against women;

- Encourage active engagement and contribution from men and boys in the prevention of violence—Positive role of men and boys, to contribute actively to preventing all forms of violence covered by the scope of this Convention;
- Introduce programs and activities for the empowerment of women, and address the specific needs of people in vulnerable situations from a human rights standpoint;
- Setting up programs aimed at teaching perpetrators of domestic violence to adopt non-violent behavior in interpersonal relationships with a view to preventing further violence and changing violent behavioral patterns, especially for sex offenders (Art 16).

In the domain of coordinated policies on violence to women and domestic violence, which is fourth pillar of the Convention, besides prevention, protection of victims and prosecution, States Parties are to undertake the following actions:

- Research and data collection: collecting and collating data and conducting research into the prevalence of all forms of violence against women and the effectiveness of their measures, which shall be shared with the public and similar agencies in other countries for comparison and to encourage cooperation;
- Inter-agency cooperation: Ensuring that there are appropriate mechanisms in place that provide for effective cooperation among the judiciary, public prosecutors, law enforcement agencies, local and regional authorities, and NGOs;
- Support and collaboration with NGOs and civil society—they should be included alongside state bodies as valued partners in the implementation of the Istanbul Convention;
- Establishing funds for policy measures and support services for victims—adequately fund all partners involved in the implementation of the Istanbul Convention, including non-governmental organizations;
- Human rights-based policies: Putting in place victim-focused laws to prevent and combat all forms of violence against women;
- Comprehensive legislation and gender-sensitive policies: Introducing laws and supporting measures to prevent all types of violence covered in this Convention;
- Coordinated action and monitoring of implementation: Creating or designating a state body to oversee the coordination, implementation, monitoring, and evaluation of the Istanbul Convention;
- Whole societal response: The Istanbul Convention sends a clear message to society as a whole. Everybody must understand that violence against women and domestic violence will not be tolerated at all—zero tolerance.

The ultimate aim of the Convention is the prevention of all forms of violence covered by its scope. Consequently, Chapter IV regulating protection and support, contains a range of obligations to set up specialized, as well as more general, support services to meet the needs of those exposed to violence.

In the field of *protection of victims*, States Parties will have to implement the following measures:

- Protection of the rights and needs of child witnesses—the best interest of child witnesses of violence must be taken into account, and age-appropriate psychosocial counseling provided;
- Providing information on the rights of victims—Victims must be informed of their rights and know where and how to get help in a language they understand;
- Enabling of support services—Victims should have access to specialist women's support services, which are often women-to-women and dedicated to a specific type of violence. Victims should also have access to general services such as legal advice/aid, psychological counseling, financial assistance, housing, education, health care, social services, and assistance in finding employment;
- Regional and international complaint mechanisms—Victims must be informed of and have access to relevant regional and international complaint mechanisms;
- Securing victims' shelters—Victims must have access to a local, easily accessible shelter for women and children;
- Establishing rape crisis or sexual violence centers—Victims must have access to a nearby, easily accessible center providing immediate medical counseling, trauma care, and forensic services;
- Providing for reporting violence to authorities—Everyone must be encouraged to report acts of violence to the relevant authorities to prevent further incidents, and confidentiality rules should not prevent professionals from doing so, where justified;
- Implementation of emergency barring orders—these will grant police the power to remove a perpetrator of domestic violence from their home for a specific period of time and order them to stay away from the victim;
- Application of protection or restraining orders—those orders should be easily accessible for immediate protection to the victim without any cost;
- Securing safe custody and visitation rights for children—If there is a history of violence, custody and visitation decisions must prioritize the rights and safety of the child and the victim;
- Enabling free telephone helplines 24/7—victims must have access to a statewide 24/7 free and confidential telephone helpline, offering them expert advice and pointing them toward relevant services.

States Parties are obliged to provide for effective cooperation among relevant stakeholders: the judiciary, public prosecutors, law enforcement agencies, local and regional authorities, and NGOs in order to implement a comprehensive approach in victims' protection. All protection measures taken are to be based on a gendered understanding of violence against women and domestic violence. This means that services offered need to demonstrate an approach relevant to their users, which recognizes the gendered dynamics, impact, and consequences of these forms of violence and which operates within a gender equality and human rights framework.[52]

Istanbul Convention: Monitoring System, GREVIO

Monitoring mechanisms, if established by international legal norms are also very important since they provide feedback on the status of concrete implementation of those international norms in each specific country, which is obliged by those provisions. The Istanbul Convention is not a "tiger made of paper," therefore it has established two pillars for monitoring of its implementation:

- the Group of Experts on Action against Violence against Women and Domestic Violence (GREVIO), an independent expert body, on the one side and
- the Committee of the Parties, a political body composed of official representatives of the States Parties to the Convention, on the other side.

Istanbul Convention (Art. 66–70) has foreseen the establishment of an independent expert international body (GREVIO) with the aim to monitor the effective implementation of the Istanbul Convention. Chapter IX of the Convention contains provisions which aim at ensuring the effective implementation of the Convention by the Parties. The legitimacy of relevant international organizations to establish mandatory legal norms has been discussed in various essays, taking into account: "decolonization; growing awareness of the global nature of many economic, environmental and public health problems; multiplication of non-governmental organizations; globalization of mass media and the market; rapid developments in the field of biotechnology; and the emergence of new information technologies, particularly the Internet."[53] In favor of effective monitoring, in its interim report, the CAHVIO Committee stated that: "The Committee is of the opinion that a strong and independent monitoring mechanism is of utmost importance to ensure that an adequate response to this problem is given in all Parties to the Convention."[54]

The Convention sets up a group of experts on action against violence against women and domestic violence (hereafter "GREVIO"), which is an expert body composed of independent and highly qualified experts in the fields of human rights, gender equality, violence against women and domestic violence, criminal law, and in assistance to and protection of victims of violence against women and domestic violence.

GREVIO is in charge of monitoring the implementation of the Convention by the Parties. It is composed of fifteen experts. GREVIO devises questionnaires for State Parties to fill in, receives, analyzes, and evaluates information, writes reports, makes recommendations, and, where necessary, holds country visits. Gender and geographical balance, as well as multidisciplinary expertise, is taken account while setting GREVIO composition, for the purpose of effectiveness of the monitoring expert body. GREVIO formulated its own rules of procedure.

After the adoption by the Committee of Ministers of the rules of the election procedure of the GREVIO members, in November 2014,[55] the first ten members of the GREVIO group were elected by the Committee of the Parties at its first meeting on May 4, 2015.[56] GREVIO held its first meeting in September 2015 in Strasbourg.

GREVIO considers a national report on general legislative and other measures undertaken by each State Party to give effect to the provisions of this Convention, with the representatives of the Party concerned. This report is submitted by the State Party and it is based on a questionnaire developed by the GREVIO. The aim of the report is to embrace general as well as concrete measures in applying the Convention in concrete State Party of the Convention. However, GREVIO also receives so-called "shadow reports" from relevant NGOs in the State Party, providing additional information on implementation of the Convention.

Subsequent evaluation procedures are divided into rounds, the length of which is determined by GREVIO. At the beginning of each round, GREVIO selects the specific provisions on which the evaluation procedure shall be based and sends out a questionnaire (Art. 68, par 3). When adopting a questionnaire for each evaluation round, GREVIO shall take due consideration of the existing data collection and research in the Parties (Art. 68, par 7). GREVIO may receive information on the implementation of the Convention from the Council of Europe Commissioner for Human Rights, the Parliamentary Assembly, and relevant specialized bodies of the Council of Europe, as well as those established under other international instruments. Complaints presented to these bodies and their outcomes will be made available to GREVIO. This is foreseen in order to avoid unnecessary duplication of work and activities already carried out in other instances.

GREVIO is authorized to organize country visits (Art. 68, par. 9), only when needed, in two cases:

1) If the information gained is insufficient and there are no other feasible ways of reliably gaining the information, or
2) in case GREVIO receives reliable information indicating a situation where problems require immediate attention to prevent or limit the scale or number of serious violations of the Convention.

GREVIO has to carry out a dialogue with the Party concerned when preparing own report and the conclusions with recommendations. It is through such a dialogue that the provisions of the Convention will be properly implemented. GREVIO will publish its report and conclusions with recommendations. Comments by the Party concerned will be published as well. This completes the task of GREVIO with respect to that Party and the provisions concerned. The report and conclusions of GREVIO, which will be made public from their adoption, cannot be modified by the Committee of the Parties.

Special procedure is furthermore foreseen, according to which GREVIO is entitled to request the submission of a report by the Party concerned related to measures taken by that Party to prevent a serious, massive or persistent pattern of any of the acts of violence covered by the Convention. The condition for requesting a special report is that GREVIO receives reliable information indicating a situation where problems require immediate attention to prevent or limit the scale or number of serious violations of the Convention. GREVIO may designate one or more of its members to conduct an inquiry and to report urgently to the GREVIO. In very exceptional cases, this inquiry could also include a visit to the country concerned. The main role of the appointed "rapporteur(s)" should be collecting all necessary information and ascertaining the facts in relation to the specific situation. The rules of procedure of GREVIO regulates the details of the functioning of this inquiry procedure. The findings of the inquiry shall be transmitted to the Party concerned and, where appropriate, to the Committee of the Parties and the Committee of Ministers of the Council of Europe together with GREVIO comments and recommendations. It should be understood as a strong political pressure on the concerned State Party in situation of a massive violations of the Convention.

In a report based on seventeen countries in Europe, covering its work from June 2019 to December 2020, GREVIO highlights trends in the provision of services for victims and discusses these against the background of the pandemic, which has greatly increased the need for victims' support. The report shows to which extent the pandemic has brought to light pre-existing gaps concerning specialist services, impacting negatively on women's and girls' ability to access specialist support services for the different forms of violence.[57] The Mid-term Horizontal Review of GREVIO of all seventeen baseline evaluation reports, dated on May 10, 2021, illustrates the findings of GREVIO, article by article of the Convention. Challenges in efficient implementation of the Convention indicate the need to ensure the Convention's aims reach all women and girls. *The emerging trend is the lack of intersectional approach to women protection.* Therefore, more comprehensive documents on gender-based violence against women are necessary.

GREVIO's general recommendation is furthermore directed to the need for inter-institutional cooperation between governments and NGOs. In addition, sufficient financial resources are needed for state duties' implementation in effective fight against gender-based violence to women and domestic violence. Without sufficient relevant state funding, GREVIO notes the limited degree of commitment of States Parties of the Convention.

GREVIO welcomed the law in Portugal, which obliged online ministries to inform on transparent gender-sensitive budget lines.[58] It is a state obligation to respond to all forms of violence against women and for women and girls in all their diversity. Although none of the seventeen analyzed countries, parties of the Convention, have yet applied completely gender equality principles, GREVIO notes promising practices (Spain, Sweden, etc.).

The Convention also establishes a Committee of the Parties (Art. 67), composed of the official representatives of the Parties to the Convention, which is a political body supplementing a monitoring system of the Convention. This pillar of monitoring enables equal participation of all States Parties in the decision-making process and in the monitoring procedure of the Convention. The Committee of the Parties strengthens cooperation between the Parties and between them and GREVIO, to ensure the proper and effective implementation of the Convention. The Committee of the Parties established its own rules of procedure.

Committee of the Parties may adopt recommendations indicating the measures to be taken by the Party concerned to implement GREVIO's conclusions, if necessary setting a date for submitting information on their implementation, and promoting cooperation to ensure the proper implementation of the Convention. This mechanism secures the respect of the independence of GREVIO in its monitoring function, while introducing a high-level political dimension to the dialogue between the Parties.

Drawing inspiration from Article 21 (1) of the UN CEDAW Convention, Article 69 provides for the possibility of GREVIO to adopt, where appropriate, general recommendations on the implementation of this Convention. General recommendations have a common meaning for all Parties and concern articles or themes that are included in this Convention. They are not country-specific. *Although these general recommendations are not legally binding, they serve as an important reference for States Parties by developing a greater understanding of the different topics in the Convention. General recommendations are to offer clear guidance that contributes to an effective implementation of the provisions contained in the Convention.*

GREVIO has issued *General Recommendation No. 1 on the digital dimension of violence against women* (adopted on October 20, 2021, published on November 24, 2021). In monitoring the implementation of the Istanbul Convention, GREVIO has identified that the digital dimension of violence against women is often overlooked in domestic laws and policies. In its General Recommendation No. 1, it outlines the problem of both gender-based violence against women committed online and facilitated by technology. The COVID-19 pandemic that started in 2020 has further amplified this issue. Based on the four pillars of the Istanbul Convention—Prevention, Protection, Prosecution, and Coordinated Policies—General Recommendation No. 1 proposes specific actions to be taken in all four areas. It coins the term "the digital dimension of violence against women" as comprehensive enough to comprise both online acts of violence and those perpetrated through technology, including technology yet to be developed.

Non-consensual image or video sharing, coercion and threats, including rape threats, sexualized bullying and other forms of intimidation, online sexual harassment, impersonation, online stalking or stalking via the Internet of Things, as well as psychological abuse and economic harm perpetrated via digital means against women and girls, all come under the above definition of the digital dimension of violence against women. Digital forms of gender-based violence against women have a serious impact on women's and girls' lives, including psychological and physical health, their livelihoods, their physical safety, and their reputation.[59]

Generally seen, treaty bodies, despite producing only non-binding acts and recommendations, have proved to be effective mechanisms in order to guarantee respect for treaty obligations.[60] Provisions of Article 70 foresee the role of national parliaments in monitoring the implementation of this Convention. In paragraphs 1 and 2, there is an obligation for Parties to the Convention to invite national parliaments to participate in the monitoring (par. 1) and to submit the reports of GREVIO to them for consultation (par. 2). Implementing the Convention, in many cases, requires legislative changes. Therefore, it is of vital importance to involve national parliaments in assessing the implementation of the Convention.

The Parliamentary Assembly shall be invited to regularly discuss the implementation of the Convention (Art. 70, par 3). With this provision, the important role that the Parliamentary Assembly played in placing the issue of violence against women on the political agenda both of the Council of Europe and of its member states is recognized. The CoE Assembly's participation in the monitoring of this Convention significantly enhances its results, bearing in mind the Assembly's long-standing commitment to this issue and the high number of recommendations adopted in this field. "By breaking this silence, by reducing the social tolerance and inhibition, and by increasing identification and reporting of domestic violence against women we will also be taking steps to progressively melt the iceberg of domestic violence. This is an important challenge for western societies (even after more than 25 years of activism in the field of intimate partner violence), but this challenge is even greater in other cultures where violence against women is seen as a natural phenomenon based in deep rooted beliefs and attitudes."[61]

EU APPROACH: EU DIRECTIVE (2023) OF THE EUROPEAN PARLIAMENT AND THE COUNCIL ON COMBATING VIOLENCE AGAINST WOMEN AND DOMESTIC VIOLENCE

The combination of gender-based discrimination and inequality with other forms of discrimination (economic, political, etc.) can result in specific forms of violence against women, also can affect women's experiences with violence and their later needs. The primary legislation of the European Union (EU) lays the foundation for the adoption of secondary legislation, in the form of provisions of Article 2 of the EU Treaty from Lisbon (2009), in which the equality of women and men is included in the values on which the Union rests.

Many authors consider that the defining of EU values, along with the legally binding EU Charter of Fundamental Rights (Article 6 of the EU Treaty), represents a particular contribution of the Lisbon Treaty on the EU and that the stated values are part of the very essence of the EU.[62] In addition, in Article 3, it was proclaimed that the EU will promote the equality of women and men and that the goal of the EU is to promote the equality of women and men in all its activities. Besides, in Article 10 of the Treaty on the Functioning of the EU, it is stipulated that the EU, in defining and implementing policies and activities, is focused on the fight against discrimination based on gender, among other things.[63] The EU's determination to fight discrimination based on gender is expressed in the powers of the Council of Ministers and the European Parliament to adopt anti-discriminatory measures at the EU level.

According to Article 19 of the Treaty on the functioning of the EU[64] the Council may, without prejudice to the other provisions of the Treaty, within the competences assigned to the Union by the Treaties, decide unanimously in accordance with a special legislative procedure and with the prior consent of the European Parliament, to take appropriate actions to combat discrimination based on gender, racial or ethnic origin, religion or belief, disability, age or sexual orientation. In addition, the EU Treaty authorizes the European Parliament and the Council to adopt measures to prevent human trafficking, especially trafficking in women and children, who are most often the victims of that serious crime, within the framework of the common migration policy. The Treaty also empowers the European Parliament and the Council, through the adoption of directives, to establish minimum rules regarding criminal offenses and sanctions in the field of serious crime with a cross-border dimension, which includes human trafficking and sexual exploitation of women and children (Art. 83, paragraph 1, Treaty on the Functioning of the EU).

In the context of the economic dimension of the equality of women and men, that is, more widely seen as a gender equality, the Treaty in Article 153 authorizes the Union to support and supplement Member States in the area of equal opportunities for women and men in the labor market and treatment in the workplace. However, according to recent research by European Confederation of Trade Unions (ECTU), from February 2021, there is a need for urgent action on dismantling violence and harassment in the world of work against women, who are the prevalent victims, especially during the COVID-19 pandemic.[65] Another research by European foundation for living and working conditions improving (2007) indicated the presence of mobbing, that is, harassment at work toward women in all Member States, which caused an increased percentage of sick leave with subsequent costs of healing and rehabilitation.[66] In theory,[67] the causes of mobbing are identified as the existence of a conflict situation in the workplace, during longer period, whose intensity is being multiplied.

Furthermore, each Member State is obliged to ensure the application of the principle of equal pay for men and women for equal work, or for work of equal value, pursuant to Article 157 of the Treaty on the Functioning of the EU. For the legal aspects of gender equality, the EU Charter on Fundamental Rights is of great legal importance, since it establishes equality before the law and prohibits any discrimination based, *inter alia*, on gender.

In the European Union (EU), the commitment to fight against gender-based violence, to support and protect the victims and to hold the perpetrators accountable, has recently been reinforced by soft law instruments, such as the Gender Equality Strategy 2020–2025[68] and the Communication of the European Commission from 2021 on hate speech and hate crime,[69] which also deals with some specific gender-based crimes against women.

The EU has only recently begun to focus on the issue of violence against women using binding legal instruments, and the starting point is the decision to sign the Istanbul Convention in 2016. *After a lengthy internal procedure, the Union officially became a contracting party to the Istanbul Convention in June 2023.*[70] The EU includes 14 of the 20 countries that are ranked highest in the world in terms of achieving gender equality. Despite this, around 22 percent of women in the EU have experienced intimate partner violence, according to available data.[71]

By acceding to the Convention, the EU obtains an important tool for combating violence against women and domestic violence, which reaffirms the central importance of the Convention, being a cornerstone of international legal standards in this area. *The Istanbul Convention of the Council of Europe for the European Union entered into force on October 1,* 2023. Although not all Member States ratified the Convention (at the time of writing this book), twenty-one of them did (at the time of writing this book).[72]

By ratifying the Istanbul Convention, the EU guarantees that minimum criminal law standards are applied in the fight against violence against women and domestic violence throughout the Union, and the message is that dealing with these forms of violence is a priority. The European Parliament, in its Resolution of February 15, 2023, called on the remaining six EU member states (Bulgaria, the Czech Republic, Hungary, Latvia, Lithuania, and Slovakia) to ratify the Istanbul Convention of the Council of Europe without delay.

Due to the specific division of competences between Member States on the one side, and the EU institutions on the other, the largest number of acts of secondary legislation in the field of gender equality, especially its economic dimension, are directives. These are legal acts that do not have direct legal effect in the Member States, but they incorporate them with their acts into the national legal order. Directives define the goals to be achieved in a certain area, while leaving the choice of methods and form of their implementation to the Member States.[73]

In the field of combating violence against women and domestic violence, the ratification of the Istanbul Convention was the driving force behind the formulation of the Proposal for an EU Directive in this area. *The EU Directive was adopted on 24th April 2024 with the aim to mutually harmonize the national legislation of the Member States and thus strengthen the role of the EU as a member of the Istanbul Convention*, which makes it responsible for its implementation, through the realization of the rights and obligations of the EU institutions and the Member States that are signatories to the Convention.[74]

The Directive on the fight against violence against women and domestic violence[75] was prepared as a kind of supplement to the Istanbul Convention, not as a replacement for it. That is, it has partial content overlap, but the Convention remains "an essential tool for the EU strategy to combat gender-based violence."[76] The adoption of this legal document was followed by strong conceptual differences in the understandings of Member States about the definition of rape. Many EU countries oppose the inclusion of this criminal offense in the Directive, with the essential element being the absence of free consent, as formulated in the Istanbul Convention. Disagreement focuses mainly on the existence of a legal basis in the Treaties providing the EU with the power to impose such a definition. The Directive is based on the combined provisions of Article 82(2) and Article 83(1) of the Treaty on the Functioning of the EU. Article 82(2) of the Treaty provides the legal basis for the establishment of minimum standards regarding the rights of victims of crime necessary to facilitate the mutual recognition of judgments and other court decisions, as well as to improve police and judicial cooperation in criminal matters for issues with a cross-border dimension. Article 83(1) of the Treaty provides the legal basis for minimum standards related to the definition of criminal offenses and sanctions related to the sexual exploitation of women and children and cybercrime.

Certain EU members believe that defining rape based on the absence of free consent would lead to major problems in court proceedings when proving this criminal offense. The traditional approach to defining rape in national legislation in the EU is based on the assumption of violence, threats, or the impossibility for rape victims to resist the aggression. However, new cases of rape proved this approach to be seriously deficient. The narrow definition of rape based on force and coercion does not take into account the fact that a reaction known as 'frozen fright' or 'tonic immobility,' and not active physical resistance, is rape victims' most common response.

The importance of this Directive is contained in the fact that before this Directive, there was no EU legislation that specifically and explicitly deals with violence against women and domestic violence. Positive secondary EU legislation that existed before the Directive, can only be indirectly applied to violence against women and domestic violence, and therefore it was estimated as not being efficient.[77] According to relevant assessments, the current EU legislation has proven to be an ineffective tool for preventing and combating violence against women and domestic violence.[78]

Among the valid directives, the Directive on the rights of victims (2012) is particularly significant,[79] as it establishes a mechanism for mutual recognition of protection measures in criminal matters between Member States and sets minimum standards for victims' rights in all EU Member States, including the right to access to justice, protection, and support. This means that member states can expand the set of victims' rights in order to ensure a higher level of protection. Member States are required to ensure that victims of domestic violence receive appropriate protection and support, including access to legal aid, medical care, counseling, and emergency services. According to paragraphs (11) and (13), the Directive sets minimum rules and applies in relation to criminal offenses committed in the Union and to criminal proceedings conducted in the EU. It grants rights to victims of extraterritorial crimes only in relation to criminal proceedings conducted in the EU. Child victims should be considered and treated as full bearers of the rights set forth in this Directive and should have the right to enjoy the rights provided in the

Directive, in a manner that takes into account their ability to form their own views (paragraph 14). When applying the Directive, it is primarily based on the principle of protecting the best interests of children, in accordance with the EU Charter on Fundamental Rights and the UN Convention on the Rights of the Child, adopted on November 20, 1989.

Directive 2011/99/EU on the European Protection Order (EPO, 2011)[80] is another important act of secondary legislation of the EU with indirect application in the domain of violence against women and domestic violence. This directive establishes a mechanism that enables the recognition between Member States of protective measures issued in criminal proceedings. A new protection measure is issued according to a simplified and accelerated procedure in another Member State to which the subject travels or moves. When it comes to protective measures issued as part of civil litigation in the Member State where the subject is a resident, that is, has a permanent residence, then the person can refer to Regulation (EU) no. 606/2013 on mutual recognition of protection measures in civil matters.[81] This regulation establishes a mechanism of direct recognition between member states of protection measures issued in civil litigation, through a certificate, which a person presents to the competent authorities in order to prove their rights.

The new Directive on combating violence against women and domestic violence prohibits forced marriage and female genital mutilation and has specific rules on cybercrimes, such as cyberflashing and cyberstalking. Victims will have improved access to justice and health care, including sexual and reproductive services, while the legislation will include provisions to prevent rape. The advantage of the Directive on the fight against violence against women and domestic violence, compared with the Istanbul Convention, is that it sets minimum standards for the Member States within the area of EU jurisdiction, including the criminalization of the criminal act of cyber violence, which is not specifically covered by the Istanbul Convention. Cyber violence against women and girls includes a range of different forms of violence perpetrated through information and communication technology (ICT) tools, based on gender or a combination of gender and other factors (e.g., race, age, disability, sexuality, profession, or personal beliefs).

Cyberstalking is a modern form of violence, which is often perpetrated against family members or former partners, in order to intensify coercive control and surveillance, but special provisions on this are rarely present in the domestic legal systems of the Member States. Therefore, minimum rules on cyberstalking should be established. In addition, cyber-harassment includes attacks, such as threats, insults, or other offensive behavior toward individuals, especially women and girls, which usually occur through social media or other online services. This modern form of violence has a particularly negative effect on women active in public life, such as politicians, journalists, and human rights activists. Although cyber-harassment can have the ultimate effect of silencing women by hindering their participation in social and political life and finally, by undermining the principles of democracy, as protected by the EU Treaty, currently this form of violence is very rarely regulated in the criminal regulations of the Member States. Disclosing private information online without consent is prohibited, as is "cyber-flashing" in the Directive.

EU Directive does not prevent the Member States, especially those that are already contracting parties to the Istanbul Convention, from maintaining and applying higher standards in the fight against violence against women and domestic violence. In addition, the directives have proven to be the most optimal and flexible means of harmonizing the national legal systems of the EU Member States in the specific areas that they regulated.[82] The Directive envisages codifying minimum standards in EU law for the criminalization of certain forms of violence against women, to protect victims and improve access to justice, to support victims and ensure coordination between competent services, in order to prevent such crimes. Member States should take measures to prevent the cultivation of harmful gender stereotypes, to eradicate the idea of women's inferiority or the stereotypical roles of women and men, and preventive measures should furthermore be implemented in formal education.

It is crucial to address gender stereotypes, starting with early childhood education and childcare, because children are exposed to gender roles from an early age, which later shape their self-perception and influence their social, academic, and professional choices in life. Member States should regularly conduct surveys to collect data and forward them to the Commission, enabling it to effectively monitor the development of the situation in the fight against violence against women and domestic violence in the Member States with a view to further progress. Member States have three years to implement the provisions of the Directive.

In accordance with the position of international human rights organizations, including the Council of Europe, the Commission proposed the criminalization of rape in the Proposal for a Directive. Article 5(1) of the Proposal defines rape as punishable behavior: "a) engaging in an act with a woman without her consent, which implies vaginal, anal or oral penetration of a sexual nature, with any part of the body or object, without her consent; b) to force a woman to engage in an act with another person, which includes vaginal, anal or oral penetration of a sexual nature, without her consent, with any body part or object."[83]

It is significant that the Proposal for the Directive referred to a sexual act without the woman's consent, and not to the use of force, threat or coercion when it comes to the crime of rape. This approach aims to overcome the fact that, although rape is criminalized in all EU member states, many of them require the use of force, threat or coercion to make rape punishable. Only the approach that defines rape when the sexual act is without the woman's consent achieves full protection of the sexual integrity of female victims. Therefore, in order to ensure equal protection of female victims in these cases throughout the European Union, it is necessary to establish a minimum standard in the definition of rape as an act without the consent of a woman, which is a constitutive element of the criminal offense of rape of women.

However, a difficult political agreement was reached in February 2024, after the criminalization of rape had been removed from the final text of the Directive. This had been the main stumbling block during the negotiations, with the EU Council objecting to the criminalization of rape as being outside the EU's legal remit, while the Parliament and Commission held the opposite view. The agreement also obliges Member States to take rape prevention measures and to raise awareness of the central role of consent. Instead of the criminalization of rape, the Directive contains actions to prevent rape and increase understanding of consent.

The Directive, in addition to the above, also criminalizes the sharing of intimate images without consent. Some Member States already punish this crime, which can be particularly harmful to the concerned person due to the way it is easily, quickly, and widely distributed.

Female genital mutilation is explicitly dealt with in criminal law in only fifteen Member States,[84] while other Member States regulate it with general criminal offenses, such as bodily harm, mutilation, and criminal offenses against health. This primitive practice causes irreparable harm to victims and is used to exercise social control over the sexuality of women and girls, as well as to preserve and confirm male dominance over them. Consequently, female genital mutilation and forced marriages are considered as crimes in the Directive.

It is important to point out the importance of the issue of secondary victimization of the victim. This question is increasingly being highlighted by the European Court of Human Rights, emphasizing the inadequacy of the internal regulations of the member states and the fact that this problem is a consequence of the functioning of a culture characterized by gender stereotypes. Only appropriate education and professional training can reverse the trend of this phenomenon, while the inability to detect signs of violence, along with sexist prejudices, delays interventions or prevents careful judicial evaluation of cases, leading to dire consequences. Consequently, the Directive foresees specialized assistance for victims in order to be treated in a gender-sensitive manner.

Strengthening victims' access to justice and rights to appropriate protection also includes:

- providing an individual needs assessment for protection and support tailored to the specific needs of victims of violence against women or domestic violence;
- providing specific safeguards for child victims of violence against women or domestic violence;
- ensuring protection through emergency barring and protection orders;
- ensuring that victims can effectively claim compensation from the offender;
- ensuring the removal of online content in relation to offenses of cyber violence, and the possibility of judicial redress for the affected users; and
- ensuring that government bodies exist to assist, advise, and to represent victims in court proceedings in matters of violence against women or domestic violence.

NOTES

1. Roman jurist Publius Iuventius Celsus (*Iustinian, Digesta 1, 1, 1, pr.),* Law is the art of (applying the principles of) the good and the just.

2. Arab Strategy for Combating Violence against Women 2011 – 2020, "Arab Women's Right to a Life Free from Violence," Arab Women Organization, prepared by H. A. Ghazaleh, http://www.arabwomenorg.org/content/publications/vaweng.pdf, 28.12.2023.

3. M. A. S. Salampessy, L. Rizky, I. Achdyana, "The Effectiveness of The Convention on the Rights of the Child (CRC) Regime by UNICEF in Encouraging the Implementation of Child Protection in Southeast Asian Countries," *Journal of Advance in Social Sciences and Policy*, 1/2022.

4. R. Francisco, "The Inter-American Human Rights System and Violence against Women," *International Human Rights Clinic at Santa Clara Law School*, May 2015, 92, http:// law.scu.edu/wp-content/uploads/150602-Santa-Clara-VAWIA HRS-Report-FINAL.pdf, 12.12.2023.

5. https://vawnet.org/material/inter-american-convention-prevention-punishment-and-eradication-violence-against-women, 29.11.2023.

6. CEDAW, General Recommendation 19, UN GAOR, 1992, Doc. No. A/47/38.

7. IACHR Series C No. 4/1988, para. 188.

8. P. Spieler, "The Maria da Penha Case and the Inter-American Commission on Human Rights: Contributions to the Debate on Domestic Violence Against Women in Brazil," *Indiana Journal of Global Legal Studies*, 1/2011, 137–142, http://www.repository.law.indiana.edu/ijgls/vol18/iss1/, 27.11.2023.

9. "What is MESECVI?," Organization of American States, http://www.oas.org/en/mesecvi/ about.asp, 14.11.2023.

10. African Union, "Protocol to the African Charter on Human And Peoples' Rights on the Rights of Women in Africa, Preamble,https://au.int/sites/default/files

/treaties/37077-treaty-0027__protocol_to_the_african_charter_on_human_and_peoples_rights_on_the_rights_ of_women_in_ africa_e.pdf, 25.11.2023.

11. F. Viljoen, "An Introduction to the Protocol to the African Charter on Human and Peoples' Rights on the Rights of Women in Africa," *Washington & Lee Journal of Civil Rights and Social Justice*, 22/2009, https://scholarlycommons.law.wlu.edu/cgi/viewcontent.cgi?article=1291&context=crsj, 17.11.2023.

12. R. Manjoo, "Report of the Special Rapporteur on Violence Against Women, its Causes and Consequences," 29th session HRC, A/HRC/29/27, Advanced Edited Version, June 10, 2015, paragraph 16, https://www.refworld.org/docid/5583f5234.html, 27.11.2023.

13. Ibid.

14. https://www.undp.org/africa/press-releases/implementation-maputo-protocol-boosted-training-situation-rights-women-and-girls-africa?, 30.11.2023.

15. UN Economic and Social Commission for Western Asia (ESCWA), "Women: Arab Horizon 2030," E/ESCWA/ECW/2017, 4.

16. Declaration of the Council of Europe on the equality of women and men as a basic criterion of democracy (Fourth Ministerial Conference on the Equality of Women and Men, Istanbul 1997).

17. Prof. Dr. Gordana Gasmi, the author of this book, was a member of the expert CAHVIO Committee of the Council of Europe, which drafted the text of the Istanbul Convention during the two-year negotiations in the CAHVIO Committee from 2009 till 2011. In 2011, she became the Council of Europe expert in the field of human rights and gender equality, and she held numerous seminars for public officials in countries of Europe, Asia, and Africa. The CAHVIO Committee, formed by a decision of the Committee of Ministers of the CoE in December 2008, started its work in April 2009 on the basis of the mandate entrusted by the CoE Committee of Ministers.

18. www.coe.int/ PREMS 128621 GBR 2574 Rec 1 GREVIO WEB 16x24 FINAL, 26.11.2023.

19. https://www.ohchr.org/en/statements/2022/03/using-international-and-regional-legal-framework-stop-all-forms-violence-against, 26.11.2023.

20. https://search.coe.int/cm/Pages/result_details.aspx?ObjectID=09000016805e2612, 26.11.2023.

21. https://www.coe.int/en/web/portal/-/the-european-union-deposited-the-instrument-of-approval-of-the-istanbul-convention-, 24.11.2023.

22. G. Gasmi, "Global Significance of European Standards of Women Human Rights' Protection in Domain of Gender Based and Domestic Violence," *Fiat Iustitia Review of Juridical Studies*, 1/2019, Faculty of Law, *Dimitrie Cantemir*, University – Bucharest, Cluj Napoca, Romania, 125–140.

23. G. Gasmi, D. Prlja, A. Jerotić, "European Leading Legal Principles of Combating Gender-based Violence—Istanbul Convention," *Perspectives of implementation of European Standards in Serbian Legal System* (ed. Stevan Lilić), Law Faculty, University of Belgrade, Serbia, 2017, 336.

24. G. Gasmi, "New European Legal Standards in the Area of Women Human Rights," *Efficiency of Legal Norms I* (eds. E. M. Fodor, P. Popovici, C. Buzdugan), Law Faculty, Cluj—Napoca, Romania, 2012, 145.

25. M. Draškić, "Do We Need Another Law on Protection Against Domestic Violence?," *Perspectives of Implementation of European Standards in the Serbian Legal System*, Vol. 6 (ed. S. Lilic), Collected Articles, Belgrade, Serbia, 2016, 41.

26. GREVIO – monitoring mechanism of the Istanbul Convention in the form of the independent expert body (15 members).

27. D. C. G. Scotto, "Defining 'Gender' Across Europe: A Linguistic Analysis of the Definition, Translation, and Interpretation of the Word 'Gender' from the Beijing Declaration to the Istanbul Convention," *International Journal for the Semiotics of Law*, 11/2022, https://doi.org/10.1007/s11196-022-09944-z,

28. Examples include coercion to surrender, forgery, theft of possessions, and improper use of guardianship or power of attorney. M. Huecker, A. Malik, K. King, W. Smock, *Kentucky Domestic Violence* (book), StatPearls Publishing, Treasure Island, Florida, January 2024.

29. Ibid.

30. Explanatory Report to the Council of Europe Convention on preventing and combating violence against women and domestic violence, 2011, https://rm.coe.int/ic-and-explanatory-report/16808d24c6, 22.01.2024.

31. Ignjatovic, *Violence Against Women in Intimate Partnership Relations*, 231.

32. C. Chinkin, "A Critique of the Public/Private Dimension," *European Journal of International Law*, 10/1999, 387, 389.

33. G. Gasmi, "Tenth Anniversary of the Istanbul Convention of the Council of Europe – Relevant Aspects," *Science and Society*, 1/2021, 39. The American Convention on Human Rights, also known as the Pact of San José, is an international human rights instrument. It was adopted in San José, Costa Rica, on November 22, 1969. It came into force after the eleventh instrument of ratification (that of Grenada) was deposited on July 18, 1978. The bodies responsible for monitoring compliance with the Convention are the Inter-American Commission on Human Rights and the Inter-American Court of Human Rights, both of which are organs of the Organization of American States (OAS).

34. Analysis of the case *Opuz v. Turkey,* 2009, will be provided in chapter 5.

35. Official title of the European Convention, in further text: European Convention on Human Rights (1950, ECHR). Implementation of ECHR is monitored by the European Court of Human Rights (ECtHR), based in Strasbourg, France.

36. Andorra, Cyprus, Malta, Monaco, Poland, Romania, Serbia, Slovenia.

37. G. Gasmi, "European Legal Standards on Gender Equality," *Efficiency of Legal Norms II*, Law Faculty Cluj-Napoca, Romania, 2013, https://www.dimitriecantemir.ro/?page_id=2749.

38. "*Article 4—Fundamental rights, equality and non-discrimination*

1 Parties shall take the necessary legislative and other measures to promote and protect the right of everyone, particularly women, to live free from violence in both the public and the private sphere.

2 Parties condemn all forms of discrimination against women and take, without delay, the necessary legislative and other measures to prevent it, in particular by:

- embodying in their national constitutions or other appropriate legislation the principle of equality between women and men and ensuring the practical realization of this principle;

- prohibiting discrimination against women, including through the use of sanctions where appropriate;
- abolishing laws and practices which discriminate against women.

3 The implementation of the provisions of this Convention by the Parties, in particular measures to protect the rights of victims, shall be secured without discrimination on any ground such as sex, gender, race, color, language, religion, political or other opinion, national or social origin, association with a national minority, property, birth, sexual orientation, gender identity, age, state of health, disability, marital status, migrant or refugee status, or other status.

4 Special measures that are necessary to prevent and protect women from gender-based violence shall not be considered discrimination under the terms of this Convention." CoE Istanbul Convention

39. G. Gasmi, "Principles of Non-discrimination and Conscientious Fulfillment of the State's Obligations—Theoretical View of the Council of Europe Istanbul Convention and the Practice of the European Court of Human Rights," *Kultura Polisa*, 1/2016, 154.

40. Ibid.

41. European Convention on Human Rights, "ARTICLE 14

Prohibition of discrimination: The enjoyment of the rights and freedoms set forth in this Convention shall be secured without discrimination on any ground such as sex, race, color, language, religion, political or other opinion, national or social origin, association with a national minority, property, birth or other status." https://www.refworld.org/legal/agreements/coe/1950/en/18688, 23.01.2024.

42. G. Gasmi, D. Prlja, A. Jerotić, "European Leading Legal Principles of Combating Gender-Based Violence—Istanbul Convention," 320–333.

43. European Convention on Human Rights, "ARTICLE 6, Right to a fair trial:

1. In the determination of his civil rights and obligations or of any criminal charge against him, everyone is entitled to a fair and public hearing within a reasonable time by an independent and impartial tribunal established by law. Judgment shall be pronounced publicly but the press and public may be excluded from all or part of the trial in the interests of morals, public order or national security in a democratic society, where the interests of juveniles or the protection of the private life of the parties so require, or to the extent strictly necessary in the opinion of the court in special circumstances where publicity would prejudice the interests of justice.

Everyone charged with a criminal offense shall be presumed innocent until proven guilty according to law.

Everyone charged with a criminal offense has the following minimum rights:

to be informed promptly, in a language which he understands, and in detail, of the nature and cause of the accusation against him,

to have adequate time and facilities for the preparation of his defense,

to defend himself in person or through legal assistance of his own choosing, or, if he has no sufficient means to pay for legal assistance, to be given it free when the interests of justice so require, to examine or have examined witnesses against him, and to obtain the attendance and examination of witnesses on his behalf under the same conditions as witnesses against him, and

to have the free assistance of an interpreter if he cannot understand or speak the language used in court.

https://www.refworld.org/legal/agreements/coe/1950/en/18688, 23.01.2024

44. F. Varvaro, "Treatment of the Battered Woman: Effective Response of the Emergency Department," *American College of Emergency Physicians*, 11/1989, 8–13.

45. D. Belknap, K. D. McCall, "Women Battering and Police Referrals," *Journal of Criminal Justice*, 22/1994, 223–236.

46. *"Article 54—Investigations and evidence*

Parties shall take the necessary legislative or other measures to ensure that, in any civil or criminal proceedings, evidence relating to the sexual history and conduct of the victim shall be permitted only when it is relevant and necessary."

47. S. Braschi, "Protecting Women from Violence: the Impact of International Human Rights Law," *Criminal Justice in the Prism of Human Rights* (X AIDP International Symposium for Young Penalists, Bologna, Italy, 27–October 28, 2022) (eds. Francesco Mazzacuva, Miren Odriozola Gurrutxaga, Nicola Recchia), Alessandra Santangelo, 118.

48. Ibid.

49. "Article 57 – Legal aid

Parties shall provide for the right to legal assistance and to free legal aid for victims under the conditions provided by their internal law.

50. *"Article 56 – Measures of protection*

Parties shall take the necessary legislative or other measures to protect the rights and interests of victims, including their special needs as witnesses, at all stages of investigations and judicial proceedings, in particular by:

providing for their protection, as well as that of their families and witnesses, from intimidation, retaliation and repeat victimization;

ensuring that victims are informed, at least in cases where the victims and their families might be in danger, when the perpetrator escapes or is released temporarily or definitively;

informing them, under the conditions provided for by internal law, of their rights and the services at their disposal and the follow-up given to their complaint, the charges, the general progress of the investigation or proceedings, and their role therein, as well as the outcome of their case;

enabling victims, in a manner consistent with the procedural rules of internal law, to be heard, to supply evidence, and have their views, needs, and concerns presented, directly or through an intermediary, and considered;

providing victims with appropriate support services so that their rights and interests are duly presented and taken into account;

ensuring that measures may be adopted to protect the privacy and image of the victim;

ensuring that contact between victims and perpetrators within court and law enforcement agency premises is avoided where possible;

providing victims with independent and competent interpreters when victims are parties to proceedings or when they are supplying evidence;

enabling victims to testify, according to the rules provided by their internal law, in the courtroom without being present or at least without the presence of the alleged perpetrator, notably through the use of appropriate communication technologies where available.

A child victim and child witness of violence against women and domestic violence shall be afforded, where appropriate, special protection measures, taking into account the best interests of the child." (CoE Istanbul Convention).

51. More details in: M. Hester, S. J. Lilley, "Preventing Violence against Women: Article 12 of the Istanbul Conventionhttps://rm.coe.int/CoERMPublicCommonSearchServices/DisplayDCTMContent?documentId=090000168046e1f0 22.01.2024.

52. Council of Europe, "Convention on Preventing and Combating Violence Against Women and Domestic Violence," Explanatory Report, CM (2011)49 add final, 07.04.2011, 36.

53. *J. M. Coicaud, V. Heiskanen*, eds, *Legitimacy of International Organizations*, United Nations University Press, Tokyo, Japan, 2006.

54. "Council of Europe Convention on Preventing and Combating Violence Against Women and Domestic Violence," 93.

55. Resolution CM/Res (2014)43 on rules of the election procedure of the members of the Group of Experts on Action against Violence against Women and Domestic Violence (GREVIO). The Committee of Ministers is composed of the Ministers of all 46 States Members of the Council of Europe.

56. The Committee of the Parties refers to the representatives of the States Parties to the Istanbul Convention.

57. Council of Europe, CoE (2021), Second General Report on GREVIO Activities covering the period from June 2019 to December 2020, 64–65.

58. J. Nelles, *Executive Secretary to the Istanbul Convention, at the Belgrade CoE Conference "The Istanbul Convention: 10 Years On!,"* held on May 7, 2021.

59. https://www.coe.int/en/web/istanbul-convention/-/grevio-publishes-its-general-recommendation-no-1, 28.11.2023.

60. N. S. Rodley, "The Role and Impact of Treaty Bodies," *The Oxford Handbook of International Human Rights Law* (ed. Dinah Shelton), Oxford University Press, Oxford, 2013, about the UN human rights treaty bodies, 621.

61. E. Gracia, "Unreported Cases of Domestic Violence against Women" (fn. 17), 536, 537.

62. J. C. Piris, *The Lisbon Treaty—A Legal and Political Analysis*, Cambridge University Press, Cambridge, 2010, 71–72.

63. Official Journal of the European Union (EU), 115, Vol. 51, 09/05/2008, Consolidated versions of the Treaty on the EU and the Treaty on the Functioning of the EU.

64. Article 19

Without prejudice to the other provisions of the Treaties and within the limits of the powers conferred by them upon the Union, the Council, acting unanimously in accordance with a special legislative procedure and after obtaining the consent of the European Parliament, may take appropriate action to combat discrimination based on sex, racial or ethnic origin, religion or belief, disability, age or sexual orientation.

By way of derogation from paragraph 1, the European Parliament and the Council, acting in accordance with the ordinary legislative procedure, may adopt the basic principles of Union incentive measures, excluding any harmonization of the laws and regulations of the Member States, to support action taken by the Member States in order to contribute to the achievement of the objectives referred to in paragraph 1.

Treaty on the functioning of the EU, Official Journal 115, Vol. 51, 09/05/2008, P. 0056–0056.

65. "The pandemic has created additional threats for women at work, whether it's violence from customers and clients who refuse to comply with COVID-19 safety rules, new forms of sexual harassment onlineonline, or an increase of cases of domestic violence when working at home." Ester Linch, "Deputy General Secretary of ECTU," *Convention 190 of the International Labor Organization, on Violence and Harassment in the World of Work (2019)* (eds. S. Paunović, R. Kosanović), Confederation of Autonomous Trade Unions of Serbia, Belgrade, 2021, 22.

66. Ibid., 32, 33.

67. Leymann considers mobbing as "negative communication treatment, which is directed against a person (with one or more others) occurring very often and in longer terms being identified as a relationship between the perpetrator and the victim." At the same time, this whole long process occurs in the workplace. (Leymann, *Mobbing: Psychoterror am Arbeitsplatz und wie man sich dagegen wehren kann*, Rowohlt, Reinbek, 1993, 192p, ISBN 3-499-13351-2, 21), quoted according to: A. Divincova, B. Sivakova, "Mobbing at Workplace and its Impact on Employee Performance," *Human Resources Management & Ergonomics, Vol. VIII*, 2/2014, 21.

68. Communication from the Commission to the European Parliament, the Council, the European Economic and Social Committee and the Committee of the Regions, A Union of Equality: Gender Equality Strategy 2020–2025, of March 5, 2020, COM (2020) 152 final.

69. Communication from the Commission to the European Parliament and the Council, A more inclusive and protective Europe: extending the list of EU crimes to hate speech and hate crime, of December 9, 2021, COM(2021) 777 final.

70. Council Decision (EU) 2023/1075 on the conclusion, on behalf of the European Union, of the Council of Europe Convention on preventing and combating violence against women and domestic violence with regard to institutions and public administration of the Union, OJ L 143I, June 2, 2023, 1; Council Decision (EU) 2023/1076 on the conclusion, on behalf of the European Union, of the Council of Europe Convention on preventing and combating violence against women and

domestic violence with regard to matters related to judicial cooperation in criminal matters, asylum and non-refoulement, OJ L 143I, June 2, 2023, 4.

71. https://www.coe.int/en/web/portal/-/the-european-union-deposited-the-instrument-of-approval-of-the-istanbul-convention-, 4.12.2023.

72. These are the following EU members (at the time of writing this book): Austria, Belgium, Croatia, Cyprus, Denmark, Estonia, Finland, France, Germany, Greece, Ireland, Italy, Luxembourg, Malta, Netherlands, Poland, Portugal, Romania, Slovenia, Spain, and Sweden. At the time of writing this book, the Istanbul Convention has 38 contracting parties, of which 37 are member states of the Council of Europe (out of 46 member states) and the EU.

73. G. Gasmi, Quo vadis *EU? – Relevant Legal and Institutional Factors*, Institute of Comparative Law, Belgrade, 2016, 101–104, 109.

74. E. Bergamini, "Combating Violence Against Women and Domestic Violence – From the Istanbul Convention to the EU Framework: The Proposal for an EU Directive," *Freedom, Security & Justice: European Legal Studies*, ISSN 2532–2079, 2/2023, 21–41, doi:10.26321/E.BERGAMINI.02.2023.03.

75. COM (2022) 105 final.

76. European Parliament Resolution of February 15, 2023, on the Proposal for a Council decision on the conclusion, by the European Union, of the Council of Europe Convention on preventing and combating violence against women and Domestic Violence (COM (2016)0109 - 2016/0062R(NLE)), point 29.

77. Victims' Rights Directive (Directive 2012/29/EU of the European Parliament and the Council of October 25, 2012 on establishing minimum standards on the rights, support and protection of victims of crime, and replacing Council Framework Decision 2001/220/JHA),

Directive against the sexual abuse of minors (Directive 2011/93/EU of the European Parliament and of the Council of December 13, 2011, on combating the sexual abuse and the sexual exploitation of children and child pornography, and replacing Council Framework Decision 2004/68/JHA) and Anti-trafficking in human beings directive (Directive 2011/36/EU of the European Parliament and the Council of April 5, 2011, on preventing and combating trafficking in human beings and protecting its victims, and replacing Council Framework Decision 2002/629/JHA).

78. M. Picchi, "Violence Against Women and Domestic Violence: The European Commission's Directive Proposal," *Athens Journal of Law*, 8(4)/October 2022, 395–408.

79. Victims' Rights Directive (Directive 2012/29/EU of the European Parliament and the Council of October 25, 2012, on establishing minimum standards on the rights, support and protection of victims of crime, and replacing Council Framework Decision 2001/220/JHA), OJ L 315/57, 14.11.2012, https://eur-lex.europa.eu/eli/dir/2012/29/oj, 12.12.2023.

80. Directive 2011/99/EU on the European Protection Order (EPO), OJ L 338/2 from 21.12.2011, on https://eur-lex.europa.eu/legal-content/EN/TXT/?uri=CELEX:32011L 0099, 12.12.2023.

81. Regulation (EU) no. 606/2013 on mutual recognition of protection measures in civil matters, OJ L 181/4 from 29.06.2013, on https://eur-lex.europa.eu/legal-content/EN/TXT/PDF/?uri=CELEX:32013R0606, 12.12.2023.
82. Gasmi, "*Quo Vadis* EU?," 109.
83. COM (2022) 105 final.
84. Picchi, "Violence Against Women and Domestic Violence," 401.

Chapter 5

Relevant Judgments of European Court of Human Rights in the Area of Violence against Women

MOTTO OF LIFE: WIPE EVERY TEAR FROM EVERY EYE[1]

Aware of the particularly traumatic nature of crimes of the violence against women, the European standards in the CoE Istanbul Convention sought to ease the burden that lengthy criminal investigations and proceedings place on the victim, while at the same time ensuring that the perpetrators are brought to justice. The goal is to enable the conduct of criminal investigations and proceedings without placing the burden of initiating proceedings and securing a conviction on the victim. Paragraph 1 of Article 55 of the Istanbul Convention on *ex officio* proceedings obligates member states to ensure that investigations of various categories of criminal offenses "will not fully depend" on the complaint or a report submitted by the victim, and that the procedure can continue even if the victim withdraws her statement or report.

However, there are also opposite views in literature, promoting that the current U.S. system of public prosecution should be reformed in favor of a model in which the victim could decide whether to pursue a criminal case and what punishment (if any) her assailant would receive.[2] There are furthermore views that modern approaches to prosecuting the perpetrators of intimate-partner assault and homicide are unsound. State actors tend to ignore the reasons victims do not cooperate with the criminal legal system, as well as to impose one-size-fits-all sentences that are ill-suited to some victim-offender relationships and detrimental to marginalized communities.[3] However, private prosecution proved to be ineffective due to the social context of victim-blaming and a victim's fear of retaliation by the offender, which caused feminist calls for mandatory state intervention in domestic violence cases where women are prevalent victims.

Prevalent numbers of various forms of violence against women are perpetrated by family members or intimate partners, that is, by well-known perpetrators. The result is that women who experienced such violence feels shame mixed with loyalty and even love, as well as helplessness, which altogether cause low numbers of reporting and, subsequently, less court convictions.

Consequently, States Parties should investigate in a proactive way in order to gather evidence such as substantial evidence, testimonies of witnesses, medical expertise, and so on, in order to make sure that proceedings may be carried out even if the victim withdraws her or his statement or complaint, at least with regard to serious offenses, such as physical violence resulting in death or bodily harm. Especially, acts resulting in severe bodily harm or deprivation of life must be addressed promptly and directly by competent authorities. Good practice examples have shown that women who are supported or assisted by a specialist support service during investigations and proceedings are more likely to file a complaint and testify and are better equipped to take on the emotionally challenging task of actively contributing to the outcome of proceedings. It is of vital importance to psychologically and emotionally prepare women who experienced violence to endure testifying in front of the accused, as well as to accompany them to court.

The number of women victims of violence has not diminished notwithstanding the increasing number of acts addressing the issue, adopted at the international and national level. Effectiveness of relevant international rules, such as in the case of the Istanbul Convention, is directly linked with the institutional capacities of specific countries that apply the CoE Convention's provisions.

More precisely, national law enforcement agencies, judiciary, and other relevant stakeholders should dispose with significant capacities to cope with violence against women and domestic violence.

Principles that should be met in an effective national court system to ensure access to justice are:

(a) Be *just* in the results it delivers;
(b) Be *fair* in the way it treats litigants;
(c) Offer appropriate procedures at a reasonable *cost;*
(d) Deal with cases with reasonable *speed*;
(e) Be *understandable* to those who use it;
(f) Be *responsive* to the needs of those who use it;
(g) Provide as much *certainty* as the nature of the particular case allows; and
(h) Be *effective*: adequately resourced and organized.

Judicial decisions of international courts, which are a subsidiary means for the determination of customary international law, demonstrate such development. Decisions of international courts and tribunals, in particular those of the International Court of Justice, concerning the existence and content of rules of customary international law are a subsidiary means for the determination of such rules. Regard may be had, as appropriate, to decisions of national courts concerning the existence and content of rules of customary international law as a subsidiary means for the determination of such rules.[4]

Examples include the European Court of Human Rights (ECtHR), *Opuz v. Turkey* (application No 33401/02), judgment of June 9, 2009, in which the Court was influenced by what it referred to as "the evolution of norms and principles in international law" (para. 164) through a range of international and comparative materials on violence against women (more detailed in further text). The ECtHR, based in Strasbourg, is an international court set up in 1959. It rules on individual or State applications alleging violations of the civil and political rights set out in the European Convention on Human Rights.[5] Since 1998, it has sat as a full-time court, and individuals can apply to it directly. The Court has examined hundreds of thousands of applications since it was set up. Its judgments are binding on the countries concerned and have led governments to alter their legislation and administrative practices in a wide range of areas. The Court's case law makes the European Convention on Human Rights a modern and powerful living instrument for meeting new challenges and consolidating the rule of law and democracy in Europe.[6] The European Convention on Human Rights is an international treaty under which the member States of the Council of Europe promise to secure fundamental civil and political rights, not only to their own citizens but also to everyone within their jurisdiction. The European Convention, which was signed on November 4, 1950, in Rome, entered into force in 1953. The European Convention secures in particular:

- the right to life,
- the right to a fair hearing,
- the right to respect for private and family life,
- freedom of expression,
- freedom of thought, conscience, and religion,
- non-discrimination and
- the protection of property.

Member States of the Council of Europe have adopted various Protocols to the Convention aimed at improving and strengthening the supervisory mechanism initially created. The most recent is Protocol No. 16 to the European

Convention, which entered into force on August 1, 2018, allowing the Court (ECtHR) to deliver advisory opinions.

The Convention prohibits in particular: (a) torture and inhuman or degrading treatment or punishment, (b) slavery and forced labor, (c) the death penalty, (d) arbitrary and unlawful detention, and (e) discrimination in the enjoyment of the rights and freedoms set out in the Convention.

Another positive example is the Inter-American Court of Human Rights case, González et al. ("Cotton Field") v. Mexico, judgment of November 16, 2009. Gonzalez, Monreal, and *Monarrez v. Mexico* is also referred to as the "Cotton Field" or "Campo Algodonero" case. This is because on November 6, 2001, Claudia, Esmeralda and Laura's bodies were discovered in the cotton fields of Ciudad Juarez. Five other women were also found murdered in the same field. In the investigations that followed, public officials continued to deny the young women justice. After receiving continual threats from Ciudad Juarez officials to withdraw their complaints, the mothers of Claudia, Esmeralda and Laura brought their case to the Inter-American Commission on Human Rights (which was eventually referred to the Inter-American Court on Human Rights). Through the mothers' testimonies, the work of advocates and data delivered by civil society organizations, a systematic pattern of violence against women and widespread discrimination was presented to the Court. The Office of the Special Prosecutor for Crimes related to the Murders of Women in the Municipality of Juarez reports that 4,456 women were reported to have disappeared between 1993 and 2005, most of them between the ages of fifteen and twenty-five. Through its analysis, the Court decided that Mexico was responsible for violating Claudia, Esmeralda and Laura Bernice's human rights.

The Court recognized that the disappearances and murders of Claudia, Esmeralda and Laura were gender-based and perpetrated in the known context of violence against women in Ciudad Juarez. While not all violations committed against women constitute a violation of the Belém do Pará Convention, these murders were influenced by a culture of discrimination against women, as evidenced by reports from the IACHR Rapporteur on the Rights of Women, the UN Committee on the Elimination of Discrimination against Women, and Amnesty International.

Accepting that the acts taken against this woman and two girls under eighteen were, in fact, gender-based violence, Article 7 of the Belém do Pará Convention required Mexico to exercise due diligence in preventing, investigating, and punishing them. In examining Mexico's actions to investigate Claudia, Esmeralda and Laura's murders, the Court found several deficiencies. These included irregularities in the handling of evidence, fabrication of perpetrators, delayed investigations, the absence of inquiries that accounted for the general environment of VAW in Ciudad Juarez, and the lack of investigation against public officials for serious negligence. Through its analysis, the Court concluded that Mexico had failed to conduct a conscientious and effective investigation into the murders. Mexico's judicial ineffectiveness demonstrated the impunity that existed in each case. Transformative reparations are required to eliminate structural causes of violence against women, concluded the Inter-American Court on Human Rights.

The supervisory functions of the Inter-American System are two-pronged. In the first place, such functions fall under the capacities of the Inter-American Court insofar as States Parties, as well as the Inter-American Commission of Women (CIM), may request Advisory Opinions from the Court regarding the interpretation of the Convention (Belém do Pará, Article 11). In the second place, such functions fall under the capacities of the Inter-American Commission of Human Rights (IACHR) insofar as it has the faculty to receive and transmit complaints of a State Party's violations of the obligations established in Article 7 of the Convention. Such complaints may be presented by any person, group of people, or nongovernmental entity legally recognized in one or more States of the Organization of American States (OAS): "Any person or group of persons, or any nongovernmental entity legally recognized in one or more member states of the Organization, may lodge petitions with the Inter-American Commission on Human Rights containing denunciations or complaints of violations of Article 7 of this Convention by a State Party, and the Commission shall consider such claims in accordance with the norms and procedures established by the American Convention on Human Rights and the Statutes and Regulations of the Inter-American Commission on Human Rights for lodging and considering petitions" (Belém do Pará, Article 12). It is important to note that features of Article 12 includes the advisory mechanism of the Belém do Pará Convention, similar to the Istanbul Convention of the Council of Europe.[7]

Optimal concept of law enforcement and judicial proceedings is based on the following:

- Effective police investigation—to respond immediately to calls for assistance and manage dangerous situations appropriately;
- Effective public prosecution—will not be dependent upon a report or complaint by the victim and may even continue if the victim withdraws their statement or complaint;
- Consideration of aggravating circumstances—victim being in an intimate or close relation, crimes against a vulnerable person or in the presence of a child, extreme levels of violence, threat of weapons, or previous convictions for crimes of a similar nature;

- Legislation criminalizing violence against women—States Parties will ensure that culture, tradition, or so-called honor reasons are not regarded as a justification for violence;
- Dissuasive sanctions for perpetrators—imprisonment, extradition, monitoring and supervision, and withdrawal of parental rights;
- Coordinated risk assessments—in cooperation with relevant agencies and institutions, taking repeat offenses and access to firearms into account;
- Protection of child victims and witnesses—special protection measures; children victims of sexual violence, forced marriage, female genital mutilation, and forced abortion or sterilization will be able to initiate legal action for a sufficient amount of time after they have reached adulthood;
- No victim-blaming investigations and judicial proceedings;
- Victims' protection during investigation and judicial proceedings—from intimidation, retaliation, and repeat victimization; alternative options to resolve disputes such as mediation between victim and perpetrator will not be mandatory; the victim will be informed of any escape or release of a perpetrator.

LUSTITIA EST OMNIUM ET DOMINA ET REGINA VIRTUTUM (JUSTICE IS THE MISTRESS AND QUEEN OF ALL VIRTUES)

European legal standards in fighting violence against women and domestic violence ensure:

- That violence against women is criminalized and appropriately punished;
- That excuses on the grounds of culture, custom, religion, or so-called honor reasons are unacceptable for any act of violence;
- That victims have access to special protection measures during investigation and judicial proceedings;[8]
- That law enforcement agencies respond immediately to calls for assistance and manage dangerous situations adequately.

International legal transplants are one of the main sources of legal changes in national legal systems,[9] preferably in a more advanced and prosperous manner to provide for optimal protection of human rights and the rule of law. Consequently, the importance of the European legal standards in the area of the fight against gender-based violence and domestic violence that are set up by the CoE Istanbul Convention, is exactly in moving the boundaries of national legal systems. At the same time, the globally widespread negative gender stereotypes can be more easily dismantled. Nonetheless, in 94 percent of episodes of domestic violence reported to the police, the victim was a woman, and nine out of ten reported perpetrators are men.

"The rule of law requires not only that laws are passed, but that they are equally enforced and independently adjudicated, free from bias or discrimination."[10]

ECtHR Case of *Bevacqua and S. V. Bulgaria,* 2008

Factual background:

In March 2000, Valentina Nikolaeva Bevacqua left her marital home in Bulgaria with her young son, after years of suffering abuse at the hands of her husband, and moved into her parents' apartment. She filed for divorce the same day and sought an interim custody order. Despite clear evidence of abuse, every stage of the justice chain failed.

It took more than a year for the authorities to take appropriate action, placing Valentina and her son in serious danger. Her estranged husband battered her and forcibly took their son away for extended periods. With each new incident, she filed complaints with the prosecutor's office and approached forensic examiners to obtain medical documentation.

On every occasion, the authorities demonstrated a lack of any sense of urgency in addressing the problem. Valentina complained to the Ministry of the Interior that the police had done little to assist her in obtaining custody of her son and had not taken necessary measures to protect him. She was told that there was nothing the police could do about a "private dispute." The courts did not address her requests for interim measures and enforced a two-month reconciliation period prior to the divorce proceeding. Valentina finally obtained a divorce and custody of her son in May 2001. When she went to her former home to collect her belongings, she was again attacked by her ex-husband. She lodged a complaint with the prosecution authorities, but they refused to initiate criminal proceedings against him.

European Court for Human Rights (ECtHR) reasoning:

In 2001, supported by the legal NGOs, the Bulgarian Gender Research Foundation and Interights, Valentina and her son brought their case to the European Court of Human Rights (ECtHR). She alleged that Bulgarian officials violated their rights to respect for private and family life, including their physical and psychological integrity, under the European Convention on Human Rights.

Previously, both the ECtHR and European governments had interpreted the Convention to mean that family relationships and those between private individuals are matters beyond the purview of the state.

In this case, however, the Court reasoned that respecting private and family life may include a duty to maintain and apply in practice an adequate legal framework affording protection against acts of violence by private individuals. When the Court finally handed down the judgment in 2008, it found the State of Bulgaria in violation of the Convention for failing to implement these positive obligations.

This case and those that followed revolutionized the understanding of domestic violence, from a private act committed with widespread impunity to a human rights violation that States have a responsibility to combat.

In particular, it contributed to the emergence of a due diligence standard to assess whether States have carried out their duty to provide a functioning justice chain to respond to domestic violence. Pre-empting the ECtHR judgment, in 2005 the Government of Bulgaria passed comprehensive legislation, placing responsibility on the State to prevent domestic violence and assist victims.

The law, which was drafted in close collaboration with the Bulgarian Gender Research Foundation, includes provisions to grant temporary custody of children and for emergency protection orders. In 2007, guidelines for police officers were issued, and a national database of domestic violence cases was established. Women's organizations have been very active in lobbying for adequate funding for the implementation of the law, spurred on by Valentina's case. Valentina Nikolaeva Bevacqua showed extraordinary perseverance in her quest for justice, facing enormous obstacles from an unresponsive system and a dysfunctional justice chain.

Millions of women like her face two major barriers when navigating the formal justice system. On the one hand, extensive social barriers discourage them from coming forward and pursuing cases. On the other hand, justice systems lack capacity, resulting in distant courtrooms, unaffordable costs, and service providers who are not responsive to women's needs.

ECtHR Case of *Opuz v. Turkey*, 2009

Factual background:

The case originated in an application (no. 33401/02) against the Republic of Turkey lodged with the Court under Article 34 of the Convention for the Protection of Human Rights and Fundamental Freedoms ("the Convention") by a Turkish national, Mrs. Nahide Opuz ("the applicant"), on July 15, 2002.

The applicant alleged, in particular, that the State authorities had failed to protect her and her mother from domestic violence, which had resulted in the death of her mother and her own ill-treatment.

In the period of 1995–2002, H.O. attacked very seriously six times his wife and her mother very seriously six times, with severe health consequences that were life-threatening.

Investigation was stopped three times due to the victim giving up on filing the suit and two times because of the lack of evidence.

Case resulted in the shooting the applicant's mother by H.O.'s firearm and her instant death in 2002. It was the final consequence of long-term, repeated domestic violence.

European Court for Human Rights (ECtHR) reasoning:

The Court has invoked numerous international legal instruments. Relevant international and comparative law—The UN CEDAW Convention defines discrimination against women as "any distinction, exclusion or restriction made on the basis of sex which has the effect or purpose of impairing or nullifying the recognition, enjoyment or exercise by women, irrespective of their marital status, on a basis of equality of men and women, of human rights and fundamental freedoms in the political, economic, social, cultural, civil or any other field."

The UN Committee on the Elimination of All Forms of Discrimination against Women (hereinafter "the CEDAW Committee") has found that "gender-based violence is a form of discrimination that seriously inhibits women's ability to enjoy rights and freedoms on a basis of equality with men" and is thus prohibited under Article 1 of CEDAW. Within the general category of gender-based violence, the Committee includes violence by "private act" and "family violence." (Committee's General Recommendation No. 19 on "Violence Against Women," (1992) UN doc. CEDAW/C/1992/L.1/Add.15)

Consequently, gender-based violence triggers duties in States. The General Recommendation No. 19 sets out a catalogue of such duties. They include a duty on States to "take all legal and other measures that are necessary to provide effective protection of women against gender-based violence, including penal sanctions, civil remedies, and compensatory provisions to protect women against all kinds of violence."

ECHR brought the judgment that Turkey has violated art. 2, 3, and 14 of the European Convention on Human Rights: right to life, interdiction of torture, and ban of discrimination. The legal basis for the ultimate attribution of responsibility to a State for private acts relies on

State failure to comply with the duty to ensure human rights protection, as set out in Article 1 (1) of the American Convention on Human Rights (1969).

Consequently, the ECtHR stated: "For a state's positive obligation to arise, it must be established that the authorities knew or ought to have known at the time of the existence of a real and immediate risk to the life of an identified individual from the criminal acts of a third party and that they failed to take measures within the scope of their powers which, judged reasonably, might have been expected to avoid that risk."

In these circumstances, the Court (ECtHR) concludes that the national authorities of Turkey cannot be considered to have displayed due diligence. They therefore failed in their positive obligation to protect the right to life of the applicant's mother within the meaning of Article 2 of the Convention.[11]

The Court (ECtHR) concludes that there has been a violation of Article 3[12] of the Convention as a result of the State authorities' failure to take protective measures in the form of effective deterrence against serious breaches of the applicant's personal integrity by her husband. At the legal disposal of the Turkish authorities were the following measures: prohibiting approaching the victim, prohibition of harassment of any kind (including by telephone), handing over weapons to the police even if the perpetrator of violence legally owns them, prohibition of coming home under the influence of alcohol or drugs, and so on, but none of them were applied.

As regards the non-pecuniary damage, the Court notes that the applicant has undoubtedly suffered anguish and distress on account of the killing of her mother and the authorities' failure to undertake sufficient measures to prevent the domestic violence perpetrated by her husband and to give him deterrent punishment. Ruling on an equitable basis, the Court awards the applicant EUR 30,000 in respect of the damage sustained by her as a result of violations of Articles 2, 3, and 14 of the Convention. The Court considered it reasonable to award the sum of EUR 6,500 for costs and expenses for the proceedings before the Court, less EUR 1,494 received by way of legal aid from the Council of Europe.

This is the revolutionary judgment of the Court, where it has emphasized the duty of a State to pursue an effective investigation with due diligence and to undertake preventive operational measures even before the trial begins. The Court brought this judgment in line with previous similar cases, such as *L.C.B. v. the United Kingdom*,[13] *Osman v. the United Kingdom*,[14] *E. And Others v. the United Kingdom*,[15] *Bevacqua and S. v. Bulgaria*, 71127/01,[16] *K.A. and A.D. v. Belgium*.[17] The Court also followed the CEDAW Committee decisions in cases *Ms A.T. v. Hungary*[18] and *Fatma Yildirim v. Austria*.[19]

Especially important is the relation between the right to respect for private and family life (Art. 8)[20] on the one side and the right to life (Art. 2) and the prohibition of torture and/or degrading treatment (Art. 3) on the other. Bearing in mind that violence against women and girls is not a private matter, the Court concluded that there is no room for extensive interpretation of Article 8 on respect for private and family life, since the protection of life and physical integrity of a victim is a priority. Additionally, the Court pointed to the fact that the failure of a State to effectively protect the life of a victim and to prevent gender-based violence against women is a form of clear discrimination against women. This represents a violation of the Article 14 of the European Convention.

ECtHR Case of *Branko Tomašić and Others v. Croatia*, 2009

Factual background:

M. M. served his sentence in Varaždin Prison and was released on July 3, 2006. On August 15, 2006, he shot M. T., their daughter V. T., and himself. Before the shooting, he was spotted by M. T.'s neighbor carrying an automatic gun and leaving his bicycle in the adjacent woods. The neighbor immediately called the police. The police arrived at the scene twenty minutes later, just after the tragic event.

M. M.'s medical record from prison, submitted by the Government, does not indicate any psychiatric or psychotherapeutic treatment.

On November 6, 2006, the applicants—close cousins of the murdered woman and her daughter – submitted a proposal to the State Attorney for a settlement of their claim for non-pecuniary damages related to the deaths of M. T. and V. T. They alleged failures by the competent authorities to take adequate steps to protect the lives of M. T. and V. T. and inadequacy of the investigation into the circumstances of their deaths. They sought 1,105,000 Croatian kunas (HRK) in compensation and HRK 13,481 for costs. They received no reply.

Before the tragic event, on January 2, 2006 M. M. had come to the Social Welfare Center and claimed that he had a bomb and would "throw it at his former wife [meaning M. T.] and child." On February 3, 2006, M. M. was detained following the instigation of criminal proceedings against him in the Čakovec Municipal Court on January 27, 2006. A psychiatric opinion obtained during the proceedings stated that on January 2, 2006 M .M. had claimed before the employees of the Welfare Center that he had a bomb and that his threats had been meant seriously. He had repeated the same claim on January 19, 2006, before police officers from the Međumurje (local) Police.

On March 15, 2006, the Municipal Court found M. M. guilty of threatening M. T. on several occasions during the period between July and December 30, 2005, and decided on five months of imprisonment with a security measure of compulsory psychiatric treatment.

Nonetheless, mandatory psychotherapeutic treatment in the prison was not applied, despite serious psychological problems of M. M. being recognized during the criminal proceedings through psychiatric expertise. Furthermore, no assessment of M. M.'s psychological condition was made before his release from prison to assess the risk of carrying out previous threats to kill his former wife M. T. and their daughter V. T.

European Court for Human Rights (ECtHR) reasoning:

The applicants made a two-fold complaint under Article 2 of the Convention. They contended, first, that the State had failed to comply with its positive obligations to prevent the deaths of M. T. and V. T., and secondly that the State had failed to conduct a thorough investigation into the possible responsibility of its agents for the deaths of M. T. and V. T.

Article 2 of the European Convention on HR reads as follows:

"1. Everyone's right to life shall be protected by law. No one shall be deprived of his life intentionally save in the execution of a sentence of a court following his conviction of a crime for which this penalty is provided by law.
2. Deprivation of life shall not be regarded as inflicted in contravention of this article when it results from the use of force which is no more than absolutely necessary:
    (a) in defense of any person from unlawful violence;
    (b) in order to effect a lawful arrest or to prevent the escape of a person lawfully detained;
    (c) in action lawfully taken for the purpose of quelling a riot or insurrection."

However, notwithstanding the chances of success of a potential civil action concerning the lawfulness of the acts of the relevant authorities, the Court notes that in any event, the issue here is not a question of whether the authorities acted unlawfully or whether there was any individual responsibility of a State official on whatever grounds. Much more broadly, the central question of the case is the alleged deficiencies in the national system for the protection of the lives of others from acts of dangerous criminals, who have been identified as such by the relevant authorities, and the treatment of such individuals, including the legal framework within which the competent authorities are to operate and the mechanisms provided for.

In this connection the Court notes that the Government has not shown that these issues, and in particular the applicants' complaint under Article 2 of the Convention related to the insufficiencies of domestic law and practice preceding the deaths of M. T. and V. T., could be examined in any proceedings relied on by the Government.

The Court cannot see how an additional criminal complaint about the same issues lodged by the applicants might have led to a different outcome. In this connection, the Court reiterates that in cases concerning a death in circumstances that might give rise to the State's responsibility, the authorities must act on their own motion (*proprio motu*) once the matter has come to their attention. They cannot leave it to the initiative of the next-of-kin either to lodge a formal complaint or to take responsibility for the conduct of any investigative procedures (see, for example, *McKerr v. the United Kingdom*, no. 28883/95, § 111, ECHR 2001-III, and *Slimani v. France*, no. 57671/00, § 29, ECHR 2004-IX, extracts).

Substantive aspect of Article 2 of the Convention—general principles: the Court reiterates that Article 2 enjoins the State to take appropriate steps to safeguard the lives of those within its jurisdiction (see *L.C.B. v. the United Kingdom*, June 9, 1998, Reports of Judgments and Decisions 1998-III, § 36). This involves a primary duty on the State to secure the right to life by putting in place effective criminal-law provisions to deter the commission of offenses against the person backed up by law-enforcement machinery for the prevention, suppression and punishment of breaches of such provisions (see *Nachova and Others v. Bulgaria* [GC], nos. 43577/98 and 43579/98, § 160, ECHR 2005-VII).

A positive obligation of the state will arise where it has been established that the authorities knew or ought to have known at the time of the existence of a real and immediate risk to the life of an identified individual from the criminal acts of a third party and that they failed to take measures within the scope of their powers which, judged reasonably, might have been expected to avoid that risk (see Osman, cited above, § 116; *Paul and Audrey Edwards v. the United Kingdom*, no. 46477/99, § 55, ECtHR 2002-III; and *Bromiley v. the United Kingdom* (dec.), no. 33747/96, November 23, 1999).

Since no adequate psychiatric treatment was provided to M. M. in the prison, there was also no assessment of his condition immediately prior to his release from prison with a view to assessing the risk that, once at large, he might carry out his previous threats against the lives of M. T. and V. T.

The Court finds such a failure particularly striking given that his threats had been taken seriously by domestic courts and that the prior psychiatric report expressly stated that there was a strong likelihood that he might repeat the same or similar offenses. Even more, the Court found that the authorities knew or should have known that the perpetrator was dangerous because his threats were taken seriously in previous proceedings. Therefore, there was a positive duty of the State to implement preventive measures to avoid the risk of endangering the lives of victims, but those measures had not been applied.

The Court notes that it has found that the authorities, in relation to the death of the applicants' two close relatives, breached the European Convention (Art. 2). In these circumstances, the Court considers that the applicants must have sustained non-pecuniary damage. Ruling on an equitable basis and having regard to the awards made in comparable cases, it awards the applicants EUR 40,000 jointly under that head, plus any tax that may be chargeable to them, and 1300 EUR for costs and expenses for the proceedings before the Court.

Despite the provisions of Article 35 on admissibility criteria, that is, that the Court may only deal with the matter after all domestic remedies have been exhausted, in this case, the Court found that this rule is not absolute nor eligible for automatic application. The Court has to be guided, besides formal legal instruments in a concrete country, also by the general legal and political context, as well as by specific personal circumstances related to the applicant.

OTHER ECtHR CASES ON VIOLENCE AGAINST WOMEN AND GIRLS

ECtHR CASE OF *KONTROVA V. SLOVAKIA* (2007)

Factual background:

On November 2, 2002, the applicant filed a criminal complaint against her husband for assaulting her and beating her with an electric cable. The police later assisted her in withdrawing her complaint when she returned to the police station accompanied by her husband. On December 31, 2002, her husband shot dead their daughter and son, born in 1997 and 2001. The applicant received no compensation.

European Court for Human Rights (ECtHR) reasoning:

The European Court of Human Rights found a violation of Article 2 (right to life) of the European Convention on Human Rights, concerning the authorities' failure to protect the children's lives, and a violation of Article 13 (right to an effective remedy)[21] of the Convention, concerning the impossibility for their mother to obtain compensation.

EcTHR Case of *E. S. and Others V. Slovakia* (2009)

Factual background:

In 2001, the first applicant left her husband and lodged a criminal complaint against him for ill-treating her and her children (the three other applicants) and sexually abusing one of their daughters. He was convicted of violence and sexual abuse two years later.

The first applicant's request for her husband to be ordered to leave their home was dismissed; the court found that it did not have the power to restrict her husband's access to the property, and she could only end the tenancy when divorced. The applicants were therefore forced to move away from their friends and family.

European Court for Human Rights (ECtHR) reasoning:

The Court found that Slovakia had failed to provide the applicant and her children with the immediate protection required against their husband's and father's violence, in an inhuman violation of the Article 3 (prohibition of torture or degrading treatment) and Article 8 (right to respect for private and family life) of the Convention.[22]

ECtHR Case of A. v. Croatia (2010)

Factual background:

The applicant's now ex-husband (suffering from post-traumatic stress disorder, paranoia, anxiety, and epilepsy) allegedly subjected her to repeated physical violence causing bodily injury and death threats over many years and also regularly abused her in front of their young daughter.

After going into hiding, the applicant requested a court order preventing her ex-husband from stalking or harassing her. It was refused on the grounds that she had not shown an immediate risk to her life.

European Court for Human Rights (ECtHR) reasoning:

The Court found a violation of the Article 8 (right to respect for private and family life) of the Convention in that the Croatian authorities had failed to implement many of the measures ordered by the courts to protect the applicant or deal with her ex-husband's psychiatric problems, which appeared to be at the root of his violent behaviour. It was also unclear whether he had undergone any psychiatric treatment.

The Court further declared the applicant's complaint under Article 14 (prohibition of discrimination)[23] of the Convention inadmissible, on the ground, in particular, that she had not given sufficient evidence (such as reports or statistics) to prove that the measures or practices adopted in Croatia against domestic violence, or the effects of such measures or practices, were discriminatory.

ECtHR Case of E.m. v. Romania (2012)

Factual background:

The applicant alleged in particular that the investigation into her criminal complaint of domestic violence committed in the presence of her daughter, aged one and a half, had not been effective. The Romanian courts had dismissed the applicant's complaints on the grounds that her allegations that she had been subjected to violence by her husband had not been proven.

European Court for Human Rights (ECtHR) reasoning:

The Court held that there had been a violation of the Article 3 (prohibition of torture or inhuman or degrading treatment) of the European Convention on basic human rights and fundamental freedoms under its procedural limb, finding that the manner in which the investigation had been conducted had not afforded the applicant the effective protection required by Article 3.

ECtHR observed in particular that, when making the first of her complaints, the applicant had requested assistance and protection from the authorities for herself and her daughter against her husband's aggressive conduct. Despite the fact that the statutory framework provided for cooperation between the various authorities and for non-judicial measures to identify and ensure action was taken in respect of domestic violence, and although the medical certificate provided *prima facie* evidence of the applicant's allegations, it did not appear from the case file that any steps had been taken to that end.

ECtHR Case of *Irene Wilson v. The United Kingdom* (2012)

Factual background:

This case concerned the complaint by a victim of domestic violence about the authorities' handling of the criminal proceedings against her husband for grievous bodily harm and her allegation that the suspended sentence given to him was too lenient.

European Court for Human Rights (ECtHR) reasoning:

The Court declared the application inadmissible (manifestly ill-founded), finding that the Northern Irish authorities had not failed in their duty to protect the applicant's rights under Article 8 (right to respect for private and family life) of the European Convention on basic human rights and fundamental freedoms.

ECtHR observed in particular that the applicant only brought one complaint to the attention of the authorities: that incident was then promptly investigated, her husband arrested and charged, and the ensuing criminal proceedings conducted with due expedition. The applicant had not made any other specific allegations of violence to the Court.

ECtHR Case of *Eremia and Others v. The Republic of Moldova* (2013)

Factual background:

The first applicant and her two daughters complained about the Moldovan authorities' failure to protect them from the violent and abusive behavior of their husband and father, who is a police officer.

European Court for Human Rights (ECtHR) reasoning:

The Court found a violation of the Article 3 (prohibition of inhuman and degrading treatment) of the Convention in respect of the first applicant, a violation of the Article 8 (right to respect for private and family life) of the Convention in respect of her two daughters, and a violation of the Article 14 (prohibition of discrimination) read in conjunction with the Article 3 of the European Convention in respect of the first applicant.

ECtHR held in particular that, despite their knowledge of the abuse, the authorities had failed to take effective measures against the first applicant's husband and to protect his wife from further domestic violence.

ECtHR furthermore considered that, despite the detrimental psychological effects of her daughters witnessing their father's violence against their mother in the family home, little or no action had been taken to prevent the recurrence of such behavior.

Finally, the Court found that the authorities' attitude had amounted to condoning violence and had been discriminatory toward the first applicant as a woman.

ECtHR Case of M.g. V. Turkey (2016)

Factual background:

The applicant, M.G., is a Turkish national who was born in 1973 and lives in Istanbul (Turkey). On July 18, 2006, M.G. lodged a complaint against her husband with the public prosecutor, stating that she had fled from her home on account of the domestic violence to which she had been subjected since the beginning of her marriage in 1997. A report detailing M.G.'s injuries was drawn up by the institute for forensic medicine. She was referred to the psychiatric department of the Medical Faculty of Istanbul University, which also submitted a document to the prosecutor's office, indicating that she was suffering from depressive disorder and chronic post-traumatic stress resulting from her experiences. Her husband denied the accusations against him; he was questioned on December 15, 2006, and on February 22, 2012, he was charged with injuring his wife.

In the meantime, on August 31, 2006, M.G. instituted divorce proceedings in the family affairs court and requested protection measures, which were granted by the court. The divorce was pronounced on September 24, 2007, and parental responsibility was awarded to M.G.; however, the children were placed under the protection of social services. On November 1, 2012, October 10, 2013, and June 19, 2014, M.G. again applied to the family affairs court, requesting preventive measures in respect of her former husband and alleging that he was constantly threatening her with violence and death. The court granted her requests, including ordering the ex-husband not to approach M.G.'s home or disturb her by communicating with her.

On March 6, 2014, the foundation "Purple Roof," which had provided refuge to M.G. and her children, submitted a social welfare report, specifying in particular that she was living under a continual threat and that her safety was still endangered.

European Court for Human Rights (ECtHR) reasoning:

European Court of Human Rights held, unanimously, that there had been: a violation of the Article 3 (prohibition of torture and inhuman or degrading treatment) of the European Convention on Human Rights, and a violation of the Article 14 (prohibition of discrimination), taken in conjunction with the Article 3.

The case concerned the domestic violence experienced by M.G. during her marriage, the threats made against her following her divorce, and the subsequent proceedings. The Court reiterated that it had already found that a State's failure, even where unintentional, to protect women against domestic violence breached their right to equal protection under the law. It also emphasized that, under Article 3 of the Istanbul Convention, the term "violence against women" was to be understood as a violation of human rights and a form of discrimination against women. In this connection, it noted that, in the circumstances of the present case, the general and discriminatory judicial passivity in Turkey was such as to create a climate that was conducive to domestic violence.

The Court found, in particular that the authorities had taken a passive attitude, in that the criminal proceedings had been opened more than five years and six months after M.G. had lodged a complaint against her husband and that the proceedings were apparently still pending.

The Court also held that after the divorce was pronounced (on September 24, 2007) and until the entry into force of a new Law (no. 6284) on March 20, 2012, the legislative framework in place did not guarantee that M.G., a divorcée, could benefit from protection measures, and noted that for many years after applying to the national courts, she had been forced to live in fear of her ex-husband's conduct. In line with Article 41 of the European Convention (just satisfaction),[24] the Court held that Turkey was to pay the applicant 19,500 euros (EUR) in respect of non-pecuniary damage and EUR 4,000 in respect of costs and expenses.

LESSONS LEARNED

Violence against women in the family context is a form of continuing violence and abuse, a situation of repeated victimization, where the victim (woman, girl) is vulnerable precisely because she shares a home with her abuser and has a sense of loyalty, or even love, toward him.[25] Landmark case law of the European Court of Human Rights (ECHR) pointed out that violence against women is a form of unlawful discrimination and a severe violation of women's human rights.

Violence against women and other forms of domestic violence are not private matters. In most countries, people are nowadays increasingly aware that gender-based violence against women and domestic violence are negative and dangerous social phenomena, and not just isolated, individual private problems. This is a fact, especially if we take into account the accompanying devastating effects of domestic and gender-based violence.[26]

For centuries, the invisibility of violence against women and girls was maintained by treating it as a private situation. Thus, the intervention of the state was prevented and assistance to the victim was made impossible. For centuries, the idea of a dichotomy between the private and public spheres concealed the subordination of women to men and was therefore an expression of a patriarchal worldview. The modern worldview rejects the belief that the division into private and public spheres inevitably stems from the natural characteristics of women and men.[27]

The binding force of ECtHR judgments represents an important influence in terms of the modernization of national legislation. Thus, a single judgment may have an impact on the whole population of a State. In addition, a State that is found to have committed a violation of the European Convention is required to provide compensation for the damage sustained by the applicant and, as far as possible, remedy any consequences of the violation. The State must also ensure that no similar violation occurs.

In twelve member States of the CoE, namely in Albania, Austria, Bosnia and Herzegovina, Estonia, Greece, Great Britain, Italy, Poland, Portugal, San Marino, Spain, and Switzerland, the authorities are required to continue criminal proceedings despite the victim's withdrawal of the complaint in cases of domestic violence. Another lesson learned is that the perpetrator is responsible for the violence, not the victim.

In twenty-seven member states of the Council of Europe, namely in Andorra, Armenia, Azerbaijan, Belgium, Bulgaria, Cyprus, the Czech Republic, Denmark, England and Wales, Finland, the FYR of Macedonia, France, Georgia, Germany, Hungary, Ireland, Latvia, Luxembourg, Malta, Moldova, the Netherlands, the Russian Federation, Serbia, Slovakia, Sweden, Turkey, and Ukraine, the authorities have a margin of discretion in deciding whether to pursue criminal proceedings against perpetrators of domestic violence.

A significant number of European legal systems make a distinction between crimes which are privately prosecutable (and for which the victim's complaint is a prerequisite) and those which are publicly prosecutable (usually more serious offenses for which prosecution is considered to be in the public interest).

The Court (ECtHR) reiterates that the first sentence of Article 2 § 1 enjoins the State not only to refrain from the intentional and unlawful taking of life but also to take appropriate steps to safeguard the lives of those within its jurisdiction (see *L.C.B. v. the United Kingdom*, June 9, 1998). The ECtHR emphasizes the particular vulnerability of the victims of domestic violence and thus urges active State involvement for their protection (*Bevacqua and S. v. Bulgaria*, 2008, para. 65; *T. M. and C. M. v. the Republic of Moldova*, 2014, para. 46). The whole course of criminal proceedings in the Opuz case highlights the degree of vulnerability of victims of domestic violence in the process.[28]

This involves a primary duty on the State to secure the right to life by putting in place effective criminal-law provisions to deter the commission of offenses against the person backed up by law-enforcement machinery for the prevention, suppression and punishment of breaches of such provisions. It also extends, in appropriate circumstances, to a positive obligation on the authorities to take preventive operational measures to protect an individual whose life is at risk from the criminal acts of another individual (see *Osman v. the United Kingdom*, October 28, 1998, § 115, *Reports* 1998-VIII, cited in *Kontrová v. Slovakia*, no. 7510/04, § 49, ECHR 2007 - extracts).

The Court notes at the outset that there seems to be no general consensus among States regarding the pursuance of the criminal prosecution against perpetrators of domestic violence and violence against women when the victim withdraws her complaint.

The Court observes that there are certain factors that can be taken into account in deciding to pursue the prosecution:

- The seriousness of the offense;
- Whether the victim's injuries are physical or psychological;
- If the defendant used a weapon;
- If the defendant has made any threats since the attack;
- If the defendant planned the attack;
- The effect (including psychological) on any children living in the household;
- The chances of the defendant offending again;
- The continuing threat to the health and safety of the victim or anyone else who is, or could become, involved;
- The current state of the victim's relationship with the defendant; the effect on that relationship of continuing with the prosecution against the victim's wishes;
- The history of the relationship, particularly if there had been any other violence in the past; and
- The defendant's criminal history, particularly any previously committed violence.

In relation to criminal prosecution against perpetrators, there is very important ECtHR assessment: "When a State makes little or no effort to stop a certain form of private violence, it tacitly condones that violence.

This complicity transforms what would otherwise be wholly private conduct into a constructive act of the State" (*Bevacqua v Bulgaria*, European Court of Human Rights, 2008).

One promising approach to reducing attrition in the justice chain is to integrate services through a "one-stop shop."

Another best model practice is the functioning of specialized courts. When they have adequate resources, specialized domestic violence courts can help to ensure accountability and victim protection and safety by streamlining navigation of the system, providing facilities such as closed session hearings, and increasing the expertise of judges and other personnel. Specialized domestic violence courts have been introduced in Brazil, Nepal, Spain, the United Kingdom, several states in the United States, Uruguay, Canada, and the Bolivarian Republic of Venezuela. Globally, women account for 27 percent of all judges. Women's representation in the judiciary approaches 50 percent in Central and Eastern Europe and Central Asia, but in South Asia, progress is less encouraging. Women's representation in supreme, constitutional, and regional courts also varies widely: Serbia, Rwanda, Slovenia, Canada, and the former Yugoslav Republic of Macedonia have the highest proportion of women judges.[29]

Women's representation in the judiciary is a matter of equality and fairness, but it is also important for maintaining public confidence in the justice system. There is evidence that women judges can create more conducive environments for women in courts and can make a difference in outcomes. One study in the United States found that women judges were 11 percent more likely to rule in favor of the plaintiff in employment discrimination cases.[30]

ECtHR landmark legal cases have established that governments' due diligence obligations mean they are not only responsible for enacting legislation that guarantees women's rights, but also for ensuring that these laws are implemented through a functioning justice chain that is gender responsive. Gender responsiveness in the judiciary can be performed through sensitizing judges through targeted training and bringing them into contact with the women they are dealing with and that can help to eliminate biased decision-making and increase optimal responsiveness to women. This is even more important bearing in mind that certain gender roles[31] and behavior can contribute to make violence against women acceptable. According to the CoE Istanbul Convention, the term gender explains that there are socially constructed roles, behaviors, activities, and attributes that a given society considers appropriate for women and men.

The question can be posed: what is the purpose of court proceedings and convictions in cases of violence against women? Main aim is certainly the protection of women's human rights, especially the right to live free from violence and to protect their dignity from discrimination, as well as protection from torture or other inhumane treatment. On the other side, the objective can be found furthermore in ensuring legal security and the rule of law through the effective functioning of the judicial system at the international, but also at national level. Legal security is a philosophical concept of modern thinking. Natural law theory, legal positivism, and legal humanism design the notion of security in law. The concept of legal security in the human right context consists of human security (security of person) and social security and security of the legal system.[32]

The long-term effectiveness of the system for the protection of human rights established on the basis of the European Convention primarily depends on the ability of the Court to quickly resolve the cases submitted to it. All applicants should exhaust all domestic remedies before applying to the European Court of Human Rights. Therefore, the provisions of Article 13[33] of the European Convention are closely related to Article 35 (1).[34] Furthermore, the effectiveness of the system depends as well on the capacity of member states of the Council of Europe to tackle effectively violations of human rights and fundamental freedoms. This is even more important, bearing in mind that, despite differences in legal systems, member states of the Council of Europe share a common history and similar problems in the implementation of the European Convention. This fact inspired the adoption of the Brussels Declaration of March 2015[35] stating that member states, the European Court of Human Rights, and the Committee of Ministers of the Council of Europe share responsibility for the long-term effectiveness of the European Convention.

Brussels Declaration promoted the subsidiarity principle in the implementation of the European Convention, which assumes effective implementation of the convictions of the European Court of Human rights at national level (Art. 46).[36] However, it is important to note that the European Convention did not explicitly mention the subsidiarity principle. This principle had been developing gradually. In the Belgian Linguistic case (1968), the European Court of Human Rights has emphasized that it "cannot assume the role of the competent domestic state authorities, because it would thereby lose sight of the subsidiary nature of the international mechanism for the collective exercise of rights established by the Convention."[37]

The subsidiarity principle has been particularly accentuated in the ECtHR case *Gherghina v. Romania* (2015): "the basic characteristic of the protection mechanism established by the Convention is that it is subsidiary in the national human rights protection systems. The Court deals with the supervision of the implementation of the obligations that the signatory states perform in accordance with the Convention. The Court should not assume the role of the state party, whose responsibility is to ensure respect and protection of fundamental rights and freedoms at the national level, which are guaranteed by the Convention."[38] Besides ECtHR decisions, the subsidiarity principle has been regulated in Protocol No. 15 on Amendments to the European Convention (June 24, 2013, Council of Europe Agreement Series No. 213). However, the subsidiarity principle is limited by the request for basic rights and freedoms to be effective, which calls for the Court's intervention, being monitoring mechanism. If the Court would be passive, there would be a denial of justice and the European Convention guarantees would not be operational.

In the area of cases devoted to violence against women and domestic violence, very important is the principle of evolutionary interpretation of the European Convention by the Court. Precisely, European Convention is a vivid instrument to be interpreted in the light of contemporary circumstances. This assumes that the Court can develop and improve its attitude toward specific rights that are guaranteed in the Convention. Furthermore, the result of this principle is that certain issues, which have been left to States Parties' jurisdiction to decide in total discretionary manner, can be called for reconsideration by the European Court. The practice of the European Court, as analyzed above, confirms this principle.

Finally, lessons learned from ECtHR cases are related to the execution of the Court convictions in the national systems of State Parties of the European Convention in line with Article 46 (1): "The High Contracting Parties undertake to abide by the final judgment of the Court in any case to which they are parties." The Committee of Ministers will supervise the execution of the final judgment of the Court. States signatories of the Convention are obliged to implement the final judgment of the Court at all levels of power. Legislator has to adopt laws that are in accordance with the European Convention. Executive power has to apply laws in a way compatible with the European Convention's provisions, as well as to adopt harmonized by-laws. National judiciary is in the best position to ensure respect for the basic rights and freedoms that are guaranteed in the European Convention.

NOTES

1. Mahatma Gandhi, 1869–1948, was one of the founders of the modern Indian state and an influential supporter of satyagraha (non-violent protest) on the way to the realization of the revolution.

2. Capers Bennett, Against Prosecutors, 105 CORNELL L. REV. 1561, 1587 (2020). Capers also discusses giving greater sentencing discretion to juries. See id. at 1607.

3. Ramsey, Carolyn. "Against Domestic Violence: Public and Private Prosecution of Batterers, University of Colorado Law School, Colorado Law Scholarly Commons *California Law Review Online Symposium*, 13:45/2022, https://scholar.law.colorado.edu/faculty-articles. 23.11.2023.

4. UN GA, Report of the International Law Commission, Sixty-eighth session (May 2–June 10 and July 4–August 12, 2016), General Assembly Official Records Seventy-first session Supplement No. 10 (A/71/10), Chapter V: Identification of customary international law, sect. C, conclusion 13, 2016.

5. https://www.echr.coe.int/documents/convention_eng.pdf, 25.01.2024.

6. https://www.echr.coe.int/Documents/Court_in_brief_ENG.pdf, 30.01.2024.

7. E. Sarac, M. Cinar, "Main features of the Inter-American Convention on Violence Against Women," *Universita degli studi Firenze*, 4/2021.

8. Chapter 6 of the CoE Istanbul Convention.

9. E. Buscaglia, W. E. Ratliff, *Law and Economics in Developing Countries*, Hoover Press, USA, 2000, 31.

10. UN WOMEN, "Progress of the World's Women 2011–12, In Pursuit of JUSTICE," 2012.

11. ARTICLE 2, Right to life Everyone's right to life shall be protected by law. No one shall be deprived of his life intentionally save in the execution of a sentence of a court following his conviction of a crime for which this penalty is provided by law.

Deprivation of life shall not be regarded as inflicted in contravention of this Article when it results from the use of force which is no more than absolutely necessary:

(a) in defense of any person from unlawful violence;
(b) in order to effect a lawful arrest or to prevent the escape of a person lawfully detained;
(c) in action lawfully taken for the purpose of quelling a riot or insurrection.

(European Convention for the Protection of Human Rights and Fundamental Freedoms, 1953).

12. ARTICLE 3, Prohibition of torture

No one shall be subjected to torture or to inhuman or degrading treatment or punishment.

(European Convention for the Protection of Human Rights and Fundamental Freedoms, 1953).

13. *L.C.B. v. the United Kingdom*, 1998-III.

14. *Osman v. the United Kingdom*, 23452/94, 1998-III, no. 95.

15. *E. And Others v. the United Kingdom*, 332218/96.

16. *Bevacqua and S. v. Bulgaria*, 71127/01.

17. *K.A. and A.D.v. Belgium*, 42758/98 and 45558/99, 2005.

18. *Ms A.T. v. Hungary*, January 26, 2005, A 60/38 (Part I).

19. *Fatma Yildirim v. Austria*, August 6, 2007.

20. ARTICLE 8 Right to respect for private and family life

1 Everyone has the right to respect for his private and family life, his home and his correspondence.

There2 There shall be no interference by a public authority with the exercise of this right except such as is in accordance with the law and is necessary in a democratic society in the interests of national security, public safety or the economic well-being of the country, for the prevention of disorder or crime, for the protection of health or morals, or for the protection of the rights and freedoms of others.

(European Convention for the Protection of Human Rights and Fundamental Freedoms, 1953).

21. ARTICLE 13, Right to an effective remedy

Everyone whose rights and freedoms as set forth in this Convention are violated shall have an effective remedy before a national authority notwithstanding that the violation has been committed by persons acting in an official capacity.

(European Convention for the Protection of Human Rights and Fundamental Freedoms, 1953).

22. ARTICLE 8, Right to respect for private and family life

1 Everyone has the right to respect for his private and family life, his home and his correspondence.

2 There shall be no interference by a public authority with the exercise of this right except such as is in accordance with the law and is necessary in a democratic society in the interests of national security, public safety or the economic well-being of the country, for the prevention of disorder or crime, for the protection of health or morals, or for the protection of the rights and freedoms of others.

(European Convention for the Protection of Human Rights and Fundamental Freedoms, 1953).

23. ARTICLE 14, Prohibition of discrimination

The enjoyment of the rights and freedoms set forth in this Convention shall be secured without discrimination on any ground such as sex, race, colour, language, religion, political or other opinion, national or social origin, association with a national minority, property, birth or other status.

(European Convention for the Protection of Human Rights and Fundamental Freedoms, 1953).

24. ARTICLE 41 Just satisfaction

If the Court finds that there has been a violation of the Convention or the Protocols thereto, and if the internal law of the High Contracting Party concerned allows only partial reparation to be made, the Court shall, if necessary, afford just satisfaction to the injured party.

(European Convention for the Protection of Human Rights and Fundamental Freedoms, 1953).

25. E. Kelly, 2003, in Ignjatovic, *Violence Against Women in Intimate Partnership*, 21.

26. The World's Women 2010, *Trends and Statistics*, United Nations, New York, 2010, Department of Economic and Social Affairs, 131.

27. Z. Mršević, *Violence and Us—Towards a Society Without Violence*, Institute of Social Sciences, Belgrade, 2014, 55.

28. Erbas Rahime, "Effective Criminal Investigations for Women Victims of Domestic Violence: The Approach of the ECtHR," *Women's Studies International Forum*, 86/2021, 1.

29. UN WOMEN, "Progress of the World's Women 2011–12, In Pursuit of JUSTICE," 2012, 37.

30. Ibid., 38.

31. The CoE Istanbul Convention (Art. 3, c).

32. C. B. Ivaylova, "Legal Security as a Principle in Law-making," *Globalization, the State and the Individual*, 2/2017, 23–29.

33. ARTICLE 13, Right to an effective remedy

Everyone whose rights and freedoms as set forth in this Convention are violated shall have an effective remedy before a national authority notwithstanding that the violation has been committed by persons acting in an official capacity.

34. ARTICLE 35, Admissibility criteria The Court may only deal with the matter after all domestic remedies have been exhausted, according to the generally recognized rules of international law, and within a period of four months from the date on which the final decision was taken.

35. The Brussels Declaration of March 2015 from the Conference at high level: "Implementation of the European Convention on Human Rights, Our Common Responsibility," March 27, 2015, http://www.echr.coe.int/Documents/BrusselsDeclaration_ENG.pdf, 23.10.2023.

36. ARTICLE 46, Binding force and execution of judgments

1e The High Contracting Parties undertake to abide by the final judgment of the Court in any case to which they are parties.

2e final judgment of the Court shall be transmitted to the Committee of Ministers, which shall supervise its execution.

3 If the Committee of Ministers considers that the supervision of the execution of a final judgment is hindered by a problem of interpretation of the judgment, it may refer the matter to the Court for a ruling on the question of interpretation. A referral decision shall require a majority vote of two-thirds of the representatives entitled to sit on the Committee.

4f If the Committee of Ministers considers that a High Contracting Party refuses to abide by a final judgment in a case to which it is a party, it may, after serving formal notice on that Party and by a decision adopted by a majority vote of two-thirds of the representatives entitled to sit on the committee, refer to the Court the question of whether that Party has failed to fulfilll its obligation under paragraph 1.

5f If the Court finds a violation of paragraph 1, it shall refer the case to the Committee of Ministers for consideration of the measures to be taken. If the

Court finds no violation of paragraph 1, it shall refer the case to the Committee of Ministers, which shall close its examination of the case.

37. Quoted by: K. Turković, "Strengthening partnership in the effective implementation of the European Convention on Human Rights," *Effective Implementation of National Remedies in Proceedings before Domestic Judicial Authorities in the Balkans and the Subsidiary Role of the European Court of Human Rights, Council of Europe*, 2017, 15.

38. *Gherghina v. Romania* No. 42219/07, par.83, July 9, 2015.

Chapter 6

Concluding Remarks

Violence against women and girls is the most brutal reflection of gender inequality. For centuries, the invisibility of violence against women and girls was maintained by treating it as a private situation. Thus, the intervention of the state had been prevented, and assistance to the victim was made impossible. On a global level, in most countries, people are nowadays increasingly aware that gender-based violence to women and domestic violence are negative and dangerous social phenomena with devastating effects, and not just isolated, individual private problems. Violence against women is worldwide; it is happening in both developed and developing countries, no matter of the religion or political ideology. Therefore, in most of the countries, gender-based and domestic violence is legally classified in the category of criminal offenses.

Generally seen, the majority of people are fascinated by violence, we are surrounded by violence, but the answer why is that so is in the domain of the socio-pathology.[1] Domestic violence is deeply rooted in society. Among the victims of domestic violence, women are predominant, as evidenced by the empirical results of relevant research at the global level. Since it takes place in the private sphere, it is very often is difficult to recognize and punish in relation to other forms of public violence. Hence, the agencies and services responsible for providing assistance to victims face different forms of hiding the truth in the four walls. Punishment occurs only in cases of prolonged manifestation of gender-based violence in a cruel way, with sometimes fatal consequences.

Each 25th November every year is marked as the International Day for the Elimination of Violence against Women at a global level. The International Day for the Elimination of Violence Against Women marks the launch of the campaign (November 25–December 10)—an initiative of sixteen days of activism concluding on the day that commemorates International Human Rights Day (10 December). This campaign, led by the UN Secretary-General and UN Women since 2008, aims to prevent and eliminate violence against women and girls around the world, calling for global action to increase awareness, promote advocacy, and create opportunities for discussion on challenges and solutions. The Global 16 Days Campaign, launched by the Center for Women's Global Leadership and feminists from around the world at the first Women's Global Leadership Institute in 1991, has been used worldwide to call for the elimination of gender-based violence against women.

Gender-based violence to women is defined as gender-based violence "directed to a woman just because she is a woman or affecting women disproportionately." Violence to women is a devastating social problem, as it prevents women to fully enjoy their human rights and fundamental freedoms, which furthermore negatively influences negatively to the development of the whole society in every state.

Normative recognition of women's human rights, especially the right to live free from violence, has been performed in universal international conventions and in resolutions and declarations, as well as in regional conventions and declarations.

International conventions are treaties signed between two or more nations that act as an international agreements. A treaty is a binding agreement between nation-states that forms the basis for international law. Authority for the enforcement of these treaties is provided by each signing party's adherence to the treaty. Conventions generally have built-in mechanisms to ensure compliance, such as procedures for inspections. These treaties also include methods to enforce non-compliance, such as economic sanctions. Generally speaking, outside of internal mechanisms, states could resort to external enforcement methods through other escalations, including the threat of military action.

UN CEDAW Convention is the most widely ratified fundamental human rights treaty that addresses the rights of women and the responsibilities of states toward ensuring them, including their right to be free from violence. It accentuates that discrimination against women can be multi-layered due to their experience of multiple forms of discrimination based on race, migration status, disability, and other factors. The CEDAW Convention is resilient and relevant to the fight to end violence against women, including to address sexual and gender-based violence during times of conflict.[2] It can be assessed that the CEDAW Convention became more effective with the adoption and implementation of the Optional Protocol in the twenty-first century. The CEDAW Committee's General Recommendations No. 19 (1992) and No. 35 (2017) have built upon the principle of women's equality and provide detailed recommendations, including on legal measures, prevention, protection, prosecution and punishment, reparations, and monitoring. The Committee's rich body of jurisprudence provides states parties with detailed guidance on how to respond to gender-based violence against women. Together with the country-specific and thematic reporting of the UN Special Rapporteur on violence against women, its causes and consequences, states are offered roadmaps to realize women and girls' right to live a life free from violence. However, gender equality is still far from being a reality for many women and girls the world over. The international and regional legal frameworks offer the tools needed to eliminate all forms of discrimination and violence against women and girls. Although criminal sanctions alone cannot change the complicated set of behavioral patterns that constitute domestic violence,[3] criminal prosecution has an evident deterrent effect.

Efficiency of legal regulations in international public law is a multidimensional issue and depends on the various vital national various interests of different countries that are mirrored and included in international norms and conventions. To the extent to which the negotiations on setting legal standards led by different states were successful, to the same extent the implementation of those legal norms will be effective. Furthermore, the effectiveness of provisions in international universal and regional conventions highly depends on the monitoring mechanism to follow their implementation and to issue adequate guidelines to state signatories.

Example of the Istanbul Convention of the Council of Europe indicates the complexity of those negotiations even at the expert level, while formulating relevant legal norms in the area of fighting violence against women and domestic violence. Reasons for such complexity lie in multicultural beliefs and often stereotype way in treatment of domestic violence and gender-based violence, even in modern states based on the rule of law and democracy. Preventing violence, protecting its victims, and prosecuting the perpetrators together with coordinated national policies are the cornerstones of the Istanbul Convention. It also seeks to change the hearts and minds of individuals by calling on all members of society, in particular men and boys, to change attitudes.

If we ask ourselves what would be the final goal of the effective regional legal standards set up by the Istanbul Convention, the answer is for sure: zero tolerance toward gender-based violence and toward domestic violence. Immediate and long-term health care, adequate counseling, timely police response, access to justice, and safe accommodation and shelter can help women and girls to exit from the vicious circle of violence and begin to recover.

The Istanbul Convention is the first international treaty specifically tackling violence from a gender perspective. It recognizes "the structural nature of violence against women" and "that domestic violence affects women disproportionately," while recognizing that men may also be victims of such violence. The Convention aims to tackle violence in a holistic manner by including obligations structured around four main pillars: (1) integrated policies; (2) prevention of all forms of violence; (3) protection of victims from further violence; and (4) prosecution of perpetrators. The Declaration of the Committee of the Parties to the Council of Europe Istanbul Convention on Preventing and Combating Violence against Women and Domestic Violence, on the tenth anniversary of the opening for signature of the Istanbul Convention of May 6, 2021, reiterates "the essential role of the Istanbul Convention in preventing and combating violence against women and domestic violence, as the most far-reaching and comprehensive set of standards to tackle this issue." Furthermore, the Declaration "acknowledges the major contribution of the Istanbul Convention monitoring mechanism in preventing and combating violence against women and domestic violence by providing tailored-made guidance as well as opportunities for states parties to learn from each other and exchange on best practices." On the other (dark) side, there are some obstacles to the prevention and elimination of all forms of violence covered by the Istanbul Convention, including challenges arising from the COVID-19 pandemic. Especially harmful is the spreading of false narratives about the Istanbul Convention and the attempt to weaken the multilateral and legally binding international system protecting women against violence. Consequently, the Declaration urges states parties to intensify their efforts to promote and fully implement the Istanbul Convention in order to realize its potential and holistic approach, and to protect and promote the right of women and girls to live a life free and to protect and promote the right of women and girls to live a life free from violence, including for women and girls facing multiple and intersecting forms of discrimination.

However, equally important are the Convention standards and principles on the one side and relevant national norms, on the other. At complex road in achieving gender equality and the effective protection of women and girls from gender-based violence, the Istanbul Convention plays emancipatory role. Strategic legal significance of the Istanbul Convention is represented in the fact that it defines violence against women as severe discrimination and a violation of women's human rights. Although the Convention was born under the auspices of the Council of Europe, it bears global importance through setting modern legal standards and by its openness for accession by non-members of the Council of Europe. The Istanbul Convention aims for zero tolerance of gender-based and domestic violence in each society and therefore it foresees implementation of national prevention measures in this domain. Special value of the Convention legal standards in the area of fight against gender-based violence and domestic violence, is in its contribution to dismantling globally widespread negative gender stereotypes, which are one of the main causes of violence against women.

Convention represents a renewed aspiration toward establishing essential equality between women and men, aimed at removing deeply rooted unequal power relations between them. Its monitoring mechanism proves to be a *spiritus movens* in guiding governments to apply efficient measures and policies to respond to violence against women. Ratification of the Convention had the effect of triggering amendments to the existing legislation and/or the adoption of new legal measures in States Parties, as national reports to GREVIO proved. Fulfilling the commitments taken under this Convention is crucial for it to reach its comprehensive potential. However, it is a long road, since more has to be achieved, such as in the implementation of Article 36 related to the definition of sexual violence based on the lack of consent. Besides, in many countries, domestic violence shelters should be more present, as well as services of support to victims.

Relevant lessons learned are the following:

- For tackling violence against women and girls, it is necessary to constantly improve the legislative framework;
- For an effective fight against sexual violence, it is necessary to sharpen prosecution rates;
- For reporting gender-based violence and domestic violence cases, it is highly recommended to improve trust in the criminal justice system;
- For a comprehensive approach to dismantling violence against women and girls, it is necessary to address intersectionality and understand how to support the most vulnerable groups;
- For prevention purposes and achieving zero tolerance, it is unavoidable to permanently undertake campaigns raising awareness and preventing gender-based violence through education. It is vital to improve identification skills and appropriate responses to the disclosure of intimate partner violence in the health sector;
- For raising general human security in public, and especially the safety of women and girls, it is recommendable to strengthen the police mandate and multisector cooperation of responsible stakeholders.

In the forthcoming period, effective public awareness campaigns should also focus on the invisible part of the iceberg of domestic violence against women, pointing out that it is the result not only of the victim's silence, but also of the explicit tolerance of the victims' social milieu. Therefore, it can be concluded that social response and responsibility in issues of gender-based and domestic violence, together with the effective implementation of relevant international universal and regional norms and national legislation, would have a deterrent effect for perpetrators. In the near future, national policy measures against gender-based and domestic violence should be based on greater research results on societal values toward intimate partner violence expressed through threats, intimidation, and coercion[4] in view of reporting, victim-blaming, tolerance, and complete silence. More resources are to be directed to the permanent fight against gender-based and domestic violence in law enforcement, health settings, support programs for the victims, and prevention measures, in line with the international universal and regional legal standards.

Soft law international instruments are created with the intention of being non-binding, but they still have legal significance. Norms from the arsenal of soft law can, given their flexibility, provide adequate and quick answers to solve problems. Soft law has another specific advantage. Namely, it is oriented *pro futuro*, because its instruments pave the way for hard law, which often *post factum* defines the legal framework for a specific situation that has already been brought under control and/or directed in the desired direction by applying soft law instruments. Soft law emerged spontaneously as a consequence of the need to simplify and speed up the process of creating law in order to more efficiently regulate problems that, due to their nature, require a quick response. Exactly at this point the legal importance and effectiveness of the international declarations and conventions regulating women's human rights and combating violence against women, are mirroring the real degree of human rights protection together with the prevention of violence against women in each country. Soft law furthermore has the position of creating a consensus among member states of a concrete international organization on minimum common principles of future relevant legislation.

Violence against women and girls is a human rights violation, and the immediate and long-term physical, sexual, and mental consequences for women and girls can be devastating, including death. Violence negatively affects women's general well-being and prevents women from fully participating in society. It impacts their families, their community, and the country at large. It has tremendous costs, from greater strains on health care to legal expenses and losses in productivity.[5]

At least 155 countries have passed laws on domestic violence, and 140 have legislation on sexual harassment in the workplace.[6] The main problem is not the normative solutions in international law, but the (un)willingness of states to apply these standards. Criminalization and prosecution of such acts when committed against a current or former spouse or partner should be secured without exceptions. The legal future of these revolutionary laws hinges on a difficult question: how can courts protect victims without curtailing the rights of defendants? Bearing in mind this open question, the answer can be found in improving cultural customs and social norms rather than exclusively in legal frameworks, because the essence of human rights violations lies, *inter alia*, in unequal distribution of power in society. Of course, modern legal frameworks are important for driving such social change toward the elimination of all forms of violence against women, especially sexual violence, but only if legislation bears emancipatory implications.[7]

Causes of the negative situation are: maintenance of the patriarchal model of family relations in a prevalent number of states, the double burden of women and unpaid housework, together with poverty in many countries. Not enough is done to prevent violence against women, and when it does occur, it often goes unpunished. Despite the magnitude of deaths resulting from gender-based violence to women and the massive scale on which the non-fatal consequences of violence affect women, as well as children and elderly people, there are important gaps in data that undermine violence prevention efforts. According to relevant analysis,[8] fully 60 percent of countries do not have usable data, globally seen.

The term "essential services" refers to a set of core services that respond to the immediate and long-term needs and well-being, of women and girls who have experienced violence. Such services include the health sector, police and justice, and social services. With a minimum and coordinated response among them, essential services can respond to some of the most common forms of violence against women, such as sexual violence and intimate partner violence, in diverse contexts and circumstances. Despite commitments by various governments, many women and girls around the world still lack access to quality, multisectoral services essential for their safety, protection, and recovery, especially those who already suffer multiple forms of discrimination. Even when basic services exist, they are typically underfunded, understaffed, or not of high quality.

Only 40 percent of women seek help of any sort after experiencing violence, and less than 10 percent go to the police[9] and therefore a high level of impunity is present at the global level. Women's reluctance to seek help is linked to the widespread acceptability of violence against women in their close surroundings. In many countries, both women and men believe that wife-beating is justified in certain circumstances. However, attitudes toward violence are beginning to change. In almost all countries with available information for more than one year, the level of both women's and men's acceptance of violence has diminished over time.[10]

Women are the most prevalent victims of intimate partner violence, which refers to behavior by an intimate partner or ex-partner that causes physical, sexual, or psychological harm, including physical aggression, sexual coercion, psychological abuse, and controlling behaviors. It can also occur among heterosexual or same-sex couples and does not require sexual intimacy. Intimate partner violence is often hidden, and only a small percentage of victims seek help from responsible victim assistance providers. Intimate partner violence against women is an important risk factor for HIV, other sexually transmitted diseases, unwanted pregnancies, and other reproductive health problems. Women exposed to intimate partner violence are almost twice as likely to have an alcohol use disorder, two times more likely to experience depression, and have an increased risk for suicide attempts compared to women who have not been exposed to partner violence. Intimate partner violence can negatively affect children in households where it occurs. Promoting gender equity, creating a climate of non-tolerance for violence, and starting prevention efforts at a young age are some of the key strategies for preventing all forms of violence against women and girls. Rigorous assessments of social and cultural norms-change strategies are still necessary to value their impact. Those strategies remain an important tool to inform and create cultural shifts in what is acceptable and unacceptable behavior and in promoting norms supportive of healthy, non-violent, and gender-equitable relationships. Microfinance combined with gender equity training is to be targeted particularly to women living in poor communities and is designed to economically empower them and address gender norms, cultural beliefs, and communication. It is one of the few strategies with documented evidence showing reductions in partner violence.

More than 125 million girls and women alive today have been subjected to female genital mutilation across countries in Africa and the Middle East, where this specific form of violence against women is concentrated. Prevalence tends to be lower among younger women, indicating a decline in this harmful practice. However, it remains commonplace in a number of these countries, with overall prevalence rates of over 80 percent.[11]

During the COVID-19 pandemic, there has been a shadow pandemic: an increase of violence to women and girls. UN Women has been working on the prevention of violence and access to essential services, such as health, justice and policing, social services, helplines, and coordination of these services, to provide support to those who have experienced and/or witnessed violence. Since the pandemic began, 45 percent of women reported that they or a woman they know has experienced a form of violence to women and girls; seven in ten women said they think that verbal or physical abuse by a partner has become more common; six in ten felt that sexual harassment in public spaces has worsened; one in four women say that household conflicts have become more frequent and feel more unsafe in their home.[12] Uncertainties surrounding security, health, and finances, coupled with confined living situations, are giving rise to experiences of violence in the domestic sphere, particularly directed toward women and children. Restrictions on mobility and reduced accessibility of support services have exacerbated the problem. Recent reports exploring the effects of the COVID-19 pandemic suggest that violence against women has increased in countries where stay-at-home measures have been widely adopted in response to the pandemic.[13]

The legal practice of the European Court of Human Rights and the UN Committee on the Elimination of Discrimination Against Women (CEDAW), as well as the analysis conducted by the Special Rapporteur on violence against women, highlights some gaps common to the States in terms of the application of protective injunctions.

Identification of those gaps facilitates the development of best practices for the implementation of mechanisms of protective injunctions:

- mechanisms for issuing the protective injunctions (warnings, restraining orders, protective orders) should enable their immediate issuance—in emergency cases and in the absence of the offender (*ex parte*);
- authorities, especially law enforcement agencies, should mandatorily inform the victims of domestic violence about their right to apply for a protective injunction;
- compliance with protective orders should be effectively ensured, and offenders should be administratively liable for violation of restraining orders, and criminally liable for violation of the provisions of the protective order;
- protective injunctions should focus on safety provisions and protection of victims, rather than the treatment of offenders;
- the period of the protective injunctions should be sufficient, and they should contain enforceable instructions that ensure maximum safety of the victim;
- the bodies of the justice system should coordinate their actions and exchange information on the issued protective injunctions (coordination between criminal courts and family courts, as well as between courts and police, is especially important).

However, current research results indicate that many victims who want to apply for a restraining or protection order are not ready to press criminal charges, which would lead to a criminal investigation and possibly criminal proceedings against the perpetrator.[14] Apply for a restraining or protection order should therefore not be made dependent on the institution of criminal proceedings against the same perpetrator. Similarly, they should not be made dependent on the institution of divorce proceedings.

Global binding norms on ending violence to women and girls are still lacking (at the time of writing this book). The idea of a global binding norm on violence against women and girls was first introduced in 1996 by the first UN Special Rapporteur on violence against women, its causes and consequences, in her report to the Commission on Human Rights. In recent period (2020), the Every Woman international coalition of NGOs launched the initiative

"Safer Sooner—Toward a Global Binding Norm to End Violence Against Women and Girls."[15]

Regional treaties on violence against women—the Convention of Belém do Pará in the Americas, the Maputo Protocol in Africa, and the Istanbul Convention in Europe—are successful in minimizing the normative gap. However, these regional standards do not apply globally. Women outside these regions, such as Asia and the Middle East, lack access to binding legal standards specific to violence against women. Therefore, people in 152 nations have joined the call for a global treaty to end violence against women and girls.

The proposed global binding norms are to:

- Mandate comprehensive national legal reform to remove harmful laws that perpetuate violence—for example, in the United States, domestic violence rates dropped 67 percent in eighteen years following the enactment of national reform through the Violence Against Women Act in 1994;[16]
- Prioritize laws and policy-making to protect women and girls from all forms of violence, in all spheres;
- Require the training of, and hold accountable, members of enforcement and implementing agencies, including the security and justice sectors, to ensure public authorities enforce laws;
- Mandate health system responses as developed by the World Health Organization's Global Plan of Action to strengthen the role of health systems within a national multisector response to address interpersonal violence;
- Ensure services for survivors;
- Provide prevention education;
- Develop data and monitoring that are measurable and objective;
- Create a globally applicable instrument;
- Close the enforcement gap with an innovative narrative and metrics-based approach;
- Catalyze funding for implementation;
- Lower rates of violence and costs associated with violence;
- Support the fulfillment of Sustainable Development Goal Number 5; and
- Strengthen women's rights movements globally.[17]

In the absence of global binding norms, the Convention on preventing and combating violence against women and domestic violence of the Council of Europe (CoE Istanbul Convention) is a regional legally binding instrument, but it has global significance due to its comprehensiveness and it is open for accession also to non-members of the CoE.

Commitments to the human rights of women must address root causes,[18] which are primarily structural conditions in many societies that perpetuate the disadvantages and unequal power relations resulting in vulnerability to abuses of women's human rights in the first place.

We need a decisive turning point on women's safety, spurred by horrific acts of violence around the world, including the brutal gang rape and murder of a young woman in India in 2012 and the abduction of schoolgirls in Nigeria by Boko Haram.

"Women are dying. There is no time left to wait. If not us, who? If not now, when?" Marina Pisklakova-Parker, PhD, member of the Steering Committee of the Every Woman Treaty.

NOTES

1. "The violence is intriguing. Universally doomed, and yet it is everywhere. Most of us are both fascinated and horrified by it. It is a fundamental ingredient of our entertainment (children's stories, world literature, film industry) and an essential addition to many of our social institutions. In most parts of the world, it is extremely common in family life, religious affairs and political history." R. Litke, "Violence & Power," *International Social Science Journal*, 132/1992, 173.

2. https://www.ohchr.org/en/statements/2022/03/using-international-and-regional-legal-framework-stop-all-forms-violence-against, 26.07.2023.

3. R. Lewis, R. P. Dobash, R. E. Dobash, et al., "Protection, Prevention, Rehabilitation or Justice? Women's Use of the Law to Challenge Domestic Violence," *International Review of Victimology*, 7/2000, 181.

4. T. Ignjatovic, *Violence Against Women in Intimate Partnership.*

5. UN WOMEN, https://www.unwomen.org/en/what-we-do/ending-violence-against-women, 19.01.2024.

6. International Bank for Reconstruction and Development / The World Bank, "Women, Business and the Law," 2020, https://openknowledge.worldbank.org/bitstream/handle/10986/32639/9781464815324.pdf, 20.01.2024.

7. G. Gasmi, Ž. Nikač, "Sexual and Gender-Based Violence in Serbia," 127–152.

8. WHO, UNDP, UNODC, *Global Status Report on Violence Prevention*, 2014, 20.

9. UN, "World's Women 2015 Trends and Statistics," Department of Economic and Social Affairs, ST/ESA/STAT/SER.K/20, 2015.

10. Ibid.

11. Ibid.

12. UN Women, "Measuring the Shadow Pandemic: Violence against Women during COVID-19," 2021, 5.

13. UN Women (2020). Impact of COVID-19 on violence against women and girls and service provision: UN Women rapid assessment and findings, https://www.unwomen.org/en/digital-library/publications/2020/05/impact-of- covid-19-onviolence-against-women-and-girls-and-service-provision, 05. 01.2024.

14. S. M. S. Dearwater, J. H. Coben, J. C. Campbell, et al., "Prevalence of Intimate Partner Abuse in Women Treated at Community Hospital Emergency Departments," *The Journal of American Medical Association*, 5/1998, 433–438.

15. Diverse coalition of more than 1,700 women's rights advocates, including 840 organizations, in 128 countries working for a safer world for women and girls worldwide, https://everywoman.org/, 24.01.2024.

16. U.S. Department of Justice, "Nonfatal Domestic Violence, 2003–2012," U.S. Department of Justice, 2014, 3.

17. Ibid.

18. Niamh Reilly, "Women, Gender, and International Human Rights: Overview," *International Human Rights of Women* (ed. Niamh Reilly), Springer, Singapore, 2019, 1–18.

Bibliography

African Union, "Protocol to the African Charter on Human and Peoples' Rights on the Rights of Women in Africa", *Preamble*, https://au.int/sites/default/files/treaties /37077-treaty-0027_-_protocol_to_the_african_charter_on_human_and_peoples _rights_on_the_rights_ of_women_in_ africa_e.pdf, 25.08.2023.

Álvaro N. V., "Five Models of Legal Science", *Revus. Journal for Constitutional Theory and Philosophy of Law*, 19/2013.

Andonović S., Prlja D., *Basics of the Right to Protection of Personal Data*, monograph, Institute of Comparative Law, Belgrade, 2020.

Arab Strategy for Combating Violence against Women 2011 – 2020, "Arab Women's Right to a Life Free from Violence", *Arab Women Organization*, prepared by H. Ghazaleh, http://www.arabwomenorg.org/content/publications/vaweng.pdf, 28.10.2023.

Bassiouni M. C., "International Crimes: 'Jus Cogens' and 'Obligatio Erga Omnes'", *Law and Contemporary Problems*, 4/1996.

Beauchamps M., "Olympe de Gouges's Trial and the Affective Politics of Denaturalization in France", *Citizenship Studies*, 8/2016.

Belknap D., McCall K. D., "Women Battering and Police Referrals", *Journal of Criminal Justice*, 22/1994.

Benedek W., Nikolova M., *Understanding Human Rights*, European Center for Training and Research on Human Rights and Democracy, Graz, 2003.

Bergbohm K., "Jurisprudence and the Philosophy of Law", 1892.

Bevacqua and S. v. Bulgaria, 71127/01.

Braschi S., "Protecting Women from Violence: the Impact of International Human Rights Law", *Criminal Justice in the Prism of Human Rights* (eds. Mazzacuva F., Miren Odriozola Gurrutxaga, Nicola Recchia, Alessandra Santangelo), X AIDP International Symposium for Young Penalists, Bologna, Italy, October 27–28, 2022.

Buscaglia E., Ratliff W. E., *Law and Economics in Developing Countries*, Hoover Press, USA, 2000.

Capers Bennett, "Against Prosecutors", *Cornell Law Review,* 105/2020, 1561, 1587.

Čavoški K., Vasić R., *Introduction to Law*, Law Faculty, Belgrade State University, Belgrade, 2006.

CEDAW, *General Recommendation 19*, UN GAOR, 1992, Doc. No. A/47/38.

CEDAW, *General Recommendation 35*, CEDAW/C/GC/35.

CEDAW, *General Recommendation No. 38 on Trafficking in Women and Girls in the Context of Global Migration*, CEDAW/C/GC/38, November 2020, 20.

Chinkin C., "A Critique of the Public/Private Dimension", *European Journal of International Law*, 10/1999.

Coicaud J. M., Heiskanen V., eds., *Legitimacy of International Organizations*, United Nations University Press, 2006.

Council of Europe, "Convention on Preventing and Combating Violence Against Women and Domestic Violence", *Explanatory Report*, CM (2011)49 add final, 07. 04. 2011.

Council of Europe, "Make Equality in Law a Reality in Fact - Compilation of Recommendations of the Committee of Ministers in the Field of Equality Between Women and Men", Directorate of Communication (F-67075 Strasbourg Cedex), 2011.

Council of Europe, "Teaching Resources 'the European Convention on Human Rights - Rights and Freedoms in Practice'", https://edoc.coe.int/en/educational-tools/5327-teaching-resources-the-european-convention-on-human-rights-rights-and-freedoms-in-practice.html, July 2013.

Council of Europe, CoE, Second General Report on GREVIO'S Activities covering period from June 2019 to December 2020, 2021.

Davis A. Y., "Women and Capitalism: Dialectics of Oppression and Liberation", *The Black Feminist Reader* (eds. J. James and D. Sharpley-Whiting), Oxford, John Wiley and Sons Ltd., 2000.

Dearwater S. M. S. et al., "Prevalence of Intimate Partner Abuse in Women Treated at Community Hospital Emergency Departments", *The Journal of American Medical Association*, 5/1998.

Declaration of the United Nations Conference on the Human Environment, June 16, 1972, Stockholm (A/CONF.48/14/Rev.1).

Diligenski A., Prlja D., Cerović D., *GDPR Data Protection Right*, Institute of Comparative Law, Belgrade, 2018.

Dimitrijević V., Paunović M., *Human Rights*, Belgrade Center for Human Rights, Belgrade, 1997.

Divincova A., Sivakova B., "Mobbing at Workplace and its Impact on Employee Performance", *Human Resources Management & Ergonomics*, Vol. VIII, 2/2014.

Djurdjev D., "Soft Law in European Community Law", *Collection of Proceedings, Law Faculty Novi Sad*, 1/2013.

Dokmanović M., "Žene i ekonomske promene 2000-2005", *Journal for Political Theory and Research on Globalization, Development and Gender Issues*, 2006, http://www.globalizacija.com/doc_sr/s0082tra.htm.

Doung K. A., "Human Trafficking in a Globalized World: Gender Aspects of the Issue and Anti-Trafficking Politics", *Journal of Research in Gender Studies*, 2(1)/2012.

Draškić M., "Do We Need Another Law on Protection Against Domestic Violence?", *Perspectives of Implementation of European Standards in the Serbian Legal System*, Vol. 6 (ed. S. Lilic), Collected articles, Belgrade, 2016.

English C., *Confronting Gender Inequality*, Gender Institute, London, 2018.

Erbas R., "Effective Criminal Investigations for Women Victims of Domestic Violence: The Approach of the ECtHR", *Women's Studies International Forum,* 86/2021, 1.

European Parliament, European Parliament Resolution of April 5, 2011 on Priorities and Outline of a New EU Policy Framework to Fight Violence Against Women (2010/2209(INI), http://www.europarl.europa.eu/sides/getDoc.do?type=TA&language=EN&reference=P7-TA-2011-0127, 29.09.2023.

Evander W. H., "A Definition of Law", *Virginia Law Review*, 12/1926.

Evola M., Jungfleisch J., Marinković T., "Human Rights Law Through the Lens of the Gender Perspective", *Gender- Competent Legal Education* (eds. D. Vujadinović, M. Frohlich, T. Giegerich), Springer, 2022.

Francisco R., "The Inter-American Human Rights System and Violence Against Women", *International Human Rights Clinic at Santa Clara Law School*, May 2015, http:// law.scu.edu/wp-content/uploads/150602-Santa-Clara-VAWIAHRS-Report-FINAL.pdf, 12.07.2023.

Gajin S., *Human Rights: Legal - Systemic Framework*, Faculty of Law, University of Union, Belgrade, 2011.

Galtung J., *Human Rights - Viewed Differently*, Frankfurt/Main, 1994.

Gasmi G., *European Legal Standards on Gender Equality – Situation in Serbia*, Efficiency of Legal Norms II, Law Faculty Cluj-Napoca, Romania, 2013.

Gasmi G., "Global Significance of European Standards of Women Human Rights' Protection in Domain of Gender Based and Domestic Violence", *Fiat Iustitia Review of Juridical Studies*, 1/2019, Faculty of Law, "Dimitrie Cantemir" University – Bucharest, Cluj Napoca.

Gasmi G., "New European Legal Standards in the Area of Women Human Rights", *Efficiency of Legal Norms I* (eds. E. M. Fodor. P. Popovici, C. Buzdugan), Law Faculty, Cluj—Napoca, Romania, 2012.

Gasmi G., "Principles of Non-discrimination and Conscientious Fulfillment of the State's Obligations - Theoretical View of the Council of Europe Istanbul Convention and the Practice of the European Court of Human Rights", 1/2016.

Gasmi G., Quo Vadis *EU – Relevant Legal and Institutional Factors*, monograph, Institute for Comparative Law, Belgrade, 2016.

Gasmi G., "Tenth Anniversary of the Istanbul Convention of the Council of Europe – Relevant Aspects", *Science and Society* (*Nauka i društvo)*, 1/2021.

Gasmi G., Nikač Ž., "Sexual and Gender-Based Violence in Serbia: After the Istanbul Convention", *Global Problems in Sexual Offenses* (ed. Erbaş, Rahime), Lexington Books, London, 2022.

Gasmi G., Prlja D., Jerotić A., "European Leading Legal Principles of Combating Gender-based Violence — Istanbul Convention", *Perspectives of Implementation of European Standards in Serbian Legal System* (ed. Stevan Lilić), Law Faculty, University of Belgrade, 2017.

Gracia E., "Unreported Cases of Domestic Violence Against Women: Towards an Epidemiology of Social Silence, Tolerance, and Inhibition", *Epidemiol Community Health*, 58/2004.

Grahovac M. M., *Human Rights*, Faculty of Law, Economy and Justice, Novi Sad, 2020.

Guzman A. T., "The Design of International Agreements", *European Journal of International Law*, 4/2005.

Hester M., Lilley S. J., "Preventing Violence Against Women: Article 12 of the Istanbul Convention", https://rm.coe.int/CoERMPublicCommonSearchServices/DisplayDCTMContent?documentId=090000168046e1f0, 22.01.2024. http://www.eige.europa.eu, 22.11.2023. http://www.oas.org/en/mesecvi/about.asp, 14.01.2023. http://www.ohchr.org/EN/HRBodies/CEDAW/Pages/Recommendations.aspx, 11.07.2023.

http://www.ohchr.org/EN/ProfessionalInterest/Pages/OPCEDAW.aspx, 09.06.2023.

http://www.unfpa.org/about-us, 15.05.2023.

http://www.unwomen.org/en/about-us, 28.09.2023.

http://www.who.int, 30.09.2023.

https://www.osce.org/files/f/documents/7/5/419756_1.pdf, 09.02.2023.

https://cdn.atria.nl/ezines/web/Globalizacija.com/2006/November.pdf, 15.03.2023.

https://everywoman.org/, 24.01.2024.

https://legal-dictionary.thefreedictionary.com/natural+law, 29.02.2023.

https://search.coe.int/cm/Pages/result_details.aspx?ObjectID=09000016805e2612, 26.11.2023.

https://unece.org/statistics/news/why-we-must-urgently-close-data-gap-end-violence-against-women, 24.11.2023.

https://unstats.un.org/sdgs/report/2022/Goal-05/, 05.02.2023.

https://vawnet.org/material/inter-american-convention-prevention-punishment-and-eradication-violence-against-women, 29.09.2023.

https://www.coe.int/en/web/human-rights-convention/the-convention-in-1950, 04.03.2023.

https://www.coe.int/en/web/istanbul-convention/-/grevio-publishes-its-general-recommendation-no-1, 28.11.2023.

https://www.echr.coe.int/documents/convention_eng.pdf, 25.01.2024.

https://www.echr.coe.int/Documents/Court_in_brief_ENG.pdf, 30.01.2024.

https://www.law.cornell.edu/wex/positive_law, 26.02.2023.

https://www.ohchr.org/en/instruments-mechanisms/instruments/international-covenant-economic-social-and-cultural-rights, 28.03.2023.

https://www.ohchr.org/en/statements/2022/03/using-international-and-regional-legal-framework-stop-all-forms-violence-against, 06.11.2023.

https://www.ohchr.org/sites/default/files/ProtocolonTrafficking.pdf, 22.12.2023.

https://www.publicpolicyexchange.co.uk/?ss=em&tg=1b; Public Policy Exchange Ltd Registered in England & Wales, No. 7350384, Registered Office: 253 Grays Inn Road, London, WC1X 8QT, "Domestic Violence: Building on the Domestic Abuse Act to Better Protect and Support Victims and Survivors", Webinar, 20.10.2022.

https://www.refworld.org/docid/52d927444.html, 22.11.2023.

https://treaties.un.org, 22.12.2023.

https://www.unodc.org/documents/treaties/Special/2000_Protocol_to_Prevent_2C_Suppress_and_Punish_Trafficking_in_Persons.pdf, 11.01.2024.

https://www.un.org/womenwatch/daw/cedaw/protocol/whatis.htm, 11.07.2023.

https://www.un.org/womenwatch/daw/cedaw/text/econvention.htm#article1; 26.05.2023.

https://www.undp.org/africa/press-releases/implementation-maputo-protocol-boosted-training-situation-rights-women-and-girls-africa?, 30.09.2023.

https://www.unfpa.org/female-genital-mutilation, 29.09.2023.

https://www.unwomen.org/en/news-stories/in-focus/2022/10/in-focus-women-peace-and-security?gclid=CjwKCAiAheacBhB8EiwAItVO2-ibNHlyDEZ7wWp962YxFZOri0HR1aTgLBPiEed7HVlh3sb2VMwf_xoCyowQAvD_BwE, 18.09.2023.

https://www.unicef.org/supply/stories/inclusive-construction-keeps-girls-school-and-learning, 17.11.2023.

https://www.unwomen.org/sites/default/files/Headquarters/Attachments/Sections/Library/Publications/2020/A-75-274-SG-report-EVAWG-Infographic-and-recommendations-en.pdf, 15.05.2023.

Huecker M., Malik A., King K., Smock W., *Kentucky Domestic Violence* (book), StatPearls Publishing, January 2024.

IACHR Series C No. 4/1988, para. 188.

Ignjatovic T., *Violence Against Women in Intimate Partnership Relations: Model of Coordinated Community Response*, RZC, Belgrade, 2011.

Inter-Agency Coordination Group Against Trafficking in Persons, *The Gender Dimensions of Human Trafficking*, Issue Brief No. 4, 09/2017.

International Bank for Reconstruction and Development / The World Bank, *Women, Business and Law*, 2020, https://openknowledge.worldbank.org/bitstream/handle/10986/32639/9781464815324.pdf, 20.01.2024.

Ivaylova C. B., "Legal Security as a Principle in Lawmaking", *Globalization, the State and the Individual*, 2/2017.

K.A. and A.D.v. Belgium, 42758/98 and 45558/99, 2005.

Kelsen H., *The Pure Theory of Law*, Faculty of Law, University of Belgrade, 2007.

Kenny C., Malik N., "Trafficking Terror and Sexual Violence: Accountability for Human Trafficking and Sexual and Gender-Based Violence by Terrorist Groups under the Rome Statute", *Vanderbilt Journal of Transnational Law*, 52(1)/January 2019.

Kramer S. N., *The Sumerians: Their History, Culture, and Character*, University of Chicago Press, Chicago, 1963.

Kühnhardt L., "Human Rights, Protection of Minorities and the Nation-state in the KSZE Process", *From Politics and Recent History*, 47/1994.

Lewis R., et al., "Protection, Prevention, Rehabilitation or Justice? Women's Use of the Law to Challenge Domestic Violence", *International Review of Victimology*, 7/2000.

Lipson C., "Why are Some International Agreements Informal?", *International Law and International Relations* (eds. B. A. Simmons, Richard H. Steinberg), Cambridge University Press, Cambridge, 2006.

Litke R., "Violence & Power", *International Social Science Journal*, 132/1992.

Manjoo R., "Report of the Special Rapporteur on Violence Against Women, its Causes and Consequences", 29th session HRC, A/HRC/29/27, Advanced Edited Version, June 10, 2015, paragraph 16. https://www.refworld.org/docid/5583f5234.html, 27.09.2023.

Maškin N. A., *The History of Ancient Rome*, Naučna knjiga, Belgrade, 1987.

Mitrović D., *About Law: Selected Essays*, Faculty of Law, University of Belgrade, Dosije Studio, Beograd, 2017.

Morris C., "Law: The Art of Justice", *Encyclopedic Dictionary of Roman Law, American Philosophical Society* (ed. Adolf Berger), Beaux Arts Editions, 1992.

Mršević Z., *Violence and us - Towards a Society Without Violence*, Institute of Social Sciences, Belgrade, 2014.

Nelles J., Executive Secretary to the Istanbul Convention at the Belgrade CoE Conference "The Istanbul Convention: 10 Years On!" held on May 7, 2021.

OSCE, *Welfare and Safety of Women*, 2019.

Paunović S., Kosanović R., *Convention 190 of the International Labor Organization, on Violence and Harassment in the World of Work (2019)*, Confederation of Autonomous Trade Unions of Serbia, Belgrade, 2021, 22.

Paunović M., Krivokapić B., Krstić I., *International Human Rights*, University of Belgrade Faculty of Law, Belgrade, 2021.

Perović S., *Besede sa Kopaonika*, Beograd, 2018.

Peters A., Pagotto I., "Soft Law as a New Mode of Governance: A Legal Perspective", *NEWGOV: New Modes of Governance,* Ref. No. 04/D11, University of Basel, 2006.

Preamble to the Declaration on the Elimination of Violence against Women (A/RES/48/104), https://www.un.org/documents/ga/res/48/a48r104.htm, 23 10.2023.

Prlja D., Gasmi G., Korać V., *Human Rights and Artificial Intelligence*, Institute of Comparative Law, Belgrade, 2022.

Radbruch, G. "Legal Philosophy," in the *Legal Philosophies of Lask, Radbruch and Dabin* (Translated by Kurt Wilk), Harvard University Press, 1950.

Ramsey Carolyn, "Against Domestic Violence: Public and Private Prosecution of Batterers, University of Colorado Law School, Colorado Law Scholarly Commons", *California Law Review online Symposium*, 13:45/2022, https://scholar.law.colorado.edu/faculty-articles, 23.11.2023.

Reilly N., "Women, Gender, and International Human Rights: Overview", *International Human Rights of Women* (ed. Niamh Reilly), Springer, Singapore, 2019.

Reinhard B., *Professional Dictionary of Politics*, Kröner, Stuttgart, 1986.

Rodley N. S., "The Role and Impact of Treaty Bodies", *The Oxford Handbook of International Human Rights Law* (ed. Dinah Shelton), Oxford University Press, Oxford, 2013, about the UN human rights treaty bodies.

Rubenstein H. et al., "Time for a Change, the Need for a Binding International Treaty on Violence Against Women", *Global Rights for Women*, 4, https://globalrightsforwomen.org/treaty-paper-final-112618-1/, 07.09.2023.

Salampessy M. A. S., Rizky L., Achdyana I., "The Effectiveness of The Convention on the Rights of the Child (CRC) Regime by UNICEF in Encouraging the

Implementation of Child Protection in SoutheastAsian Countries", *Journal of Advance in Social Sciences and Policy*, 1/2022.

Sarac E., Cinar M., "Main Features of the Inter – American Convention on Violence Against Women", *Universita degli studi Firenze*, 4/2021.

Scotto D. C. G., "Defining 'Gender' Across Europe: A Linguistic Analysis of the Definition, Translation, and Interpretation of the Word 'Gender' from the Beijing Declaration to the Istanbul Convention", *International Journal for the Semiotics of Law*, 11/2022, https://doi.org/10.1007/s11196-022-09944-z.

Shaffer G., Pollack M. A., "Hard and Soft Law, Interdisciplinary Perspectives on International Law and International Relations", *The State of the Art* (eds. Jeffrey D. Lunoff, M. A. Pollack), Cambridge University Press, Cambridge, 2013.

Skjærseth J. B., Stokke O. S., Wettestad J., "Soft Law, Hard Law, and Effective Implementation of International Environmental Norms", *Global Environmental Politics*, 3/2006.

Snyder F., "Soft Law and Institutional Practice in the European Community", *The Construction of Europe* (ed. S. Martin), Kluwer Academic Publishers, 1993.

Somló, Felix, *Juristische Grundlehre* (2nd edn), Meiner, 1927, 23.

Spieler P., "The Maria da Penha Case and the Inter-American Commission on Human Rights: Contributions to the Debate on Domestic Violence Against Women in Brazil," *Indiana Journal of Global Legal Studies*, 1/2011, http://www.repository.law.indiana.edu/ijgls/vol18/iss1/, 27.11.2023.

Stojčević D., *Roman Private Law*, Belgrade, 1985.

The Brussels Declaration of March 2015 from the Conference at High Level, "Implementation of the European Convention on Human Rights, Our Common Responsibility", March 27, 2015, http://www.echr.coe.int/Documents/BrusselsDeclaration_ENG.pdf, 23.10.2023.

The World's Women 2010, *Trends and Statistics*, United Nations, New York, 2010, Department of Economic and Social Affairs.

Turković K., "Strengthening partnership in the effective implementation of the European Convention on Human Rights", *Effective Implementation of National Remedies in Proceedings Before Domestic Judicial Authorities in the Balkans and the Subsidiary Role of the European Court of Human Rights*, Council of Europe, 2017.

Turquet, Laura, and Un Women. Progress of the World's Women 2011-2012: In Pursuit of Justice. UN, n.d.

Uhde Z., "From Women's Struggles to Distorted Emancipation", *International Feminist Journal of Politics*, 3/2016.

UN Declaration on the Elimination of Violence against Women (A/RES/48/104).

United Nations Department of Economic and Social Affairs, *The World's Women 2010 : Trends and Statistics*, United Nations, New York, 2010.

UN Economic and Social Commission for Western Asia (ESCWA), "Women: Arab Horizon 2030", E/ESCWA/ECW/2017.

UN Economic Commission for Europe, ECE/AC.28/2019/6, Geneva, Item 4 of the Provisional Agenda: Key Trends on Gender Equality Across the ECE Region, 29 and 30.10.2019.

UN GS, Report of the International Law Commission, Sixty-eighth session (May 2–June 10 and July 4–August 12, 2016), General Assembly Official Records Seventy-first session Supplement No. 10 (A/71/10), Chapter V: Identification of Customary International Law, sect. C, Conclusion 13, 2016.

UN Handbook for Legislation on Violence Against Women, 2010, http://www.un.org/womenwatch/daw/vaw/handbook/Handbook%20for%20legislation%20on%20violence%20against%20women.pdf, 11.10.2023.

United Nations Office on Drugs and Crime, *Global Report on Trafficking in Persons 2022*, United Nations, New York, 2022.

UN Resolution adopted by the General Assembly on December 16, 2020 [on the report of the Third Committee (A/75/471, para. 80)] 75/161, Intensification of Efforts to Prevent and Eliminate all Forms of Violence Against Women and Girls, A/RES/75/161.

UN Resolution No 48/104.

UN Women, https://www.unwomen.org/en/what-we-do/ending-violence-against-women, 19.01.2024.

UN Women, *Impact of COVID-19 on Violence Against Women and Girls and Service Provision: UN Women Rapid Assessment and Findings*, https://www.unwomen.org/en/digital-library/publications/2020/05/impact-of-covid-19-onviolence-against-women-and-girls-and-service-provision, 05.01.2024.

UN Women, "Measuring the Shadow Pandemic: Violence against Women during COVID-19", https://data.unwomen.org/publications/vaw-rga, 2021.

UN Women, *The Beijing Declaration and Platform for Action - Beijing+5 Political Declaration and Outcome*, United Nations Entity for Gender Equality and the Empowerment of Women (UN Women), 2014.

UN, "World's Women 2015 Trends and Statistics", *Department of Economic and Social Affairs*, ST/ESA/STAT/SER.K/20, 2015.

U.S. Department of Justice, *Nonfatal Domestic Violence, 2003–2012*, U.S. Department of Justice, 2014.

Varvaro F., "Treatment of the Battered Woman: Effective Response of the Emergency Department", *American College of Emergency Physicians*, 11/1989.

Vasić R., Jovanović M., Dajović G., *Introduction to Law*, Faculty of Law, University of Belgrade, Belgrade, 2015.

Vienna Convention on the Law of Treaties (1969, entered into force in 1980, United Nations, Treaty Series, vol. 1155.

Vienna Declaration and Program of Action: https://www.ohchr.org/en/instruments-mechanisms/instruments/vienna-declaration-and-programme-action, 05.02.2024.

Viljoen F., "An Introduction to the Protocol to the African Charter on Human and Peoples' Rights on the Rights of Women in Africa", *Washington & Lee Journal of Civil Rights and Social Justice*, 22/2009, https://scholarlycommons.law, wlu.edu/cgi/viewcontent.cgi?article=1291&context=crsj, 17.07.2023.

Wehberg H., "Pacta Sunt Servanda", *The American Journal of International Law*, 4/1959.

Index

About the Author

Professor **Gordana Gasmi**, PhD, is a research associate at the Institute of Comparative Law, Belgrade (Serbia), is a full professor, and has published numerous books and scientific essays in the fields of legal theory, international law, and European law and politics. She has worked intensively with international governmental and nongovernmental organizations in a wide range of professional activities, covering research, academic, and advisory expert functions (UNDP, Council of Europe, European Union). She taught Law of the European Union, Theory of Law, Social Law, Human Rights Law, and Commercial Law at Singidunum University in Belgrade in the period 2004–2018, and she was elected to the position of full professor at Union University "Nikola Tesla" Belgrade in 2021. She is an active participant at numerous international academic conferences and is a visiting professor at the Law Faculty of Dimitrie Cantemir University, Romania. As an expert for the Council of Europe and UNDP expert, she held numerous seminars on issues of women's human rights and gender equality for public policy decision-makers and experts in many countries across Europe, Africa, and Asia. She has a great professional experience in gender equality issues. She actively participated in the negotiation process on the Istanbul Convention on preventing and combating violence against women and domestic violence at the Council of Europe in Strasbourg (France).

www.ingramcontent.com/pod-product-compliance
Lightning Source LLC
LaVergne TN
LVHW091531200926
848483LV00002B/363